Cavalry of the Sky

Books by Lynn Montross

Cavalry of the Sky   Rag, Tag and Bobtail

The Reluctant Rebels   War Through the Ages

East of Eden   Half Gods   The Talk of the Town*

Fraternity Row*   Town and Gown*

* WITH LOIS MONTROSS

CAVALRY
OF THE SKY

*The Story of U.S. Marine
Combat Helicopters*

By LYNN MONTROSS

HARPER & BROTHERS, Publishers, New York

Library of Congress catalog card number: 54-6287

This Book
Is Dedicated to the Memory
Of the U.S. Marine Helicopter Pilots and Crewmen
Who Gave Their Lives

CONTENTS

ILLUSTRATIONS

FOREWORD

In 1947 the Marine Corps realized that the devastating effects of atomic weapons called for new landing force procedures and equipment to replace those which had won so many decisive victories in World War II. As the solution, the Marine Corps committed itself to new amphibious tactics of dispersion made possible by the troop-carrying helicopter and vertical landings.

Seven years have passed. The story of the growth of Marine helicopter combat tactics and techniques during those years is told from official records by Lynn Montross in *Cavalry of the Sky*.

It is a story of creative achievement. From peacetime exercises, the Marine Corps progressed to Korean combat operations in which whole battalions were transported to the front and whole regiments supplied by helicopter. And from the helicopter of 1947, carrying two men, the Marine Corps progressed to the helicopter of 1954, lifting 26 battle-equipped troops.

It is a story in which all Marines can take pride. Nearly ten thousand men in Korea were evacuated to hospitals or rescued from behind the enemy lines by Marine helicopters. Marine battle operations were meanwhile being rendered more effective by helicopter troop lifts, supply missions, and command flights.

This is the theme of the following pages. It is a genuine contribution to the history of the Marine Corps as the Nation's force-in-readiness.

LEMUEL C. SHEPHERD, JR.

GENERAL U.S. MARINE CORPS

COMMANDANT OF THE MARINE CORPS

ACKNOWLEDGMENTS

For making the story of Marine Corps combat helicopters a history as well, much of the credit must go to Mr. Michael O'Quinlivan, who did all the basic research. His was the task of gathering from scattered and diverse sources the data and documents which furnish the foundation of the narrative. To him fell the lot of analyzing, organizing, and arranging this material for the author—as well as having always available that invaluable supplementary insight which comes to a careful student of the records and which is necessary to piece together the written words. Mr. O'Quinlivan is also responsible for the photographs and their captions, the bibliography, and the footnotes. The conciseness and clarity of these notes can be appreciated by anyone who has struggled in the bewildering morass of military documentation.

Now a word for those unsung heroes of any victory over the problems of research—the historians, librarians, and archivists who serve as mentors and guides through the mountains of records which must be sifted to get at the facts.

For making valuable background material available, special thanks go to Miss Jean Howard, Aircraft Industries Association of America, who furnished reference material compiled by the Helicopter Council; and to Mr. Arthur G. Renstrom, Division of Aeronautics, Library of Congress, who gave access to a wealth of secondary sources and use of the exhaustive helicopter bibliography in the Pacific Aeronautical Library Index maintained by the Division.

Thanks for making available official records and compilations are due as follows:

U.S. Army Air Forces—Mr. Thomas E. Blades and Mrs. Francis J. Bowen, General Reference Section; and Mrs. Pauline Wiltshire and Mrs. Blanche L. Moore, Air Force Records Section, Departmental Records Branch, Office of the Adjutant General, U.S. Army;

U.S. Air Force—Mr. B. Lindenbaum, Rotary Wing Section, Aircraft Laboratory, Wright-Patterson Air Force Base, Dayton, Ohio;

U.S. Navy and Marine Corps—Dr. Nelson M. Blake and Mr. Robert Mehl, Navy Records Section, National Archives; Mr. Paul L. Bishop, Naval Records Management Center, Alexandria, Va.; Dr. Henry M. Dater and Mr. Adrian Van Weyn, Air History Unit, Office of the Deputy Chief of Naval Operations for Air; Mr. Joel D. Thacker, Mr. Paul R. Rugen, and Mr. John H. Marley, Records and Research Section, Historical Branch, G-3; Captain Edward S. Stallknecht, USMC, Secret and Confidential Files Section, and Mr. J. E. Smith, General Files Section, all of Headquarters, U.S. Marine Corps; Major Frances B. Jackson, USMCR, and Captain Eleanor A. Driscoll, USMCR, of the Records Section, Marine Corps Educational Center, and the Secret and Confidential Files Section, respectively, Marine Corps Schools, Quantico, Va.

The author is indebted to Major George J. King, USMC, for criticizing the manuscript from the aviation viewpoint. Over-all statistics of helicopter operations in Korea were prepared by Mrs. Elizabeth L. Tierney under the direction of Major Edna Loftus Smith, Historical Office, Division of Aviation, U.S. Marine Corps.

Miss Laurene Bryant not only checked data and statistics

but also drew the preliminary maps, sketches, and diagrams. Miss Kay P. Sue typed some of the chapters, and Mr. Rowland P. Gill prepared the index.

Permission to quote from articles published by the author about the war in Korea has kindly been granted by the editors of the *Marine Corps Gazette* and the *Naval Institute Proceedings*.

Credit is due to Marine Transport Helicopter Squadron 161 for the title of this book, a translation of the Latin inscription on the striking insignia which was first introduced during that unit's Far East operations.

The author is responsible for any opinions or interpretations found in these pages. This is not an official history, though most of its material has been derived from official documents. Moreover, it would be hard to overestimate the contribution made in letters or interviews by officers of the U.S. Marine Corps whose names appear in the chapter notes as sources of the history they created.

L. M.

Washington, D.C.
February 2, 1954

Cavalry of the Sky

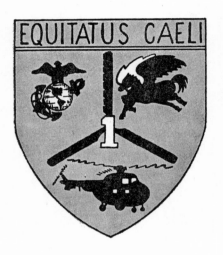

CHAPTER I

Two Generations of Marines

In the summer of 1946, only a year after the victory in the Pacific, it was a question whether the victors or vanquished had been hardest hit emotionally by the atomic bomb. Far from rejoicing over the development of the war's most potent weapon, Americans faced the future with misgivings. They could scarcely be blamed for concluding that there was no defense against atomic weapons when some of the world's most renowned generals and admirals held forth little hope in their public statements.

It was in this atmosphere of doubt that the United States Marine Corps went ahead to plan on the premise that offensive combat techniques of amphibious warfare could be worked out for the Atomic Age.

This was not the first time that the planners of the Marine Corps had differed with contemporary military thought. History repeated itself in 1946, for it was in those red brick buildings of the Marine base at Quantico, Va., that officers of the 1920's set themselves the task of creating a new system of amphibious warfare that could prevail against the accelerated firepower developed by weapons of World War I.

At that time the battleship sinkings and heavy troop casualties of the disastrous Anglo-French amphibious operation at Gallipoli in World War I were only too well remembered. These object lessons had convinced a majority of Europe's

1

generals and admirals that a major ship-to-shore attack could never be launched against modern defensive weapons without incurring ruinous losses.

It is unfortunate that the renown of the U.S. Marine Corps for physical daring should sometimes outshine an equally well-earned reputation for intellectual valor. For it took the stubborn courage of conviction in 1921 when a group of Marine officers flew in the face of world military opinion. At a time when respected English and French military writers were preaching the tactical doctrine of the all-powerful defensive, these Marine dissenters believed that the most dangerous form of the offensive could be made to succeed.

Recruiting posters of that day depicted an aggressive Leatherneck storming ashore, presumably on some foreign strand, with outthrust jaw and bayonet. But it would have been quite as fitting to show a contemplative officer of the Marine Corps Schools at Quantico—some brow-furrowed colonel bending over his desk and working out a solution to the tactical problem assigned to him.

It is hardly necessary to add that modern combat techniques are seldom if ever the result of a general's happy inspiration on the battlefield. They are more likely to be the product of an extended period of planning and testing by school and staff officers before theory is accepted as doctrine. This stage began in the summer of 1921 for Marine amphibious combat techniques which were not translated into action until the Guadalcanal landings of 1942. The two intervening decades were devoted to preparations for the greatest mission in the history of the Marine Corps.

A start was made with the official approval on July 23, 1921, of Operations Plan 712.[1] This Top Secret document remained a guide to Marine strategy in the Pacific down to World War II, insofar as the Marines were concerned with high-level strategic decisions. The plan was based on the recommendations of a brilliant young Marine officer, Major Earl H. Ellis, who predicted that Japan would strike first and win initial successes. He also foresaw that the Marine Corps would find a mission in amphibious assault landings to seize Japanese-mandated islands as bases for the fleet.

Ellis visioned an American invasion route leading from Pearl Harbor to the Marshalls, the eastern Carolines and the Palau group as the steppingstones of an advance on Japan by way of the Marianas and Bonins. He dealt with tactics as well as strategy, and his plan for an amphibious assault on Eniwetok might almost be mistaken for a report of the actual operation which took place 22 years later.[2]

Some of Ellis' proposals were incorporated into the early ORANGE plans adopted in the 1920's by the Joint Board of the Army and Navy (forerunner of the Joint Chiefs of Staff) for offensive operations in the Pacific if it came to war with Japan. And in 1927 the Board issued a directive giving the Marine Corps the mission of preparing for the conduct of landing operations.[3]

Progress was slow because of the necessity of maintaining Marine occupation forces in Haiti and Nicaragua. Not until the last month of 1933 did the Fleet Marine Force come into being as a mobile Marine striking force and integral part of the fleet under the control of the Commander in Chief, U.S. Navy.[4] So new was the modern science of amphibious warfare that even the doctrine had not yet been established, let alone procedures. Classes were dismissed at the Marine Corps Schools in Quantico, therefore, until a landing force manual could be written under pressure. Despite the exigencies of composition, the basic tenets of this hornbook were later accepted with revisions by both the Army and Navy.[5]

A tremendous task still lay ahead. Techniques and weapons had to be improvised where none had existed before. Strange landing craft and fantastic amphibian vehicles evolved under the supervision of Marine officers. Large-scale simulated Marine assault landings were made annually in fleet exercises, and thousands of amphibious specialists graduated from schools set up for that purpose. New bases were established, new units formed, and new types of ammunition developed to meet the needs of amphibious warfare.

For sheer creativeness, few chapters of military history can compare with this period of Navy and Marine Corps cooperation.

THE TEST OF WAR

It has long been a tradition that the United States is unprepared at the outbreak of every war, but this was not quite the case on December 7, 1941. Even though Fleet Marine Force techniques had not yet matured, the nation was in possession of a tactical system capable of winning a succession of decisive victories during the next four years without incurring a single major reverse. Neither the Germans nor the Japanese were ever able to repulse one of the large-scale amphibious operations which laid the Axis powers open to invasion and defeat.

These results were not achieved without growing pains. American amphibious preparedness was only relative at first, and such early landings as Guadalcanal and Tarawa left object lessons. But techniques and command relations improved with combat experience until Naval and Marine forces set a high standard of effectiveness at Saipan, Guam, Peleliu, Iwo Jima, and Okinawa.

Nor was the Pacific the only theater of amphibious operations. The African and European continents were also opened up by assault landings based upon Fleet Marine Force doctrine. Four U.S. Army infantry divisions had been trained by Marine instructors in amphibious procedures, and three of them took a leading part in the Oran, Casablanca, Port

Lyautey, Sojro, Sicily, Anzio, and Normandy landings. The other Marine-trained division gave a good account of itself in such Pacific operations as Attu, Kiska, Kwajalein, Leyte, and Okinawa.[6]

American amphibious techniques were "in all probability . . . the most far-reaching tactical innovation of the war," concluded Major General J. F. C. Fuller, English military critic and historian of World War II.[7] Even at the moment of final victory, however, top-level Marine officers faced the sobering possibility that a tactical system which took years to develop might have been outdated in seconds by the atomic bomb dropped on Hiroshima.

Any comforting doubts on this score were blighted in the summer of 1946 by a firsthand Marine report on the results of Operation CROSSROADS.[8] The U.S. Navy had charge of the tests at Bikini Lagoon, in the western Marshalls, when two atomic bombs were exploded in the midst of a fleet of obsolescent warships used as targets. Enough damage was done in these experiments to convince high-ranking Marine officers that the amphibious techniques of World War II could not cope with atomic weapons.

A cycle had been completed, and in the Marine Corps Schools at Quantico a new generation of officers tackled the problems of creating a new amphibious tactical system adapted to atomic weapons. In 1946, as in 1921, an atmosphere of pessimism prevailed in military circles. The explosion which rocked Hiroshima had shaken confidence in the future of amphibious tactics. Again a group of Marine officers disagreed, even though they conceded that the great naval concentrations of the recent past had been relegated to the wastebasket of history.

Tactical dispersion, these Marine officers insisted, was the answer to "the bomb"—a degree of dispersion which could be put into effect only by new means of landing troops.

Only two dimensions of amphibious tactics—frontal and flank attack—had been open to planners of assault landings in World War II. But Marine officers of 1946 believed that a new type of aircraft made possible a third dimension, as represented by vertical landings. This was the helicopter, which could fly straight up, straight down, forward, backward, and sidewise in either direction. The helicopter could hover, remaining motionless in air except for its spinning rotor. Or the helicopter could land "on a dime" in country too rugged for a conventional plane.

This type of rotary-wing aircraft was just nine years old, with the first practicable machine dating back to Germany in 1937. Five years later Igor Sikorsky designed the pioneer American model capable of flight for military purposes, but rotary-wing aircraft were too experimental to cut much of a figure in World War II, either in Europe or the Pacific. The Army, Navy, and Coast Guard contracted for the limited number of helicopters manufactured in the United States during the last two years of the war. But only a few reached the front, where they were used chiefly for administrative and rescue flights.

Thus the helicopter remained pretty much of an unknown quantity, militarily speaking, when officers of the Marine Corps Schools visioned it as the means of tactical dispersion made possible by vertical amphibious landings. These officers were not balked by the fact that there was no such thing at this time as a helicopter carrying more than two combat-equipped men in addition to the pilot. After all, there had not been any such thing as a usable amphibian tractor when Marines of the 1930's agreed upon concepts calling for such a vehicle. It had been necessary to encourage inventors until they developed an amphibian tractor worthy of its concepts.

This approach may seem to be putting the cart before the horse, but one of the Marine officers of 1947 defined it as "a prospective military philosophy. It consists of thinking in terms of the next war instead of the last," explained Colonel Victor H. Krulak. "This means starting with ideas, when you have nothing more tangible, and developing them into the concepts, procedures and weapons of the future."[9]

Existing means of aerial troop landings in World War II— gliders, parachutes, or transport planes—had been considered inadequate by Marine planners. But the prospective advantages of rotary-wing aircraft were summed up at a later date by a Marine jet and helicopter instructor, Major Archie J. Clapp:

"Consider the complication of defense planning when the [amphibious] attacker is capable of utilizing the third dimension. The attacker could then strike from any direction at any point and in any strength. Thus, the helicopter enables the attacker to choose the point of contact—to hit the defender where it will hurt him most.

"The speed of helicopters would permit them to depart from the ships while they were well out at sea—out of visual sight, or possibly out of radar contact range—and still be able to achieve the necessary concentration of force at the point of impact. In addition to the obvious element of surprise which this would add, the ships will have maneuvering space so that evasive action can be taken against atomic attack."[10]

The Marine Corps, last branch of the American military service to have a helicopter, became the first to institute a long-range program of working out helicopter combat techniques. In 1947 an experimental squadron, HMX-1, was formed at Quantico for the purpose of putting theory to the test. Again, as in 1933, officers of the Marine Corps Schools were assigned the task of writing a manual where none had existed before.

This doctrinal publication made it plain that helicopter troop lifts were intended to supplement and not to supplant conventional amphibious landings. The aeronautical limitations of the helicopter were such that it took faith to envision Marines landing from the sky at points several miles in the rear of the beaches. Yet when the experimental squadron was only six months old, it participated with a few Sikorsky utility machines in the amphibious command post exercises held by the Marine Corps Schools in the spring of 1948 at New River, N.C.[11]

Even at this early date, Marine pilots had made progress in such diverse missions as traffic direction, rescue work, formation flying, fighter evasive tactics, and high-speed wire laying. More realistic training in troop landings was possible in the summer of 1948 after the arrival of the first twin-rotored, ten-passenger Piasecki helicopters, soon to be dubbed the Flying Bananas.

The following spring, when the experimental squadron took part in the annual amphibious exercises at New River, the helicopters stole the show. A dramatic comparison was offered between old and new amphibious techniques as the landing boats hit Onslow Beach while carrier-borne helicopters were lifting troops five miles inland for a simulated vertical envelopment. Many of the boats had trouble in the rough seas, and others were delayed on their return. Yet the effectiveness of the helicopters, each carrying six fully equipped combat troops, was little impaired as they shuttled back and forth from the carrier to their inland objective. Cover was provided by fighter aircraft simulating smoke and strafing attacks on defensive forces.[12]

COMBAT SERVICE IN KOREA

The helicopter experimental squadron had been training pilots and enlisted personnel at Quantico for two and a half years when United Nations intervention in Korea plunged this country into the fourth most costly military effort of American history. A Marine brigade was activated at the outset for service in the Far East, and its air component included an observation squadron, VMO-6, made up of Sikorsky utility helicopters as well as light fixed-wing planes.

The 1st Provisional Marine Brigade landed in Korea on August 2, 1950, and the helicopters went into action early the next morning. Command and liaison flights, rescue missions, reconnaissance, evacuation of casualties, and drops of food and water became routine duties after August 7, when the Marines and U.S. Army units launched the earliest sustained counterattack of the United Nations forces in Korea.

The date was the anniversary of the Marine landing on Guadalcanal in 1942 which led to the first serious defeat administered to Japanese ground forces in World War II. A similar fate overtook the Communist invaders of South Korea, who were given their first reverse by the counterattacking Marine and Army forces. After two more offensive operations in South Korea, the Brigade units were absorbed into the 1st Marine Division just in time for the amphibious landing of September 15 at Inchon. The Marines seized the seaport and Kimpo Airfield, then drove inland to capture Seoul, a city of a million and a half prewar population.

This blow, combined with the converging advance of the Eighth U.S. Army, virtually knocked the Red Korean remnants out of the war. Communist China came to the rescue, and the Marines had the first large-scale fight with the new enemy after making an unopposed landing on the northeast coast of Korea. In the early winter of 1950 the 1st Marine Division was attacked by eight enemy divisions which had secretly infiltrated through the mountains while other Chinese Communist forces struck the Eighth Army in northwest Korea. Helicopters often made possible the only physical contact during the critical period between Marine units separated by enemy roadblocks. The "flying windmills" carried out command, liaison, and casualty evacuation missions in sub-zero weather when the division fought its way for 70 miles from the Chosin Reservoir area to the sea.

The summer of 1951 found the Marine Corps represented in Korea by HMR-161, the first helicopter transport squadron of history. Equipped with Sikorsky machines capable of lifting five or six fully armed troops each, this unit soon made front-page headlines in the "Punchbowl" sector of east Korea. Such combat operations as the lift of an infantry company to the front line were followed by the landing of another company at night, and the relief of a battalion with full equipment on the main line of resistance.

In 1952, after the 1st Marine Division took over a new sector in West Korea, the helicopter transport squadron continued to set precedents. While performing its regular missions, HMR-161 flew a week's supplies and ammunition to an infantry regiment at the front. Batteries of rocket launchers were transported with their crews to new firing positions, and troop movements involving as many as 2,000 men became routine operations.

While VMO-6 and HMR-161 were creating tactical history in Korea, the Marine Corps activated new helicopter squadrons for training in the United States. Troop landings from carrier-borne transport helicopters were completed on a large scale in exercises simulating amphibious assaults against an enemy using atomic weapons. During the spring of 1953, more than 2,000 Marines participated with 39 helicopters in the DESERT ROCK atomic bomb exercises held in Nevada. Even in Korea, while taking their regular turn in the line, infantry units of the 1st Marine Division trained behind the front in amphibious landings carried out by the helicopters of HMR-161.

When the firing ceased in the late summer of 1953, rotary-wing aircraft could no longer be considered experimental for military purposes. Marine helicopter combat operations which made headlines in 1951 had become such routine performances within a year that they were no longer considered news. The precepts benefited other branches of the military service, for both the Army and Air Force enlarged the scope of their helicopter operations in 1952. Rotary-wing aircraft won recognition as the standard means of evacuating seriously wounded men from the front to base hospitals or hospital ships, and hundreds of American lives were saved which would have been lost in past wars as the consequence of delayed surgical treatment.

It would perhaps be going too far to compare the aeronautical and tactical progress of the helicopter with the gains made by conventional aircraft in World War I. Helicopters in Korea were not exposed to enemy air attack, and no opportunity arose for testing them in an actual ship-to-shore assault. But the Marine Corps has not departed from the original concept of 1946, envisioning the new type of aircraft as the means of vertical amphibious landings against an enemy using atomic weapons.[13] Meanwhile the place won by the helicopter in Korea has been evaluated by Lieutenant General Gerald C. Thomas, who became Chief of Staff of the Marine Corps after commanding the 1st Marine Division while HMR-161 was carrying out its pioneer operations.

"Helicopter combat techniques and procedures were unquestionably the foremost tactical innovation of the ground conflict in Korea," said General Thomas. "Indeed, the helicopter gave clear evidence, from its first tactical employment, that a major advance in combat was at hand."[14]

CHAPTER II

Saga of the OP-1

The interest of the Marine Corps in aircraft of the helicopter type goes back some years before there was any such thing as a helicopter capable of flight for military purposes. The autogiro came first, and a group of young Marine pilots gave that early rotary-wing machine its pioneer test flights in the field.

The OP-1, as it was designated, flew no combat missions. But this Pitcairn autogiro was tested in Nicaragua for five months in 1932 by combat fliers supporting the combat ground forces of the Marine occupation troops. And its flights took it over jungle and mountain terrain infested with guerrillas.

It is not quite a coincidence that the Marines tested the OP-1 in a combat area while other Americans were at peace. There have been only two years from the outbreak of the Spanish-American War in 1898 to the end of the Korean conflict in 1953 when Marines were not on combat duty either in a war or police action. Custom has long sanctioned the tacit assumption that the Marines, as transitory naval forces, can land on foreign soil without the implication of hostilities and permanent occupation usually associated with invading troops. This explains the interventions which kept the Marine Corps engaged continuously for nearly three decades in the Caribbean and Latin America. The causes show a remarkable similarity. Elections won by bullets rather than ballots, financial manipulations, and pressure applied by European creditors—

these were the factors which led the State Department to embark upon a much-criticized policy of supervising unstable governments in a sensitive strategic area.

Our right of mediation in Latin-American affairs, based on a liberal interpretation of the Monroe Doctrine, was extended to Cuba in 1906, Nicaragua in 1912, Mexico in 1914, and Haiti and the Dominican Republic in 1915. The American occupation of Haiti continued for twenty years, and a second intervention in Nicaragua lasted from 1927 until the end of 1932.

The political aspects were no more troublesome than the military problems which had to be solved when a handful of Marines took on the job of policing large mountain and jungle areas overrun by hostile guerrillas. Tactics were freely improvised to suit the need, and the hospitality of the Marine Corps to new tools and methods resulted in the first tests ever given any rotary-wing aircraft under combat conditions.

THE HISTORICAL BACKGROUND

New as the autogiro was in 1932, man's dream of emulating the birds began long ago with the rotary principle of flight. In the fifteenth century Leonardo da Vinci sketched a flying machine (never built or tested) consisting of enormous spiral wings attached to a whirling shaft mounted on a circular base. But he did not attempt to solve the problem of propulsion, and not until the late eighteenth century did the steam engine offer some hope of an adequate source of power.

This period was an age of feverish aeronautical experimentation, and several French inventors came up with ideas for a helicopter—a name derived from the Greek *helix,* meaning spiral, and *pteron,* meaning wing.* None of them had any practical possibilities, though a spring-driven model actually

* Lexicographers tell us that derivatives from *helix* call for a short "e" (helical, helicoid, etc.) while words derived from *helios,* meaning sun, are long (heliotrope, heliometer, etc.). These distinctions are officially accepted by the Marine Corps, but many dissenters still prefer *heeli*copter to *helli*copter.

did get off the ground. Meanwhile the first successful balloon flights were taking place in France, and the thoughts of inventors turned to lighter-than-air experiments. Balloons were used for purposes of military observation by the French Revolutionary armies, though Napoleon failed to see their value at a later date. It took a peace-loving American to catch the first prophetic glimpse of warfare in a new element, for Benjamin Franklin wrote in the year 1783:

"It [the balloon] appears to be a discovery of great importance and what may possibly give a new turn to human affairs. . . . Five thousand balloons, capable of raising two men each, could not cost more than five ships of the line, and where is the prince who can afford so to cover his country with troops for its defense, so that ten thousand men descending from the clouds might not, in many places, do an infinite deal of mischief before a force could be brought together to repel them?"

This concept of airborne invasion was too advanced for its age. In 1784, however, two Frenchmen hit upon a solution for an aeronautical problem which still vexes designers of rotary-wing aircraft. Launoy, a naturalist, and Bienvenu, a mechanic, collaborated in the construction of a spring-driven toy helicopter exhibited before the French Academy of Sciences. Two rotors revolving in opposite directions were introduced to overcome torque reaction—the tendency of the body of any aircraft to turn in a direction opposite to the rotation of the airscrew. Since a single rotor applies force in one direction, the equal reaction in the opposite direction is known as torque. Launoy and Bienvenu neutralized it successfully by means of two rotors compensating each other, and the principle is utilized by present-day helicopter manufacturers.[1]

After the interest in lighter-than-air flight subsided, the early nineteenth century abounded in models of steam-driven helicopters. The first full-size machine designed to carry a man was planned by Sir George Cayley of England, but the experiment never outgrew the stage of small spring-driven models.[2] In 1842 another English inventor, W. H. Philips, built a 20-pound model powered by a diminutive steam engine and consisting of three rotors, one for lift and two for steering. But the shortcomings of this creation only added to the overwhelming burden of proof that the weight of an adequate steam engine would be too great for a helicopter large enough to carry a pilot.[3]

During the American Civil War a Confederate officer, William C. Powers, proposed a helicopter to be used for bombing as well as reconnaissance. His design was described as looking more like a plow than a flying machine. It seems to have been conspicuously lacking in aeronautical respects, but Captain Powers thought so highly of it that he abandoned the project for fear that his secret would be discovered by the enemy.[4]

Dozens of ideas for helicopters were advanced during the last half of the century, some of them so fantastic as to be incredible. In 1880, however, the most productive inventor of the age set his mind to work on the hitherto unsolved problem of providing enough power without adding too much weight. Thomas A. Edison first thought of an electric motor before deciding that it was impractical. Then he experimented with the explosive qualities of guncotton, but the result was a premature blast which rocked his laboratory to its foundations. In spite of his failure, Edison continued to believe in the helicopter principle long after the development of fixed-wing aircraft. As late as 1924 the great inventor declared that "once the helicopter was perfected, flight would revolutionize civilization."[5]

Two young bicycle mechanics of Dayton, Ohio, recalled that as boys they had constructed many toy helicopters with rotor blades of bamboo and tissue paper—replicas of the model exhibited by Launoy and Bienvenu a century before. But these

experiments did not convert Wilbur and Orville Wright to
helicopter doctrine. On the contrary, Orville explained years
later that "we learned early that the bigger the blades were,
the worse they would react in the air. . . . We thought the
helicopter more difficult: consequently, when we turned to the
development of the flying machine, our favoritism was toward
the glider methods. . . ."[6]

The ultimate result, as everyone knows, was the historic
flight at Kitty Hawk, N.C., which demonstrated in the last
month of 1903 that the gasoline internal-combustion engine
could provide enough power to propel a man through the air.
The helicopter, though first to start, had lost the race to the
machine with a propeller and rigid wings designed for airlift.

THE EARLY HELICOPTERS

It had been a close finish, for only four years later Louis
Breguet and Charles Richet of France produced the first helicopter of history to get off the ground with a pilot. The 1,000-
pound machine consisted of a rectangular framework, a 55-
horsepower Renault engine, and four rotors of five blades
each. The first flight took place in 1907, and a year later the
helicopter lifted a passenger as well as a pilot—a total of 1,600
pounds. But its best record was a flight of 64 feet at a height
of 15 feet, and it was too unstable to be practicable.[7]

The inventor abandoned his experiments with vertical flight
to become known as one of the foremost designers of fixed-
wing aircraft. This was also the experience of a young Russian
named Igor Sikorsky, who visited Paris in 1909, at the age of
20, with a burning ambition to construct a helicopter.
Financed by loans from his sister, he designed a first machine
in 1909 which vibrated alarmingly while making futile efforts
to lift itself from the ground. A year later he tested his second
helicopter, a 400-pound affair with a 25-horsepower motor and

two contrarotating rotors mounted coaxially.* Young Sikorsky succeeded this time to the extent of seeing his overgrown model rise a few feet into the air, but he soon decided to follow Breguet's example and design conventional planes.[8] Needless to add, the Russian inventor made a reputation in this field before emigrating to become an American citizen and gain new fame in the 1940's as a helicopter manufacturer.

Rotary-wing aircraft made little or no progress during World War I while the development of fixed-wing types received a tremendous impetus. The conventional plane came of age during the four war years, but in 1919 the helicopter had not bettered the records set by Breguet ten years before. The best that could be said was that a valuable store of knowledge had been acquired as a result of past experiments in the rotary-wing field.

Single-rotor, twin-rotor, and four-rotor designs had been tested. Biaxial twin rotors had been both laterally and longitudinally disposed as well as meshing each other, and coaxial rotors were an old story (see accompanying diagram). But there still was no such thing as a practicable helicopter in 1921 when the U.S. Army Air Service financed a machine designed by George de Bothezat, a Russian exile who described himself as "the world's greatest scientist and outstanding mathematician."[9]

At least he was one of the foremost authorities on vertical flight. His project was carried on with great secrecy at McCook Field, near Dayton, Ohio, until the helicopter was ready for testing in December, 1922. Weighing 3,585 pounds, and powered by a 185-horsepower Le Rhone engine, it consisted of a cross-shaped framework mounting a six-blade rotor

* One rotor above the other on the same axle, rotating in opposite directions. A glossary of aeronautical and military terms will be found in Appendix A.

BASIC DESIGNS OF THE TWIN-ROTOR HELICOPTER

COAXIAL - TWO ROTORS MOUNTED ON SAME AXLE.

BIAXIAL - TWO AXLES ON LATERAL OUTRIGGERS.

BIAXIAL (LONGITUDINAL)

BIAXIAL (MESHING)

at each of the four corners. Grotesque as the contraption appeared, it actually got off the ground and set new records by lifting four men on one flight and remaining in the air two minutes and forty-five seconds on another occasion. But the machine fell far short of military demands even after the Army advanced De Bothezat an additional $10,000 for improvements.[10]

Other inventors succeeded during the early 1920's in constructing helicopters capable of brief, ineffectual flight. Among them were Paul Hateras of Argentina, Etienne Oemichen of France, and Henry Berliner of the United States. Still others put their trust in that hybrid which came later to be known as the autogiro—a machine depending on a propeller for forward motion and an overhead rotor for vertical lift. Progress in this field had not been exhilarating until a Spanish engineer, Juan de la Cierva, succeeded on his fourth attempt in producing an autogiro that would fly. Thus, on January 9, 1923, came into being the world's first practicable rotary-wing aircraft.[11]

Any doubts as to its performance were laid at rest when Cierva's machine flew across the English Channel and covered 3,000 miles in European demonstration flights. These results were so convincing that Harold F. Pitcairn bought the American rights and started his own manufacturing plant in 1929 at Willow Grove, near Philadelphia. Wallace W. Kellett was also licensed to manufacture autogiros in this country, and the patents were sold and used in England, Germany and Austria.[12]

The word "autogiro" was originally a proprietary name, like "kodak," which soon found its way into popular usage. For the public was fascinated by the new type of aircraft after Sunday newspaper writers pictured a future in which every family would be airborne, thanks to an autogiro in the back yard. Such a millennium was far distant in 1931, however, when the U.S. Navy contracted to purchase three of the first autogiros to be turned out by Pitcairn's Willow Grove plant.[13]

THE OP-1 IN NICARAGUA

The basic difference between the two types of rotary-wing aircraft was that the autogiro depended on "autorotation"— the whirling of the rotor in flight without the aid of mechanical power. The engine was used only on the ground to start the rotor spinning, whereupon the pilot threw a clutch and transferred the power to the propeller for forward motion. On the other hand, the rotor of the helicopter was geared at all times to the engine, and the machine had neither a propeller nor the stubby wings which gave added lift to some types of the autogiro.

In terms of performance, the chief difference was that the autogiro did not have the helicopter's ability to hover or make a vertical landing, though it could give a very good imitation of both when bucking a stiff wind. Once in flight, the rotor of the autogiro required the action of the air on its blades to continue spinning, so that some forward motion was essential. If this motion ceased, the autogiro must settle, though it could land and take off in less space than a fixed-wing plane.

The Navy was interested in the possibilities of the autogiro for carrier flying, submarine detection, defense of convoys, and coast patrol and rescue missions. After the delivery of the first Pitcairn machine in the spring of 1931, it was to be tested by Navy pilots at the Anacostia Field on the outskirts of Washington. When the second autogiro arrived, the first was to be sent back to the Willow Grove factory for such experiments as the addition of landing floats and other changes to convert it into a seaplane. The third autogiro, scheduled for still later appearance, was to be flown from the factory to the Marine Corps base at Quantico for field tests in Nicaragua.[14]

In preparation, a Marine pilot and mechanic were to be sent

to Willow Grove for preliminary instruction. This duty fell to Lieutenant Edward L. Pugh and Gunnery Sergeant Harold Kaltenback.[15] But the machine was not delivered until the early spring of 1932, and it went first to Anacostia. An overhauling at that field interposed further delays, so that the Marine autogiro did not reach Quantico until May.[16]

The saga of OP-1* begins at this point. Pugh was directed to give flying lessons to Lieutenant Frank M. June, the pilot destined to become chief jockey of the unpredictable machine. A young Iowan who had graduated from the U.S. Naval Academy, June had served with Marine ground forces in Nicaragua before winning his wings at Pensacola in one of the first classes to be instructed in instrument flying.

OP-1 behaved like a half-broken broncho during the new pilot's initiation. Nearly every take-off ended in a forced landing apparently caused by stoppages in the fuel line. The engine was given a complete check by Kaltenback, who discovered that the fuel line had been clogged by such foreign objects as a toothpick and bits of rubber tubing, not to mention a valve put in backwards. These discoveries gave rise to the legend, which persists to this day, that a Navy hospital corpsman was in charge of the overhauling at Anacostia and signed the repair logbook.[17]

However this may be, OP-1 was restored to better health during June's brief period of instruction at Quantico. Next, it became Kaltenback's duty to take the machine apart for shipment by sea and reassemble it in Nicaragua.

There the autogiro drew enthusiastic crowds. As a Latin-American people, the Nicaraguans took pride in a Spanish invention; and OP-1's initial appearance was hailed by a Managua newspaper, *La Prensa*, on June 28, 1932:

"At 9:00 yesterday an autogiro flew under our skies for the first time. . . . The people of the city saw it in flight and groups

* See Appendix A for an explanation of aircraft designations.

of curious ones gathered on the plazas and open places to watch with interest the maneuvers of the bird. It has a kind of windmill of four blades on its upper side, these blades drooping slightly when the machine is on the ground. The machine now in Nicaragua, arrived practically 'knocked down' on the naval transport *Vega* two weeks ago, was brought from Corinto by rail, and was put together at Zacharias Field.[18]

The Marines, it appears, were amused by the exhibition. *La Prensa* recorded that "the other pilots . . . saluted it [the autogiro] with a chorus of laughter when they saw it land the first time with the exact precision of a game bird."[19]

Even after the novelty wore off, OP-1 continued to delight Nicaraguans who gave it affectionate nicknames. *Diario Moderno*, another Managua newspaper, noted on August 13 that "the United States autogiro which is in this capital spent part of yesterday morning going through aerial acrobatics. The 'turkey hen' was admired for a long time by the curiosity seekers."[20]

But if OP-1 afforded some diversion, it also claimed the serious attention of the Marine pilots putting it through its paces. Air was an integral part of a Marine expeditionary force, not a separate arm. Operating under the direct control of ground force officers, Marine pilots in Haiti and Nicaragua worked out many of the techniques of World War II during the 1920's. Air drops of supplies, aerial casualty evacuations, message pickups, and signaling by ground panels were an old story by that time, and Marine fliers initiated dive bombing in combat nearly two decades before Nazi aviators of the Luftwaffe were popularly credited with the "innovation."

THE OP-1 FOUND WANTING

Tests of the OP-1 were conducted throughout the summer of 1932 by a board made up of three Marine pilots. June put the autogiro in competition with an O2U-1 Corsair biplane flown by Lieutenant Paul A. Putnam.* Captain Harold C. Major acted as senior member and referee; and Lieutenant Samuel S. Jack took part occasionally, though the board report was signed by the first three.

The pilot started the autogiro by engaging a clutch connecting the engine to the rotor shaft. It took several minutes to get the four rotor blades spinning at the minimum number of revolutions per minute. Then the power was applied to the propeller; and as the machine rolled, the pilot took care to keep the tail down while leaving the ground. Otherwise, the rotor would slow down to such an extent as to endanger control and stability.

Weight-lifting tests came first. The OP-1 was flown with measured loads of sandbags representing supplies and ammunition for the ground forces. This was the payload in addition to the pilot and copilot in tandem seats and their 63 pounds of regular equipment. With a 50-pound sandbag, according to the board report, "the take-off distance averaged 90 yards and the time averaged 8 seconds into a 7-mile wind. An altitude of 500 feet was reached in 53 seconds, and 1,000 feet in 1 minute and 57 seconds. As the sand load was increased in 50-pound increments, the take-off time and distance increased only slightly but the rate of climb and performance decreased materially. When a load of 200 pounds was carried, the airplane [sic] became so loggy that it was considered unsafe. From the above it was concluded that 50 pounds was the maximum weight that could be carried efficiently."[21]

This was far short of an acceptable payload, which consisted of at least 200 to 300 pounds for Nicaraguan operations. OP-1 had such a slow cruising speed, moreover, as to handicap it for flying in formation or with an escort plane. It was a serious defect in Nicaragua, where Marine planes

* Putnam was the major in command of Marine air units on Wake when the Japanese struck in 1941.

seldom flew singly over the guerrilla-infested jungle because of their lack of radio communication.

Aside from these shortcomings, OP-1 showed good accuracy in measured landings. The wheels "were consistently placed within ten feet of a mark and the roll varied from zero to a maximum of 55 feet."[22]

Gasoline consumption "averaged 17 gallons per hour at 1,700 revolutions per minute, giving an indicated speed of 70 miles per hour and a cruising radius of approximately three hours or 200 miles." But the board added that this was "not sufficient for expeditionary duty, as flights of 300 to 400 miles are often necessary, and in many cases additional fuel is not available except at the base of operations."

The report of the three Marine pilots was forwarded to Marine Corps Headquarters in Washington on November 22, 1932, by their commanding officer, Major Francis P. Mulcahy. And their conclusion was the only verdict made possible by the summer's tests:

"It is the opinion of the undersigned that the chief value the OP-1 has on expeditionary duty is in landing to inspect small fields, whose value as landing areas has been recommended by ground troops, with a view to preparing these fields for other types; to evacuate medical sitting cases from landing areas that cannot be used by other types of planes; and to ferry important personnel to the same kind of landing areas. . . ."[23]

During the remainder of its sojourn in Nicaragua, OP-1 was used by the Marines for such missions and for instructional purposes. A number of young Corsair pilots tried their hand, including such present-day colonels as Arthur F. Binney, Frank H. Wirsig, Millard T. Shepard, Frank C. Dailey, John S. Carter, and Frank H. Schwable.

Every beginner was warned that the steel pin in the rotor shaft mechanism might be snapped off when the engine was connected, and spare pins were carried in the pilot's pocket. Several near-accidents occurred during instruction flights, but the OP-1 ended its saga with a record of never having killed anyone. This was fortunate, since the autogiro's landing peculiarities could be dangerous to a novice. When the rotor let the machine down, a sudden increase in engine power might cause a torque-induced dive requiring about 200 feet in altitude for recovery. Even at best, the rotor landed the OP-1 with a rocking motion which had the effect of seasickness on some of the victims.[24]

FURTHER AUTOGIRO TESTS

The Marine occupation of Nicaragua ended on the last day of 1932, and the autogiro was taken apart by Sergeant Kaltenback for shipment to Quantico. There is little further mention of OP-1 in Marine records until November 6, 1933, when Captain Francis E. Pierce reported to Headquarters after being detailed as artillery observer "to test the use of radio telephony on an autogiro as a spotting platform for observation of the fire of 75mm artillery."

The occasion was the annual firing of Battery C, 1st Battalion, 10th Marines, at Fort Hoyle, Md., during the first two weeks of October. Pierce found that a makeshift installation functioned perfectly in nine flights, proving "that spotting by radio telephone was entirely feasible and considerably faster than by radio telegraphy."

Again, however, OP-1 was found wanting. For Pierce concluded "that the autogiro in its present form is not satisfactory for artillery spotting due to its restricted field of vision and relatively slow speed, which makes it more susceptible to antiaircraft fire than the conventional airplane."[25]

This seems to have been OP-1's last performance. At any rate, a search through Marine records has not revealed any further mention, and it is the recollection of Marine officers that OP-1 ended by smashing up in 1934. Probably some unwary pilot neglected to keep the tail down.

The two Pitcairn autogiros purchased by the Navy also receded into the mists of history, leaving behind them a record of unsatisfactory results. A flight test report from Anacostia, dated October 24, 1931, described comparative tests of the XOP-1, as the Navy autogiro was designated, and a training plane of conventional type. The latter proved to be superior in rate and angle of climb, speed, gliding angle, and ability to get out of a small, enclosed area. The autogiro surpassed only in length of landing roll and ability to land more accurately.[26]

The Navy, according to a Material Division memorandum of March 22, 1932, had been primarily interested in reducing the stalling speed of seaplanes. But tests at Anacostia indicated that the XOP-1 had "many disadvantages" either as a seaplane or catapulted aircraft.[27]

Bureau of Aeronautics records also show that an inquiry was made as to whether the autogiro could land on the roof of the main Navy Building in Washington, which was a venerable-appearing structure even at that date. This issue was sidestepped with the explanation that the roof was too cluttered with ventilators for such stunts.[28]

One of the Navy autogiros cracked up for the second and last time in 1932, and it was decided in August of that year that the other be put in storage.[29] The Navy tried again in 1935 with a later model of Pitcairn autogiro known as the XOP-2. Tests were made in the hope of obtaining a flying ambulance capable of landing on the deck of a battleship or cruiser if special provision were made. But the new model was found unsatisfactory and even dangerous because of the vibration set up by the rotor. Two years later it was recommended that the XOP-2 be flown to Norfolk for storage, and its epitaph was an anonymous penciled comment in the margin:

"Fly it, hell! Better crate the thing and ship it."[30]

The interest of the U.S. Army Air Corps in the autogiro was revived in the spring of 1936. Tests were made during the next three years with various models of Pitcairn and Kellett machines. An autogiro school was started on April 15, 1938, at Patterson Field, Fairfield, Ohio, for training of Army Air Corps pilots and mechanics.[31] But landing accidents occurred frequently, and too many tests continued to be unsatisfactory. Lack of room and weight-lifting capacity for a minimum payload was the chief objection to Kellett as well as Pitcairn models.

Marine records show that in 1935 the Kellett autogiro was tested by June and Major. Both pilots found it an improvement over the OP-1, but the official last word of the Marine Corps was expressed by Lieutenant Colonel Roy S. Geiger in a memorandum of July 12, 1936:

"To date no type of autogiro has been demonstrated which will carry a reasonable fuel supply and military load and at the same time retain its peculiar characteristics of taking off and landing in a restricted area and hovering over a given spot. Until such time as this type of aircraft can carry a satisfactory military load and retain its flying characteristics, its use by the Marine Corps is not recommended."[32]

CHAPTER III

The Marine Amphibious Mission

Prospects for rotary-wing aircraft in general were not bright in 1936. While the autogiro was showing disappointing results in many of its tests, there was still no such thing in the world as a helicopter worth testing for military purposes.

Little apparent progress had been made since the early 1920's in this field of rotary-wing design. The best record was set in 1929 by an Italian inventor, Coradino d'Ascanio, whose coaxial, twin-rotor machine reached an altitude of 59 feet and remained in the air nearly 9 minutes while covering a distance of 3,500 feet.[1] But even though the statistics of performance were disappointing, much was contributed to the storehouse of aeronautical knowledge during these seemingly barren years. In 1924, for instance, a Dutchman named von Baumhauer constructed a helicopter using a single main rotor driven by a 200-horsepower engine and depending on a small vertical tail rotor to neutralize torque.[2] This craft was wrecked before it could be put through its paces, but the merit of the design was later demonstrated by Sikorsky helicopters.

Breguet returned to the helicopter field in 1931 with a coaxial, twin-rotor machine which had a 350-horsepower engine. Overweight proved to be a serious handicap, but the French designer was confident enough to predict the possibility of a huge helicopter flying boat capable of crossing the Atlantic.[3]

This was a brave dream, but the world had to wait two more

years for the reality of a practicable helicopter. In 1937 the news came from Germany that Dr. Heinrich Focke, the designer of Nazi military planes, had constructed a helicopter which put all past records in the shade. Reports of such feats as a flight from Bremen to Berlin were greeted with skepticism at first in other countries. But further tests left no doubt that the German inventor had left all rivals far behind. His craft, mounting twin biaxial, contrarotating three-bladed rotors on lateral outriggers, established these records:

Distance (airline), 143.069 miles;
Duration, 1 hour, 20 minutes, 49 seconds;
Altitude, 11,243.416 feet;
Speed (for 20 kilometers), 76.151 miles per hour.[4]

A dramatic exhibition of the stability of the Focke helicopter was given in 1938 when Hanna Rasch, a German aviatrix, flew it inside a large sports palace in Berlin. The outbreak of World War II the following year put an end to the exchange of ideas. Before Germany was isolated, however, an American inspected the Focke machine and brought back motion pictures shown to Army officers at Wright Field.[5] A former engineer for the Pitcairn and Kellett autogiro companies, W. Laurence LePage, had formed a partnership with Havilland H. Platt, a New York engineer who had done independent research. And it was the Platt-LePage Company which received the contract in 1940 when the U.S. Army Air Corps asked for bids on a rotary-wing aircraft for military purposes. This was the inception of the XR-1, a 4,800-pound experimental helicopter with a 450-horsepower motor and twin biaxial rotors mounted on pylons extending from each side of the fuselage behind the two tandem cockpits. The first tests were conducted in the spring of 1941, but the performance of the XR-1 fell below minimum Army Air Corps requirements.[6]

Platt and LePage made improvements and kept on trying

until their second machine, the XR-1A, made a successful flight in December, 1943.[7] Meanwhile a rival aircraft of entirely different design had won the right to be known as the first practicable American helicopter.

Igor Sikorsky, now an American citizen, returned to the rotary-wing field with ideas for a single main rotor combined with a small vertical tail rotor to neutralize torque. As early as 1938, Army Air Corps officers visited the Vought-Sikorsky plant at Stratford, Conn., to inspect the test rig which developed into the VS-300. Tests conducted by an Air Corps pilot in 1939 indicated that this machine showed more promise than any helicopter ever built before in the United States.[8]

On the strength of this performance, the Air Corps and other Government agencies agreed upon a subsidy of $50,000 toward the construction of a second Sikorsky helicopter to be designated the XR-4.* The machine was completed shortly after the Japanese attack at Pearl Harbor and tested early in 1942 with surpassing results. At last the United States had a helicopter which satisfied military requirements, and it was decided to fly the XR-4 from the Connecticut plant to Wright Field at Dayton, Ohio. The delivery flight took place from May 13 to 18, 1942. A distance of 761 airline miles was covered in 16 stages amounting to 16 hours and 10 minutes of actual flying time. Among the new records set, an unofficial world endurance time of an hour and 50 minutes was recorded.[9]

It might seem that overnight the helicopter had made the autogiro obsolescent, but there is much to be said for the contention of Harold F. Pitcairn at a later date:

"No sharp line of distinction can be drawn, because the modern helicopter largely incorporates the fundamentals of

* The XR-2 and XR-3 were Kellett autogiros.

the autogiro as originated by the late Juan de la Cierva and developed by the Autogiro Company of America. Modern helicopters employ the autogiro type of rotor. They use the autogiro control system. If the engine fails, the helicopter uses the autorotation of the autogiro to effect a landing, which is an imperative safety provision."[10]

THE WAR YEARS

The helicopter had arrived. But it had not arrived in time to play anything but a minor role in World War II.

Hitler and the Luftwaffe generals apparently did not think highly enough of the possibilities of rotary-wing aircraft to make much tactical use of Germany's advantage. During the development of the Focke-Achgelis FA-223 early in the war, a glider was built with a helicopter rotor. Designed and flown within seven weeks, this machine made successful towed flights of 110 miles per hour, but it was not employed for aerial assault landings.[11]

Another German experiment was the FA-330, a rotary-wing kite towed from the deck of a submarine by a winch and cable for observation purposes. Weighing 180 pounds without the pilot, it folded into a compact package. About 200 were built by Focke-Achgelis, but American postwar tests revealed that the pilot had little control over flights which resulted in excessive fatigue after an hour.[12]

The FA-223 helicopter appears to have been used by Hitler's forces chiefly for such operational chores as liaison, rescue, and communication. But the British Expeditionary Force was probably first to employ rotary-wing aircraft in World War II. In 1939 several Cierva C-40 autogiros were flown in France for observation missions, all of them being lost in the evacuation from Dunkirk. A small "Rota Squadron" was formed in 1943 of Cierva C-30 autogiros collected from private owners. Squadron 529 had as its chief mission the calibration of radio stations, and the unit did good work throughout the war.[13]

England had to depend on the United States for helicopters. The first two Sikorsky machines arrived in December, 1943, and others were received the following year to establish a Royal Air Force school. British helicopter techniques were still at the experimental stage, however, when the conflict ended.[14]

Not much more could be said for the development of the helicopter by the armed forces of the United States. It is a truism of military history that a new weapon is no better than the use made of it, and new techniques are not learned in a day. The tank, for instance, saw little action until the final months of World War I, though the first machines were built early in the struggle. And not until World War II did armor come into its own on the battlefield.

Few helicopters were available to the American forces until 1945, and then only in limited numbers. It is understandable, therefore, that helicopter techniques should scarcely have progressed beyond the experimental stage.

The XR-4 was followed by two improved Sikorsky machines in 1943—the YR-4 and the XR-5. The last was described as showing as much improvement over its predecessors as the B-29 bomber over the B-17. Finally, the Army and Navy co-operated to subsidize the development of the XR-6 in 1944, representing the high-water mark of American rotary-wing aeronautical progress during the war. The 225-horsepower Franklin air-cooled engine drove the main rotor and tail rotor through a shaft and gear transmission. With a gross weight of 2,600 pounds, the XR-6 could carry enough gasoline to remain aloft five hours. It could climb to 5,000 feet in seven minutes or attain a top speed of 100 miles per hour, and it had sufficient ceiling to cross the Rockies.[15]

On March 2, 1944, Colonel H. F. Gregory of the U.S. Army Air Forces set a new world record with the XR-6. Taking a passenger in the three-place cabin, he made a non-stop flight of 387 miles from Washington National Airport to Patterson Field, Ohio.[16]

One of the earliest military tests took place in the winter of 1943-44 when an Army YR-4 was taken apart and flown 4,000 miles to Alaska in a C-46 transport plane. This helicopter was equipped with pontoon gear and used for simulated rescue missions under Arctic weather conditions. The machine performed surprisingly well at low temperatures.[17]

There was nothing simulated, however, about a helicopter lifesaving mission completed at this time by a Coast Guard pilot. On January 3, 1944, a Navy destroyer blew up off Sandy Hook, N.J. Commander Frank A. Erikson, head of the Coast Guard aviation unit at Floyd Bennett Field, flew from lower Brooklyn to the Battery in a YR-4 and landed to pick up plasma which he delivered to the explosion victims at Sandy Hook. The flight took 14 minutes at a time when military planes in the New York area were grounded by low clouds, rain, and snow.[18]

The Navy's first HNS-1 was received in November, 1943. The equivalent of the Army XR-4, it was assigned to the helicopter training base at the Coast Guard Air Station, Brooklyn, under Coast Guard supervision. Other Sikorsky craft were received from time to time until the Navy had a total of 17 in February, 1945. According to a Navy report of that month, these machines were used chiefly for training, experimentation in air-sea rescue, and transfer of personnel or mail at sea.[19]

The Navy did not find its helicopters quite satisfactory for lifting purposes. Maintenance requirements were considered excessive, and vibration discouraged air speeds higher than 80 knots with the HNS-1. In spite of these drawbacks, 36 R-5 types and as many R-6's had been ordered, though delivery in any quantity was not expected before the end of 1945. No helicopters would be available in the Pacific until early in 1946, the report concluded.[20]

Army, Navy, and Coast Guard tests were conducted to find out what the helicopter could do on water as well as land. But in time of war the results were not thoroughly analyzed or collated, and there was little co-operation between the various branches of the service. The possibility of landing on the deck of a cargo ship was established, but nobody seemed clear as to what helicopter missions might be involved. And though other tests indicated that the helicopter might be useful for submarine detection, the techniques were not worked out in detail.

The fact was that the development of a practicable American helicopter had come too late for World War II. A few Sikorsky and Platt-LePage aircraft saw Army Air Corps field duty during the last months in the rear areas of such widely separated fronts as Europe, Burma, Okinawa, New Guinea, and the Philippines. Rescue, liaison, and supply missions were reported, but for the most part the U.S. combat forces seemed to regard the helicopter of 1945 as a fascinating aeronautical freak, useful for running administrative errands. It might also be noted that the "flying windmills" were such a novelty as to be frequently in demand for public relations stunts as well as the transportation of VIP's.

The helicopter, in short, was still in its tactical swaddling clothes when World War II ended, and the problems of bringing the infant up to maturity were left for the future.

THE GREATEST MARINE MISSION

At this point it might be inquired why the Marine fliers who gave the autogiro its first field tests had taken no part as yet in helicopter developments. The answer is that most of the resources of the Marine Corps from 1933 to 1945 were devoted to the greatest mission in the history of the organization—the creation and employment of a new system of amphibious assault.

So absorbing was that task, particularly during the war years, that Marine fliers had little opportunity for helicopter experiments. Yet it was this very same amphibious mission that was soon to plunge the Marine Corps into the most intensive study of helicopter combat techniques that any branch of the American armed services had attempted.

Landings on foreign shores, many of them contested, had long been a specialty of Marines, with some 280 such operations having been carried out from the American Revolution to the end of World War II. After the transition from sail to steam, doctrines of amphibious warfare had to be revised. The cruising range of warships was limited by their fuel-carrying capacity, so that the seizure and defense of advanced bases took on a new importance in strategic calculations.

This problem came up during the Spanish-American War, when Rear Admiral William P. Sampson's squadron was unable to operate even in nearby Cuban waters without a coaling and supply base. The solution was provided by a battalion of Marines, which landed with its own artillery and secured Guantanamo Bay as a base for the naval attack on the Spanish warships bottled up in Santiago harbor.

Instruction in "advanced-base work," as it was then known, was given to Marine officers and enlisted men from 1901 to 1917. Maneuvers were carried out with the fleet whenever possible, and a school was established at Philadelphia in 1911.

Although the Marines had taken a long stride toward present-day amphibious concepts, advanced-base instruction placed the emphasis on defense rather than offensive landings. In 1917 the training program was interrupted by the American participation in World War I, when Marines were sent to

France to fight as infantry. By that time, moreover, the doctrine of amphibious warfare had been discredited by the defeat of the Allied powers at Gallipoli, which was interpreted as proof that the ship-to-shore attack could not succeed against modern defensive weapons.

Winston Churchill, the brilliant, 41-year-old First Lord of the Admiralty, was the chief British sponsor for the strategy of forcing the Dardanelles by means of a great Anglo-French amphibious assault. The object was to isolate Turkey, seize Constantinople, and smash through the unlocked back door to attack Austria and Germany. Churchill also hoped to establish direct contact with Russian allies while influencing neutral Balkan nations waiting to hail the victor.

Unhappily, the plan had been weakened by compromises and evasions before a shot was fired. Then on March 18, 1915, when the British and French fleet bombarded Turkish positions on the Asiatic shore, four battleships blew up as the penalty of faulty mine-sweeping. This was the first of the preventable reverses which continued to blight the attempt after troops were finally landed at a grievous cost in casualties. The operation dragged on for month after month until the Allies accepted defeat in December by withdrawing their land and sea forces.

Actually, the Gallipoli campaign had been bungled from start to finish. The fault had not been with the conception but with the violation of fundamental principles of strategy and tactics. Allied generals and admirals found a face-saving excuse, however, by blaming the debacle on the supposed odds against any large amphibious assault succeeding in the teeth of modern firepower.

Although this verdict was widely accepted in Europe, a good many U.S. Marine officers had their doubts. Among them was Major Earl H. Ellis, who had been an instructor before the war in advanced-base doctrine at the Naval War

College in Newport, R.I. In 1921 he completed his "Advanced Base Operations in Micronesia"—a strategic plan for assaults on Japanese-mandated islands in the Pacific which was approved by Major General John A. Lejeune, Commandant of the Marine Corps. Known as Operation Plan 712, this 50,000-word Top Secret document predicted that Japan would strike first and win initial successes.

"In order to impose our will upon Japan," wrote Ellis, "it will be necessary for us to project our fleet and land forces across the Pacific and wage war in Japanese waters. To effect this requires that we have sufficient bases to support the fleet, both during its projection and afterwards."[21]

The first, second, and third phases of Ellis' plan consisted of amphibious assaults on key islands in the Marshalls, the Carolines, and the Palau group. These objectives were to provide the fleet with bases for the reinforcement of the Philippines and the advance on Japan by way of the Marianas and Bonins.

Ellis's ideas helped to shape the first ORANGE plans approved by the Joint Board of the Army and Navy for offensive operations against Japan in the event of war. Later ORANGE plans were amended to fit changing conditions, but the invasion route of U.S. forces in the Pacific during World War II was substantially the one advocated two decades before by the Marine major.

Nor did he limit himself to strategy. Tactics were worked out in detail for amphibious operations supported by naval gunfire and land-based aerial attacks. Ellis estimated that 4,000 assault troops would be needed to secure Eniwetok in the Marshalls, and this was about the size of the Marine and Army landing force which seized the atoll in 1944.[22]

As a newly promoted lieutenant colonel, Ellis was granted an extended leave of absence in 1921. Traveling ostensibly as the Japanese-speaking commercial representative of a New

York firm, he began a tour of the mandated Pacific islands which took him from the Marshalls to the Carolines and the Palau group. This was the invasion route he had visioned, but Ellis did not complete his mysterious mission. In the spring of 1923 the Japanese authorities reported the death of the 43-year-old officer from "illness" on the island of Koror in the Palaus. American newspapers hinted broadly at foul play, but the circumstances will probably never be known.[23]

THE FLEET MARINE FORCE

In 1921, after the approval of Ellis' plan, the Advanced Base Force was moved to the new Marine Corps Schools at Quantico and reorganized as the Expeditionary Force. The change of name is indicative of a swing to an offensive amphibious strategy summed up in 1923 by General Lejeune, speaking before the Naval War College:

"The seizure and occupation or destruction of enemy bases is another important function of the Expeditionary Force of the Marine Corps."[24]

Simulated Marine assault landings during fleet maneuvers of the 1920's showed that the modern science of amphibious warfare was still in its infancy. In 1927 it became the Marines' baby when the Army and Navy deposited it on their doorstep for adoption. The Joint Board of the Army and Navy stated in a directive that the Marine Corps had the mission of "special preparation in the conduct of landing operations."[25]

This preparation was delayed several years by the necessity of keeping up expeditionary forces in Haiti, Nicaragua, and China. In 1933, however, Major General John H. Russell, Assistant Commandant, urged that a mobile Marine striking force be organized. This force, as an integral part of the fleet, was to be in readiness for tactical employment under the control of the Commander in Chief, U.S. Navy. General Russell further proposed that "Expeditionary Force" be superseded by "Fleet Marine Force" as a name better expressing the new mission.[26]

After the official acceptance of these recommendations, the Marine Corps schools at Quantico became virtually a laboratory of amphibious techniques. Classes were ordered discontinued late in 1933 and the main effort devoted to the production of a new and comprehensive manual on modern amphibious assault techniques.

Valuable even if fragmentary contributions had been made in the past by both the Army and Navy. But in all the world of 1933 there was no such thing as the proposed Marine manual. There was not even much experience as a guide, since many of the techniques proposed for the new manual had never been tested under fire. Thus it is understandable that the head of one committee at Quantico admitted that his group proceeded "with fear and trembling" while "using the imagination that God gave to us."[27]

The document which emerged in 1934 was known as the *Tentative Manual on Landing Operations*. It was to be the guide for all the joint maneuvers held by the Navy and Marine Corps down to World War II. Most of its procedures were accepted with revisions in the Navy's *Fleet Training Publication 167*, issued in 1938 as official doctrine for landing operations. And that publication in turn was the model three years later for the Army's first basic field manual for landing operations.[28]

Theory went hand in hand with experiment as Fleet Marine force landing exercises were held every year with the fleet. Marine amphibious bases were set up on both the Atlantic and Pacific coasts for training programs, and the Marine Corps Schools continued to work out solutions for new problems as they arose.

When simulated landings revealed the inadequacies of existing craft, Marine officers encouraged inventors to produce something better. Thus the LCVP (landing craft, vehicle, personnel) of World War II started life as an easily retractable boat of shallow draft and protected propeller designed by Andrew J. Higgins for the use of fur trappers in the bayous of Louisiana. He continued to experiment with Marine backing until he developed a landing craft with a bow ramp for the quick discharge of troops, trucks and small tanks.[29]

The model of 1941 was put into mass production by the Navy, which had already let a contract for the first tracked landing vehicle, known as the LVT. This machine could trace its ancestry back to an amphibian vehicle invented by Donald Roebling for rescue work in the Everglades. Marine officers were sent to Florida for inspection, and their favorable reports induced the Marine Equipment Board to accept an improved design.[30]

These were only two of the strange craft and vehicles which eventually went into production. Technology came to the aid of tactics again as new types of ordnance and ammunition were developed to meet the needs of naval gunfire for amphibious operations. Schools were set up to train Navy and Marine officers as specialists in fire-control parties. When the gunnery range of Culebra Island, off Puerto Rico, proved inadequate, the Navy purchased Bloodsworth Island in Chesapeake Bay at the suggestion of the Fleet Marine Force. It became the first amphibious gunfire range to be used for that purpose alone. All types of warships could at last be given co-ordinated practice in fire support missions.[31]

Air support offered some intricate problems, since it must be closely co-ordinated with naval gunfire, shore artillery, and troop landings. Not only would planes play a vital part in observation, reconnaissance, and spotting, but also in supporting the ship-to-shore movements and securing of beachheads. Training in two-way radio communication was given to pilots, and such alternate means of communication were established as ground panels of various colors combined with wing, engine, and searchlight signals.

Marine close air support, as it was later understood, had not yet reached full stature in the 1930's. But Fleet Marine Force doctrine called for air strikes "on targets for which ground weapons are not suitable or available."[32] And Marine fliers had already learned to combine precision with boldness in tactical support of the ground forces in the jungles of Haiti and Nicaragua.[33]

The critical moment of the amphibious landing came when the assault waves approached the beaches in the teeth of enemy fire. Such were the complexities of deploying water-borne troops that only the most detailed planning and organization could save the movement from confusion. After the men hit the beaches, therefore, they passed under the control of Marines who had the mission of maintaining order. Other specialists who landed in following waves had such duties as marking the beaches, setting up a communications center, establishing contact with firing ships and fire-control parties, evacuating the wounded, directing labor parties, controlling traffic, and expediting the movement of troops inland.

As soon as beachheads were secured, the logistical phase of the ship-to-shore movement had top priority. Ammunition, food, water, and other supplies must be landed immediately to nourish the drive inland. One of the new procedures worked out for this purpose by the Fleet Marine Force was known as combat loading—the loading of a transport with all of a unit's essential equipment and supplies in such order as to be available when needed. Studies were made and booklets published with tables for planning combat loading on a basis of estimated tonnage and cargo capacity.

Not only new techniques and new weapons but even new units were created by the Fleet Marine Force. Experience pointed the way in 1941, during the exercise at New River, N.C., when a Marine rifle battalion had to be pulled out of simulated combat for the unfamiliar work of unloading boats on the beaches.[34] The object lesson was not lost on the Marine Corps, which promptly trained experts in the logistics of amphibious operations. These service troops were later organized into the shore party battalion, a unit found only in a Marine division.

Altogether, the Fleet Marine Force training program continued at full blast for nearly a decade. New Marine bases were set up on both the Atlantic and Pacific coasts. Thousands of Navy and Marine officers and men were graduated as specialists of the great sea-ground-air team which would soon hit the beaches of Japan's island fortresses in World War II. The Marine Corps, in short, had set its sights on the ideal visioned by Earl Ellis when he wrote in 1921:

"To effect a landing under the sea and shore conditions obtaining and in the face of enemy resistance requires careful training and preparation, to say the least; and this along Marine Corps lines. It is not enough that the troops be skilled infantrymen or jungle men or artillery men of high morale: they must be skilled water and jungle men who know it can be done—Marines with Marine training."[35]

OPERATION CROSSROADS

This does not mean that the Marine Corps was fully prepared for its greatest mission on the Sunday morning when Japanese bombs fell on Pearl Harbor. Much remained to be learned in combat, of course, and such early landings as Guadalcanal and Tarawa were not model amphibious operations. But the Marines did learn from experience. Not only combat techniques but also Naval and Marine command relations showed a perceptible improvement after the first few operations.

The history of the war in the Pacific could be written largely in terms of such Army landings as Kwajalein and Ie-Shima, or such Marine landings as Saipan, Peleliu, and Iwo Jima. American victories in Africa and Europe were also made possible by Army landings based upon Fleet Marine Force doctrine. Four U.S. Army divisions were trained by the Marine Corps in amphibious tactics and took part in these operations:

1st Infantry Division... Oran, Sicily, Normandy;
3d Infantry Division... Casablanca, Sicily, Anzio;
7th Infantry Division... Attu, Kiska, Kwajalein, Leyte, Okinawa;
9th Infantry Division... Port Lyautey, Sojro, Sicily, Normandy.

Other Army divisions absorbed a good deal of Marine amphibious doctrine from the Army basic field manual of 1941 for landing operations on foreign shores, a work derived chiefly even if indirectly from the Marine *Tentative Manual for Landing Operations.*[36]

Thousands of Army and Marine troops were preparing in the summer of 1945 for what would doubtless have been the greatest assault landing of all. Fortunately, the war ended before it was necessary to hit the beaches of Japan. Japan had been thoroughly beaten, her fleet sunk, her island fortresses seized by amphibious assault, and her expeditionary forces destroyed or bypassed before the two American atomic bombs devastated Hiroshima and Nagasaki. But even as the victory was being celebrated, it remained a bitter irony that the foremost American weapon of the war should have the potentialities of canceling out the foremost American tactical development! In other words, the atomic bomb threatened to make future amphibious landings too costly in terms of casualties to be militarily profitable. Thus the Marine Corps faced the dismal possibility of having to abandon its greatest mission just after scaling the peaks of fulfillment.

The only alternative—and it was the solution occurring to every Marine officer—was to revise and strengthen amphibious techniques until they could cope with "the bomb." Marine tactics had always been primarily offensive, and it was contrary to Marine traditions to admit that any defensive weapon could be invincible.

First, of course, it would be necessary to learn more about an atomic explosion and its probable effects on an assault landing. Observers were sent to the ruins of Hiroshima and Nagasaki by all branches of the armed service, and the preliminary reports were not encouraging. Meanwhile a detailed study was being made by the U.S. Strategic Bombing Survey, and the findings were released as a secret document on June 19, 1946.[37] The effective range of an atomic air burst, according to this survey, was 2,000 yards. Within that radius all human beings in the two Japanese cities had been killed or seriously injured with the exception only of those shielded by unusually strong walls. All buildings in the area except a few reinforced concrete and steel structures were completely destroyed, and secondary fires had gutted the surviving buildings. Beyond 2,000 yards the degree of damage fell off rapidly, although burns, mild radiation sickness, and injuries from flying debris occurred at ranges up to 6,000 yards.

Valuable as this survey proved, more specific information was required for military purposes. And on January 14, 1946, the American press announced that joint Army and Navy plans for two large-scale tests had been completed and submitted to the Joint Chiefs of Staff. This was the inception of Operation CROSSROADS.[38]

Vice-Admiral W. H. P. Blandy, USN, deputy Chief of Naval Operations for special weapons, was appointed to the command of Task Force One, formed to carry out the tests at Bikini Lagoon in the western Marshalls. A fleet of 73 obsolescent ships, including battleships, cruisers, and aircraft carriers, some of them captured from the Japanese and Germans, was assigned to the operation as targets. Altogether, about 100 ships and 20,000 officers and men were to take part in the tests.[39]

The possibility of the target ships being exposed to "thousand-mile-an-hour winds, hundred-foot waves, and steel-fusing temperatures" was considered by the New York *Herald Tribune*. The air burst of the first Bikini atomic bomb, however, seemed anticlimactic in comparison. Admiral Blandy issued a statement on July 2, 1946, in which he announced that the explosion had occurred on schedule the day before. Two transports were sunk, he reported, while a destroyer capsized and sank later. Another destroyer, three battleships, a light carrier, and a heavy and light cruiser and a concrete landing ship were badly damaged. About 25 other ships were slightly damaged.[40]

On the strength of evaluations five days later it appeared that the bomb had not been as much of a dud as newsmen at first supposed. Revised Navy damage estimates disclosed that 59 of the 73 ships had been struck. Five were sunk, two battered beyond repair, seven heavily damaged, five moderately damaged, nine superficially damaged, and the remaining 31 damaged to a "negligible" extent. Captain George Lyon, USN, radiological safety officer, asserted that if the Bikini target fleet had been fully manned by crews at topside battle stations, every warship would have been in a few seconds reduced to helplessness.[41]

All branches of the service had sent high-ranking observers, the Marine Corps being represented by Lieutenant General Roy S. Geiger, commanding general of the Fleet Marine Force Pacific (FMFPac). He was particularly interested in the next Bikini test, the world's first underwater explosion of an atomic bomb, scheduled for July 25, 1946. This time the target fleet of about 85 units included LST's and amphibious landing craft.

The burst sent a column of water nearly a mile into the air, capped by gas and vapor rising to a height of 9,000 feet. The battleship *Arkansas* was destroyed and the carrier *Saratoga* sank seven hours later, her bottom plates ripped apart. Within the next few days the Japanese battleship *Nagato* went to the bottom along with some lesser targets, bringing the total to eight ships sunk. Two battleships, and two cruisers were among the 20 damaged ships.[42]

Hanson W. Baldwin summed up the results of the two tests judiciously in the New York *Times* when he commented that the atomic bomb "has not yet replaced navies, armies, or air forces and the conventional weapons, and it is not likely to do so in the foreseeable future. But it is far more than just another weapon and the air burst and subsurface burst at Bikini Atoll have illustrated its potentialities."[43]

These potentialities were viewed so gravely by General Geiger that he and his chief of staff, Colonel William F. Coleman, composed a letter which became one of the historic documents of the Marine Corps. Addressed on August 21, 1946, to Lieutenant General Alexander A. Vandegrift, Commandant of the Marine Corps, the conclusions of this letter were as follows:

"Under the assumption that atomic bombs can be produced in large quantities, that they can be used in mass attacks against an enemy objective, and that our probable future enemy will be in possession of this weapon, it is my opinion that a complete review and study of our concept of amphibious operations will have to be made. It is quite evident that a small number of atomic bombs could destroy an expeditionary force as now organized, embarked, and landed. Such a force might not fare so badly on the high seas, if properly dispersed.

"Naturally, the first thought and immediate necessity is to develop countermeasures. The ones known today are air superiority, destruction of the bomb prior to reaching its objective, and destruction of enemy plants which make the bomb. Others may be developed.

"It is my opinion that future amphibious operations will be undertaken by much smaller expeditionary forces, which will be highly trained and lightly equipped, and transported by air or submarine, and movement accomplished with a greater degree of surprise and speed than has been heretofore visualized. Or that large forces must be dispersed over a much wider front than used in past operations. With an enemy in possession of atomic bombs, I cannot visualize another landing such as was executed at Normandy or Okinawa."[44]

Such conclusions could only have been disturbing to officers who had seen Marine assault landings brought to a high pitch of effectiveness on the beaches of Guam, Tinian, and Okinawa. And the final paragraph of General Geiger's letter was calculated to start a chain reaction which has been reshaping Marine Corps amphibious doctrine ever since:

"It is trusted that Marine Corps Headquarters will consider this a very serious and urgent matter and will use its most competent officers in finding a solution to develop the technique of conducting amphibious operations in the Atomic Age."

CHAPTER IV

Search for a Solution

Copies of General Geiger's letter were forwarded from Marine Corps Headquarters in Washington to a lengthy distribution list which included high-level Naval as well as Marine officers.[1] A better qualified advocate of tactical change could not have been found in the Marine Corps of 1946. For Geiger's career of nearly 40 years exemplified the close relationship between ground and air tactics which has been an ideal of the Corps ever since it acquired its first flimsy biplane in 1912.

A native of Florida and graduate of Stetson University, Roy Stanley Geiger had enlisted as a Marine private in 1907, at the age of 22, and was commissioned a second lieutenant a few months later. In 1916, after duty with the ground forces in Nicaragua, the Philippines, and China, he completed the course as a student aviator at the Naval Aeronautic Station, Pensacola, Fla. As a Marine pilot in the first World War, he was awarded the Navy Cross. He held important Marine air commands during the next two decades, and in World War II he commanded the 1st Marine Aircraft Wing on Guadalcanal. A year later Geiger's knowledge of ground as well as air tactics was recognized when he was appointed commanding general of the First Marine (later the Third) Amphibious Corps in such operations as Bougainville, Guam, and Peleliu. In the Okinawa operation he became the first Marine to command a force on the army level when he succeeded Lieutenant General Simon Bolivar Buckner, who was killed in action. And Geiger led the Tenth Army to the successful conclusion of the final campaign of World War II.

As it proved, his letter inspired by personal observation of Operation CROSSROADS was to be one of his last services to the Marine Corps. Several months later he was incapacitated by illness, and on January 23, 1947, he died at the age of 62 in the Naval Hospital at Bethesda, Md.

Before his death, he was to have the assurance that his letter had aroused the Marine Corps to immediate action. General Alexander A. Vandegrift, eighteenth Commandant, was a veteran of only two years' less service than Geiger. A native Virginian who had attended the University of Virginia, he was commissioned a second lieutenant in 1909. After service in Nicaragua, Haiti, Mexico, and China, he won the Medal of Honor as commanding general of the Marines who landed on Guadalcanal in 1942 and gave the Japanese their first serious reverse in ground warfare. The first Marine general to win four-star rank on active duty, he became commandant in 1944.

In response to the Geiger message, Vandegrift addressed a letter of his own on September 13, 1946, to a Special Board consisting of Major General Lemuel C. Shepherd, Jr., Assistant Commandant and Chief of Staff; Major General Field Harris, Assistant Commandant (Air) and Director of Marine Aviation; and Brigadier General Oliver P. Smith, Commandant of the Marine Corps Schools.

"Certainly," wrote the Commandant, "the advent of the atomic explosive may alter radically the means and methods of waging war as they existed in the last conflict, and on no concept will the impact probably be mightier than in the field of amphibious operations. Carrying the war across the oceans or Arctic wastes to an enemy armed with the atomic explosive must inevitably mean, to mention a few obvious items, tremendously greater dispersion on the land and sea and in the air, very rapid or thoroughly concealed movement coupled with the greatest possible surprise, light armament together with correspondingly increased hitting and firepower, and means of protection against atomic blasts and radioactive poisoning.

"These and other unmentioned requirements are not insuperable, but in surmounting them revolutionary measures may be required. Details are neither expected nor desirable at this time, but general principles must be determined in order to orient the effort of the Marine Corps away from the last war and toward the next."[2]

Italics have been added to lines which at that time impressed a Marine officer, Colonel Merrill B. Twining, as "conveying an appeal of the utmost gravity and immediacy."[3]

The Commandant's letter concluded: "The sense of urgency Lieutenant General Geiger expresses . . . is the feeling of the Marine Corps. Accordingly the Special Board, Commandant of the Marine Corps, is directed to propose, after thorough research and deliberation, the broad concepts and principles which the Marine Corps should follow, and the major steps which it should take, to fit it to wage successful amphibious warfare, at some future date, against an enemy armed with the atomic explosive."[4]

THE MARINE CORPS SCHOOLS

It was inevitable that the problem would be left on the doorstep of the Marine Corps Schools, which had brought the Fleet Marine Force up to maturity. Other branches of the armed service also have their professional schools, of course, but Marines like to believe that there is none to compare with the institution founded at the Quantico base in

1920, when the former Infantry School and Training School were combined under a single management.

Few Marine officers reach the rank of lieutenant colonel without having had a tour of duty at the Schools as student, instructor, or both. This makes for a spirit of cohesiveness in a Corps which has no academy of its own. Marine officers come from every college and university in the land, though a limited number of graduates from the U.S. Naval Academy are permitted each year to choose service in the Marine Corps.* Generally speaking, however, the Marine Corps Schools are the only common Alma Mater of officers who are likely to have completed the junior course as lieutenants or captains. The careers of the Special Board members could scarcely be called typical, in view of their high attainments, but the following condensed biographical sketches indicate that all three had spent several years at the Marine Corps Schools.

MAJOR GENERAL, LEMUEL C. SHEPHERD, Jr. Born in Virginia, 1896, and educated at the Virginia Military Institute. Commissioned in the Marine Corps, 1917, he was twice wounded in France during World War I. Following sea duty and shore duty in China, he returned for a course in the Marine Corps Schools. Then came field duty in Haiti and a course at the Naval War College, at Newport, R.I. In 1939 Colonel Shepherd began a second tour of duty at Quantico, starting as instructor and ending three years later as Commandant of the Marine Corps Schools. In World War II, promoted to the rank of brigadier general, he was ADC of the 1st Marine Division on Cape Gloucester, and led the 1st Provisional Marine Brigade in the amphibious assault on

---

* About 65 graduates of the Academy each year, or slightly more than 7 per cent, are granted this privilege. Preference is given to men who have served in the Marine Corps and to sons of Marines. The remaining vacancies, which are never enough to satisfy all applicants, are filled on a basis of class standings and drawing of lots.

Guam. In 1945 he commanded the 6th Marine Division on Okinawa. Returning to the United States, he was named Assistant Commandant and Chief of Staff in 1946.

MAJOR GENERAL FIELD HARRIS. Born in Kentucky, 1895, he was commissioned as a Marine second lieutenant in 1917, shortly after graduation from the U.S. Naval Academy. Three years of duty in Cuba and the Philippines were followed by a like period of Headquarters duty in Washington. In 1928 Harris finished a year's course at the Marine Corps Schools and took flight training at Pensacola. Designated a Naval Aviator in 1929, he held several Marine air commands before attending the Naval War College and returning briefly to the Marine Corps Schools. In World War II he participated as Chief of Staff or Commandant Aircraft in the Guadalcanal, Northern Solomons, and Green Island operations. After the war he was named Assistant Commandant (Air) and Director of Aviation.

BRIGADIER GENERAL OLIVER P. SMITH. Born in Texas, 1893, he graduated in 1916 from the University of California. Commissioned in the Marine Corps the following year, he was assigned to duty in Guam. Sea duty and service in Haiti led in 1931 to a year at the Army Infantry School, Fort Benning, Ga., and a first tour of duty at the Marine Corps Schools. Then came two years in Paris at the office of the U.S. Naval Attaché and courses at the École Superieure de Guerre. Upon his return in 1936, he became an instructor during the next three years at the Marine Corps Schools. His service in World War II included the command of a battalion in Iceland and a regimental command on New Britain. As assistant commander of the 1st Marine Division, he participated in the Peleliu operation, and on Okinawa he was Deputy Chief of Staff of the Tenth Army. When the operation ended, General Smith returned to the Marine Corps Schools as Commandant.

It would fill a page to list in detail the honors and decorations awarded to the three Special Board members, including medals won for bravery in action. For an extensive firsthand acquaintance with actual combat is another bond between Marine officers in addition to the Marine Corps Schools. The opportunity has seldom been lacking during the present century, owing to the "incidents" which have kept the Marines busy in undeclared little wars.

Instructors and students at Quantico in the autumn of 1946 were nearly all veterans of hard-fought amphibious operations in the Pacific during the last few years. Purple Heart ribbons were the rule rather than the exception. Yet in spite of the uniforms seen on every side, the Marine base had a strangely serene look. Time and weather had mellowed the red brick halls, grass-bordered walks, and athletic fields until they gave the appearance of a secluded campus.

Despite this peaceful atmosphere, the business of the Marine Corps Schools was to fit men for combat. The Marines in the classroom consisted of regulars and reservists, senior and junior ranks, officers and enlisted men, air and ground specialists. All the activities on this military campus had a common denominator which has been defined by Lieutenant General Franklin A. Hart, a later commandant of the Marine Corps Schools:

"The Marine Corps exists, and has existed for nearly two centuries, because of its demonstrated ability to furnish fast-moving, hard-hitting striking forces at a moment's notice. . . . The special task of the Marine Corps Schools is that of continuously retranslating the general concept of readiness into the specific terms required in a constantly changing world and reindoctrinating Marines and their associates in these new specific terms. Quantico draws its inspiration from the past but keeps its eyes firmly on the present and the future."[5]

For functional purposes the Schools were divided into the Development Center and Educational Center. The first, as its name implies, had the mission of developing the weapons, equipment, and tactical tools needed for specific tasks; and the amphibian tractor of World War II was one of its greatest achievements. The Educational Center consisted of a headquarters, eight component schools, and seven academic sections such as Aviation, Combined Arms, Logistics, and Intelligence.

The Basic School trained officer candidates for commissioned rank, and enlisted men for noncommissioned grades. Company officers attended the Junior School, while the Senior School prepared officers of higher rank for command and staff duties on the battalion, regimental, or division level. Normally, according to General Hart, "no distinction is made between air and ground officer students and their curricula include both air and ground subjects. The breadth of this educational approach has much to do with the success of the Marine air-ground team."[6]

A further claim to distinction lay in the fact that the manuals and textbooks of the Marine Corps Schools were written by students as well as instructors. As many as a score of officers might be assigned to such a project, each developing some special subject for later assembly and revision. In this manner the first comprehensive manual of landing operations was composed in 1934, with all classes of the Marine Corps Schools being dismissed for the purpose.

A reinforced battalion which comprised infantry, artillery, tanks, engineers, and amphibious vehicles was available to put doctrine to the test, and aircraft of various types were provided by the Marine Corps Air Station. It was not too far-fetched, therefore, when Marines described the Quantico base as the "tactical laboratory" of the Corps.[7]

EARLY HELICOPTER CONCEPTS

In the autumn of 1946, as might be supposed, there was no topic of more gripping interest at Quantico than atomic weapons and their threat to the Marine amphibious mission. So far, the possibilities of the helicopter as a tactical antidote had won little recognition. The Navy had other fish to fry when CNO (the Chief of Naval Operations) announced on June 6, 1946, that the Secretary of the Navy had approved a helicopter development program. The purpose was to "provide for comprehensive trial and experimentation with existing types and concomitant with advancements in future helicopter design."[8]

The Navy was represented by a single helicopter at Operation CROSSROADS the following month, with Captain Clayton C. Marcy, USN, at the controls. The original intention had been for the HOS-1A (Navy version of the YR-6) to be utilized in making radiological surveys and picking up dirt and water samples in the blast area. But the danger of a forced landing (several of which had already occurred) caused the machine to be used for lesser tasks such as shuttle service, observation, photographic errands, and radar calibration.[9]

On July 23, 1946, CNO directed the Commander of the Operational Development Force "to evaluate the helicopter for general utility duties." The project was given Priority "C" and such tests were suggested as torpedo tracking, radar alignment, air-sea rescue, and "mercy and transportation missions for the transfer of patients, medical personnel, and medical supplies from ship to ship, ship to shore, and shore to ship."[10]

Little progress was made until the Navy commissioned Squadron VX-3 on September 10, 1946. Captain Marcy, USN, and Commander Charles E. Huston, USN, were placed in command of an experimental unit at the Naval Air Station,

Lakehurst, N.J., which numbered seven other officers and 80 enlisted men with 14 utility helicopters. Operational control was maintained by the Commander of the Operational Development Force, U.S. Fleet.[11]

The Marine Corps had meanwhile launched its own helicopter development program, and in the summer of 1946 two sets of recommended missions were submitted to the Commandant. Although General Geiger's letter was written on July 29, only four days after the underwater explosion at Bikini, he made no specific mention of amphibious tasks among the following suggestions:

"Wire laying over inaccessible terrain and in cases where time is a vital factor.

"Aerial observation for field artillery.

"Messenger service in combat operations.

"Evacuation from areas where vehicles or conventional aircraft cannot be used.

"Supply to otherwise inaccessible units.

"Rapid reconnaissance by assault troops."[12]

General Smith, the Commandant of the Marine Corps Schools, evidently saw some possibilities for using the new type of aircraft in amphibious as well as general ground operations. His letter of August 9, 1946, contained these recommendations for the helicopter development program:

"Delivery of last-minute intelligence to all echelons aboard ship in approach phase of amphibious operations.

"Landing and withdrawal of small reconnaissance patrols when security is not jeopardized.

"Rapid transfer of important PW's and captured documents from forward units to higher echelons afloat and ashore.

"Air evacuation of wounded from front lines.

"Artillery spotting in addition to present liaison type aircraft."[13]

Shortly after the two generals sent in their recommendations, the Special Board came to grips with the problems posed by the Commandant's letter of September 13, 1946. As a first step, the Board appointed a Secretariat consisting of three officers on duty as instructors in the Marine Corps Schools— Colonel Merrill B. Twining, Colonel Edward C. Dyer, and Lieutenant Colonel Clair W. Shisler.[14]

The initial task assigned to the Secretariat was to conduct a detailed research into the probable effects of atomic explosions on future amphibious operations. In a memorandum of October 4, the Commandant requested Vice-Admiral Blandy, who had commanded the task force of Operation CROSSROADS, to make available to the Marine researchers all conclusions drawn from the Bikini tests, now that enough time had elapsed for the findings to be analyzed.[15]

TOP SECRET WATER COLORS

Preoccupation with this subject was not confined to the three members of the Secretariat. In all Quantico there was no more engaging topic of conversation than the possibilities of strengthening Marine amphibious techniques by the use of new types of aircraft for troop landings. But even though the threat of atomic weapons was taken seriously, these Marine officers discussed it with gusto and enthusiasm. The creative side of tactics had a fascination for veterans of the amphibious operations which penetrated Japan's island defenses, and Lieutenant Colonel Loren E. Haffner expressed his ideas pictorially. His inspiration, he recalled long later, came from Colonel Robert A. Hogaboom. A native of Mississippi who was commissioned in the Marines after graduating from the Naval Academy in 1925, Hogaboom had participated in the Kiska, Attu, Saipan, and Tinian operations. Returning for a three-year tour of duty as instructor in the Marine Corps Schools, he convinced Haffner that the helicopter could be adapted to the uses of amphibious operations of the Atomic Age.

Haffner had just "integrated" as a regular officer after having come up as a reservist. Thirty-two years old at this time, he had been born and educated in Spokane, Wash. A talented though untrained artist, he made water colors his medium for what he has described as "a fanciful ship-to-shore movement employing 'copters. . . . I painted about a dozen scenes showing a fast striking preliminary shore bombardment by small craft employing recoilless weapons, etc. Then I illustrated the ship-to-shore movement of troop-carrying 'copters rising from carrier decks and moving across beach areas and landing directly or in close proximity to enemy-held areas. The whole series of pictures was bound in a book colorfully painted on the outside with a mushroom cloud and the caption, *Ship to Shore Movement in the Atomic Age.*"[16]

Colonel Hogaboom and Colonel Thomas J. Colley of the Senior School were first to inspect the production. They agreed that it should be seen and admired by the Research Section of the Development Center.

"Three days later," added Haffner, "I was called up to the Research Section and told that my book was right along the line of Marine and Navy thinking, and they asked to retain it. The sketches that I had so casually carried around for several days were now stamped TOP SECRET, and I couldn't get my clutches on them. In fact, I never saw them again."

The disappearance is still a mystery. No trace of the water colors could be found among present-day records, and it is suspected that they may be a trophy of some Marine officers' club.

The artist continued to be in demand for his imaginative sketches of the tactical millennium. As his next venture, he painted colored slides for Colonel Hogaboom and the other Marine officers, including himself, who were scheduled to address the Armed Forces Staff College at Norfolk, Va. This episode was related by Haffner in a letter written in 1953 when he was assistant Chief of Staff G-3 of the 1st Marine Division in Korea:

"I got the idea that something should be added to the presentation that would be more futuristic than just rehashing the techniques with which we wound up the Okinawa campaign. We had about six days before we hit the road, and it was a late time to be throwing more balls into the juggling act. But I decided to have a colored slide presentation somehow.

"As there was still no tactical concept for a ship-to-shore movement employing helicopters, I decided once again to dream up a ship-to-shore technique and present a verbal dissertation to be accompanied by projected slides. I wrote the script, took two days' leave, and set up my drawing board in the living room at home. Considerable moral support was received from various visitors like Lieutenant Colonel William K. Jones, who dropped in to offer advice. In two days and nights I managed to run off a dozen or so drawings showing helicopters coming in from aircraft carriers . . . moving inland and landing reconnaissance and weapons units on top of hills; landing assault forces on or near enemy objectives; supplying and evacuating wounded from positions near the front lines; pursuing the defeated enemy by leap-froging 'copters; and finally landing supports and reserves on the secured beaches from huge assault seaplane transports."

The fantastic terrain of the slides derived from Haffner's memories of the Iceland occupation as well as his participation in the Guadalcanal, Tarawa, Saipan, and Tinian operations. At the final rehearsal, before going to Norfolk, he read his script and showed the slides to a Quantico audience which included General Smith and such helicopter enthusiasts as Lieutenant Colonel Victor H. Krulak and Lieutenant Colonel Donald McP. Weller. They agreed that the performance should be repeated for the Armed Forces Staff College. "At

Norfolk," Haffner's letter concluded, "Colonel Hogaboom wound up the two-day session with the helicopter fantasy, and the applause was loud and long. . . . I still have copies of those slides, rather crudely drawn and showing helicopters which were aerodynamically unsound. However, I believe that these drawings and presentations helped to establish our Marine pioneering status."[17]

THE SPECIAL BOARD REPORT

The Secretariat of the Special Board had meanwhile been busy. Colonel Twining made amphibious tactics his province during the weeks of research, and the aeronautical or communications problems usually fell to Colonel Dyer.[18] Both officers were graduates of the U.S. Naval Academy and the flight training course of the Naval Air Station, Pensacola, Fla. But Dyer specialized in Marine aircraft operations afterward while Twining had both staff and line duty with the ground forces.

In 1923, at the age of 21, Twining graduated from the Naval Academy, four years after an older brother finished at West Point.* Portland, Oreg., has been his legal residence throughout a long Marine career which included the Guadalcanal landing and service on General Vandegrift's staff in later amphibious operations of World War II. Returning to the United States, he became Chief of Operations and Training and subsequently the Executive Officer of the Marine Corps Schools.

Dyer was born in 1907 at Baltimore, Md. After finishing his flight training, he served in a Marine air observation squadron on the USS *Lexington* and had a two-year tour of duty in the Bureau of Aeronautics, Navy Department. In 1936, following postgraduate studies at the Naval Academy, he transferred to

* The brother, General Nathan F. Twining, was named Chief of Staff of the U.S. Air Force in 1953.

the University of California and received a Master of Science degree upon completing a course in radio engineering. During World War II he headed the Communications Section, Division of Aviation, and participated in the Leyte campaign as operations officer of the Strategic Air Force, Central Pacific. Returning from the Pacific, he became commanding officer of the Marine Corps Aviation Technical School at Quantico.

Lieutenant Colonel Clair W. Shisler, the third member of the Secretariat, was born at Canton, Ohio, in 1910. After serving six years in the Marine Corps as an enlisted man, he completed the basic training course at Quantico and was commissioned as a second lieutenant. During World War II he distinguished himself as a troop leader in such assault landings as Guam and Okinawa. Afterward he returned to the Marine Corps Schools as instructor.

Shisler acted as secretary of the Secretariat and compiled the notes of the interviews with Admiral Blandy. More than two months of concentrated research went into the project as a whole. Twining was the tactical analyst of the team, while Dyer made it his task to study the feasibility and availability of new types of aircraft. His old Annapolis classmate, Captain Marcy, USN, then commanding the new Naval helicopter experiment squadron, probably knew as much about the military possibilities of rotary-wing aircraft as any man in the country. He contributed his practical knowledge, and Dyer also consulted with Captain William V. Davis, USN, chief of the Operational Development Force.[19]

The Secretariat completed its research early in December, 1946, and summarized the findings for the approval of the three generals of the Special Board. And on the 16th the Board submitted the report to the Commandant.

Iwo Jima, the most costly of Marine amphibious operations, was cited to illustrate the probable effects of atomic explosions. About 6,775 Americans, largely Marines, had been killed in this operation, and nearly 20,000 wounded or otherwise incapacitated—a higher toll than the Federal forces suffered at Gettysburg. Yet the Special Board report made it starkly plain that the losses of Iwo Jima would have been much increased if the enemy had used atomic bombs:

"A formation of landing craft with embarked troops would be affected in the following ways by atomic explosion in the form of an airplane bomb, guided missile, or static underwater mine.

"a. Destruction of all landing craft and occupants within a radius of 2,000 yards.

"b. Swamping or capsizing of many landing craft within a radius of 4,000 yards.

"In addition, troop personnel would be exposed to flash and the radiological effect of poisoned water spray up to much greater distances. It is therefore not an exaggeration to state that a single atomic explosion during a ship-to-shore movement such as at Iwo Jima would have destroyed the combat effectiveness of two divisions, inflicting at a single blow casualties many times those actually experienced during the entire operation."

An increased dispersion of landing craft would have reduced losses, the report continued, "but only at the risk of defeat ashore through the slow piecemeal commitment of forces. This would likewise deprive the amphibious attack of its greatest characteristic—the ability to strike swiftly and in overwhelming force. It would therefore appear that some alternate means must be devised to make the initial assault landing in the force necessary for success yet without exposure to overwhelming loss from atomic attack."

Submarine troop landings were viewed as a limited and dubious alternative. Nor did an analysis of the three available means of airborne attack—parachutes, gliders, and transport planes—offer much encouragement. These methods, according to the Board report, had the following weaknesses:

"They are, to a considerable degree, dependent upon existing airstrips at the objective (for cargo aircraft), suitable landing zones (for gliders) or suitable dropping zones (for paratroops).

"They are dependent upon friendly air bases, adequately equipped and supplied to support the operation. Should these bases be at a great distance from the objective, the problems of intervening weather, navigation, and long-range fighter support all further complicate the problem."[20]

No military report is ever complete without a section labeled "conclusions," and it was here that the Special Board held forth hope for future Marine amphibious operations. "The answer," continued the report, "lies in a wide dispersion of our attack force, a rapid concentration of our landing force by means other than small boats or amphibians, and thereafter maintaining close contact with the enemy. Airborne operations by land-plane transport, by parachute or by glider are not suitable for Marine Corps employment. . . . Submarine transports will be useful but to a limited extent. The development of a combination of large flying boats and helicopters will overcome the limitations of a purely airborne method, keep the enterprise a purely naval one, and permit its rapid exploitation and support from widely dispersed and more economical surface vessels."[21]

Unfortunately, it appeared, there was no such thing in 1946 as a large transport seaplane, or "flying LST," immediately available for Marine amphibious operations. Nor was there a troop-carrying helicopter that could lift more than two or three men with combat equipment.

Old timers were reminded of the 1930's at Quantico, when Fleet Marine Force doctrine was based upon troop landings in amphibious tractors before any practicable vehicles of the sort were in existence. But it was encouraging to remember that Marine officers of those days had worked with civilian inventors until usable machines were developed according to their specifications.

The Special Board saw no hope of a Navy-designed Flying LST being produced before 1952. The Martin "Mars" was mentioned as a prospect along with a large flying boat under construction by Howard Hughes, the California millionaire who made a hobby of aircraft design. The four-motored Mars, with an empty weight of 75,000 pounds and a useful load (cargo and fuel) of 63,000 pounds, was to have a troop-carrying capacity of 133 equipped men in seats. Even more impressive were the statistics of the eight-motored Hughes prototype transport seaplane, which was designed to carry a 44-ton tank as part of its payload of 120,000 pounds. Clamshell doors and a landing ramp could be added to the design, but the Special Board did not seem very optimistic about the outlook for either the Hughes or Martin seaplane being delivered in adequate numbers "within the next five years."*

It was obvious, even at this early date, that the Board had more faith in the helicopter.[22] From an aeronautical viewpoint, there was good reason to believe that a practicable machine with a troop-lifting capacity of eight or ten men would soon be ready for delivery. Tactically speaking, the Board concluded that the helicopter offered "a practical means of overcoming the effects of dispersion while likewise reducing exposure to the amphibious attack forces. In addition, it possesses many of the advantages of the airborne attack with few attendant disadvantages. Under the method visual-

* The doubts of the Special Board were upheld by subsequent events. Although the enormous Hughes seaplane was built and tested, it did not prove satisfactory. Six Mars seaplanes—one JRM-1 and five JRM-2's—were delivered by Glenn Martin to the Navy. The first was considered experimental. One of the JRM-2's crashed, and the remaining four were still flying in 1953, though no more of this type had been built in the past six years.

ized, helicopters would be carried by transport carriers with additional machines carried by transports and LST's. The modern helicopter can take off and land vertically, using small platforms or open spaces on the decks of transport and cargo vessels. It can cruise at speeds of 100 knots or more and land vertically in any small open area on shore. Personnel can be landed in proper formation on the flanks and rear of the hostile position. Palletized supplies can be slung under the fuselage and landed in or near dumps without further handling. The speed of the helicopter renders the degree of transport dispersion at sea a matter of no disadvantage and likewise introduces a time space factor in landing that will avoid presenting at any one time a remunerative atomic target.

"The helicopter in flight is more vulnerable than a landing craft but it is considered that this disadvantage can be overcome by the provision of fighter escort and heavy saturation of enemy anti-aircraft defenses. The relatively unlimited choice of landing area is likewise a factor in reducing the probability of serious losses in landing.

"The helicopter method would be used primarily for the initial assault only. Upon seizure of a landing area from flank or rear, resort would be made to the conventional and more economic means of landing supplies and heavy equipment by means of landing ships or cargo seaplanes sufficiently dispersed to avoid presenting a profitable target. Our helicopter units will have further use subsequent to the assault in operations ashore by providing a valuable means for the movement of troops and cargo when speed is a necessary element."[23]

The report concluded with a proposed program for the development of both helicopters and transport seaplanes by the Marine Corps during the next two years. Studies as to the tactical possibilities of seaplanes were to be continued, and it was suggested that a Marine helicopter experimental squadron be organized "at the earliest practicable date . . . for the training of pilots and mechanics and for practical development of the air tactics and techniques of a ship-to-shore operation by helicopter." A further suggestion was that the Marine Corps Schools be directed to submit a tentative doctrine for helicopter employment.[24]

The Special Board report went to the Commandant on December 16, 1946. Three days later General Vandegrift sent it to the Marine Corps Schools with the comment:

"The Commandant of the Marine Corps concurs in the Board's conclusions and has directed that steps be taken to implement the development program outlined in its report."[25]

With these words the Marine Corps turned its back on the military past and committed itself to planning for the Atomic Age.

CHAPTER V

Doctrine and Experiment

Early in 1947 it grew evident that the Marine Corps Schools evaluated the helicopter more highly for tactical purposes than Flying LST types of aircraft. Not only was the large transport seaplane considered too vulnerable for future amphibious operations, but it did not lend itself readily to tactics of dispersion. Finally, there was the objection that present examples were at the experimental stage, and many of the aeronautical "bugs" had not yet been eliminated.

References to Flying LST types became more and more infrequent in Marine doctrinal writings. And by the end of 1947 the giant seaplanes were usually mentioned only in connection with such logistical missions as bringing in supplies after assault troops had been put ashore by helicopters and landing craft to secure the beachhead.

The year started hopefully, with the Commandant's endorsement of the development program being followed by the partial approval of CNO.[1] There was no imminent prospect of helicopters being delivered at Quantico, but it could never have been said that Marine officers were petty in their outlook. At a time when no rotary-wing machine in existence could lift more than the pilot and two fully equipped men, one school of Marine thought held that the most acceptable helicopter for landing amphibious combat troops was the XH-16.

This was the Air Force designation for a Piasecki transport

helicopter. All proportions of the prototype machine were fabulous as compared with anything in the rotary-wing past. Two enormous rotors in tandem were to be powered by two Pratt and Whitney engines of 1,650 horsepower each. The capacity was announced as 42 places, though a payload of 6,000 pounds would not indicate that more than 25 to 30 troops could be lifted with full equipment. A range of 175 miles and a cruising speed of 87 to 96 knots were claimed for a helicopter which interested the Air Force for its possibilities in Arctic rescue missions.

The XH-16 was still far from the testing stage, and predictions as to actual delivery remained vague even if roseate. Nevertheless, many Marine officers were in favor of developing a helicopter of true transport capacity rather than compromising with smaller machines.

This question was not settled definitely until 1949. Opinion at Quantico was also divided meanwhile as to the organization of helicopter tactical units and the numbers of aircraft required.

Here again the statistics seem optimistic in the light of later experience. One of the early doctrinal studies recommended that a Marine helicopter wing be composed of 240 aircraft, each "capable of carrying a payload of fifteen (15) fully armed troops or four thousand (4,000) pounds of cargo."

There were not at that time as many as 240 helicopters in the entire world. Yet this Marine report contemplated the "simultaneous lift of one RCT [regimental combat team], helicopter borne." And it was emphasized that "where helicopters are of lesser capacity the numbers of helicopters in helicopter units should be increased as necessary to provide for maintaining the tactical integrity of troop organizations."[2]

The doctrinal pioneers who wrote these words can only seem visionary when viewed with the infallible wisdom of retrospect. It must be remembered, however, that Marine documents of this sort are often composed on a basis of the equipment believed to be *needed* for a tactical mission, not the equipment immediately available. And in 1947 nothing seemed impossible in the field of the helicopter, which had made such astonishing progress during the past few years. Not only were the aircraft themselves strange and wonderful, but the careers of the leading designers might have been thought too incredible for fiction.

Consider the Russian émigré occupying a small furnished room in New York during the early 1920's while making a living by lecturing on mathematics to his fellow countrymen. This was Igor Sikorsky, who had designed the world's first four-motored airplane while still a subject of the Czar. Finding a refuge in America after the Russian Revolution, he returned to aircraft design and built his first plane in a Long Island farmyard. During the 1930's he made a new name for himself with his four-engine Clippers for Pan American transoceanic flights. Then, at the height of his success, he calmly announced that he was returning to his first love, the helicopter. Starting in middle age where he had left off as a youth in Russia after two failures, he experimented for five years before producing the VS-300 approved by the U.S. Army Air Corps in 1942. Within the next five years, Sikorsky was to build the world's largest helicopter plant in a Connecticut town and introduce the onion-shaped dome of his Russian Orthodox church among its early American steeples.

The rise of Lawrence D. Bell, though less spectacular, was also founded on a lifelong devotion to aviation. Beginning as an employee of Glenn L. Martin in 1912 at the age of 18, he worked up to be general manager. In 1928 he became vice-president in charge of sales for Consolidated Aircraft Company, and seven years later he organized the Bell Aircraft Corporation at Buffalo, N. Y., which manufactured the P-39 Aircobra fighter of World War II. In 1943 Bell entered the helicopter field, specializing in a light utility machine, and made his first delivery to the Navy in 1947.

The third of the leading helicopter manufacturers came up during the great industrial depression of the 1930's when pessimists lamented that opportunity had vanished in America. The son of a Polish immigrant who became a Philadelphia tailor, Frank N. Piasecki worked for the Kellett Autogiro Company, graduated in mechanical engineering from the Towne School of the University of Pennsylvania, earned a degree in aeronautical engineering at New York University, and became a Platt-LePage designer—all by the time he was 20 years old. In 1940, upon reaching voting age, this precocious young man formed an aeronautical engineering firm with five associates. Three years later a helicopter of his design became the second in this country to be publicly demonstrated in flight.

It was scarcely to be expected, in view of such accomplishments, that representatives of the Piasecki plant at Morton, Pa., should err on the dark side when making predictions either as to the performance or availability of the XH-16. But the Bureau of Aeronautics of the U.S. Navy remained to be convinced before the machine could be officially approved for purchase by the Marine Corps. And the Bureau required a great deal of convincing.

THE NAVY-MARINE TEAM

Then, as now, the general public had only a vague idea of the relationship of the Navy and Marine Corps within the Department of the Navy—that vast over-all organization headed by the Secretary of the Navy and composed of civilian as well as military personnel. No better definition has ever appeared, however, than the one given in an address by Secretary of the Navy Robert B. Anderson to the graduates of the

Marine officers' candidate course at Quantico in the early autumn of 1953.

"New organizational charts," said Mr. Anderson, "will show the Commandant of the Marine Corps as my Marine Corps command assistant, reporting directly to me in all matters directly pertaining to the Marine Corps. In matters wherein the Chief of Naval Operations acts as my naval executive, your commandant will continue to be responsible to me through him. Headquarters Marine Corps, the Marine Corps supporting establishment, and all Marine Corps forces not otherwise assigned are now fixed firmly and irrevocably within the exclusive command structure of the Marine Corps.

"The Fleet Marine Forces, being an agency of the fleet commanders, are under their operational command, but of course continue to be under the administrative control of the Commandant of the Marine Corps, who is responsible for their training and readiness."

Not all of these distinctions, to be sure, would have applied in 1947, since Navy-Marine relations have been shaped gradually by circumstances through the years. But Secretary Anderson was calling attention to the spirit and tradition of the command structure when he described the Marine Corps as "the partner of the Navy."

"Together," he continued, "they have but one reason for being: to insure the freedom of the seas in peacetime, and insure their control and use on our side in time of war.

"They are in every sense of the word a team—an indispensable team to an America dependent absolutely upon free use of the seas both in peace and in war.

"Separate but inseparable, they have throughout their long association set an example of co-operation and mutual support unexcelled anywhere in the annals of military history."[3]

Navy-Marine teamwork at its best could have been found in

the operations of the Bureau of Aeronautics, which was staffed by Marine as well as Navy flying officers. The scope of the Bureau's responsibilities has been defined in U.S. Navy Regulations as "the design, development, procurement, production, test, fitting out, maintenance, alteration, repair, and material effectiveness of all Navy and Marine Corps aircraft . . . including components and equipment thereof, and photographic and aerological equipment; the research therein; and all pertinent functions relating thereto."[4]

This meant, in less official language, that "BuAer" had the last word in virtually everything relating to Navy or Marine Corps air equipment. New types of aircraft were given the most rigorous tests, but in 1947 few standards or precepts existed as a yardstick for judging helicopters. Several high-level Naval officers of the Bureau were a bit skeptical at first as to the value of rotary-wing aircraft in future amphibious operations, but the Marine concept found a stout champion in General Field Harris. Although the Director of Marine Aviation had himself been a reluctant convert after a career devoted to conventional aircraft, he became an influential spokesman for Marine helicopter doctrine with the Bureau of Aeronautics.[5]

Not all Marine air officers of this preliminary period, for that matter, were in entire agreement with the helicopter development program. Colonel Dyer encountered "grave doubts" based not so much on disapproval of the concept as a low opinion of the aeronautical progress made by the helicopter itself.[6]

Official approval of the development program had by no means ended the labors of the Special Board and its Secretariat. The aeronautical side was mainly Dyer's responsibility, but Twining accompanied him on several visits to the Sikorsky and Piasecki plants for the purpose of acquainting the manufacturers with Marine Corps requirements. Both officers kept in close touch with BuAer.

The name of Lieutenant Colonel Samuel R. Shaw also appears in connection with Secretariat activities. A native of Cleveland, Ohio, he enlisted in the Marine Corps in 1928, at the age of 18, and entered the U.S. Naval Academy two years later. Graduating in 1934, he became a lieutenant colonel early in World War II and a troop leader in Pacific operations. In 1946, as an instructor at Quantico, he devoted much of his time to the helicopter development program.

Helicopter doctrine owed a great deal at this period to Twining's analyses and interpretations. Where rotary-wing aircraft had been described as slow in contrast to the conventional plane, he insisted that the only valid comparison was with the boats or amphibian vehicles used to land troops, or with the wheeled or tracked vehicles of supply. On this basis the helicopter was from four to ten times as fast as previous means, even though it could not compete with the fixed-wing plane for speed.

The bugbear of excessive helicopter vulnerability was also cut down to reasonable size by Twining. He pointed out that if transport helicopters needed fighter protection during a ship-to-shore movement, so did troopships, landing boats, and amphibian vehicles. And if the helicopter wasn't as fast as conventional planes, only the helicopter could maneuver its way out of danger by changing speed, reversing, darting straight up or down, and dodging sidewise. Only the helicopter, moreover, could take advantage of the terrain by flying in defilade or hovering at low altitude.[7]

PROBLEMS OF DOCTRINE

In response to the Commandant's directive, officers of the Marine Corps Schools were busy on problems of helicopter doctrine in 1947 before there was any immediate prospect of setting up an experimental squadron. The Chief of Naval Operations had given a partial approval of the Marine development program. His reservations did not imply disapprobation but simply lack of funds as a consequence of the cuts in military appropriations voted by Congress after World War II. There was also the fact that helicopters could not be delivered at Quantico throughout the entire year by plants swamped with orders.[8]

An incentive was provided at this time by a historical repetition after a lapse of two decades. Just as the Joint Board of the Army and Navy had given the Marine Corps of 1927 the mission of preparing for landing operations, so the National Security Act of 1947 made it the function of the Corps "to provide fleet marine forces of combined arms, together with supporting air components, for service with the fleet in the seizure and defense of advanced naval bases and for the conduct of such land operations as may be essential to the prosecution of a naval campaign."*

Officers of the Marine Corps Schools went ahead as best they could to work out problems of doctrine. Few of them, with the exception of Twining and Dyer, had ever been up in a helicopter. This did not detract from the zeal of men who studied various aspects of the subject according to the lights of their military experience and education.

One of the most energetic was Lieutenant Colonel Krulak, who had entered the Naval Academy in 1930 from Denver, Colo. A decorated, Purple Heart veteran of Pacific operations in World War II, his service was divided between staff and line. Late in 1945 he returned to Quantico as Assistant Director of the Senior Schools. As his contribution to the helicopter program, he wrote prolifically and had a part in assembling and collating the writings of others.

* Section 206(c) of the National Security Act of 1947.

Naval gunfire was the specialty of Colonel Weller, a Vermont graduate of the Naval Academy in 1930. After graduating from the Army artillery school at Fort Sill, he distinguished himself in the Guam and Iwo Jima operations during World War II. At Quantico afterward he became an instructor in the Naval Gunfire Section and contributed to the helicopter doctrinal studies.

Logistics problems were referred to Lieutenant Colonel Wayne H. Adams, who had enlisted in the Marine Corps from Kentucky for a year and entered the Naval Academy in 1927. Graduating in 1931, he saw service in New Caledonia, Okinawa, and China during World War II. As chief of the Logistics Section at Quantico in 1947, he took part in the helicopter discussions.

Lieutenant Colonel Fred P. Henderson, a native of Ohio, graduated in engineering from Purdue University before being commissioned as a Marine lieutenant in 1935. He was at Pearl Harbor on the Sunday morning when the Japanese attacked, and later he participated in the Guam and Okinawa operations. As a Senior Schools instructor at Quantico in 1947, he concentrated on helicopter loading and unloading problems.

Communications were the chief interest of Lieutenant Colonel George C. Ruffin, a Virginian who graduated in 1934 from the Naval Academy. He took the flight courses at Pensacola two years later and studied chemical warfare in 1940. In World War II he participated at Saipan, Tinian, and Okinawa before returning to Quantico in 1940 as an instructor in communications.

Colonel John N. Hart was another Virginian educated at the Naval Academy, where he graduated in 1925 and trained for aviation at Pensacola after becoming a Marine officer. A veteran of operations in Haiti, China, and Nicaragua, he was awarded the Distinguished Flying Cross for his participation in Pacific campaigns of World War II. As an aviation instructor at Quantico, he conducted technical research for the helicopter program.

Technical aviation advice was also contributed to the helicopter program by Lieutenant Colonel George S. Bowman, Jr., who took flight training at Pensacola soon after graduating from Louisiana State University in 1936 and being commissioned in the Marine Corps. As a Marine pilot in the Pacific, he earned the Bronze Star at Okinawa. At Quantico after the war he became an instructor in the aviation section of the Marine Corps Schools.

Lieutenant Colonel J. D. Hittle, author of *The Military Staff, Its History and Development,* was born in Michigan and graduated from Michigan State College in 1937. After both line and staff duty, he instructed in the Marine Corps Schools from 1942 to 1944 before taking part in the Iwo Jima operation. Returning to Quantico with the Legion of Merit and Purple Heart, he became secretary of the Academic Board.

These were some of the men who had a part in shaping helicopter doctrine before the Marine Corps had a helicopter to its name. As authors, they were anonymous, for the names of contributors do not appear on the severe blue covers of tactical or doctrinal works published by the Marine Corps Schools. Sometimes, indeed, their contributions were not written but oral—a word that is considered more precise than "verbal" by purists of military English.

Nor were they the only officers at Quantico who left their mark on the helicopter program in 1946 and 1947. Nobody troubled to record names for historical purposes, and official reports usually were signed only by the chairman of a committee, even though a dozen men might have contributed. This was the case when the Committee of the Academic Board presented the first report offered in response to the Commandant's directive of December 19, 1946. Entitled

"Military Requirements of Helicopter for Ship-to-Shore Movement of Troops and Cargo," it was dated February 28, 1947, and signed by Colonel Hogaboom as chairman. The first paragraph, in approved military style, stated the problem:

"On the premise that the helicopter offers a valuable means of accelerating and dispersing the ship-to-shore movement, it is recognized that complete replacement of all existing ship-to-shore conveyances may at some future date be desirable. Under such conditions, it would appear necessary that there be designed a relatively small type helicopter for transportation of assault troops, as well as a large type helicopter capable of lifting all divisional loads. However, examination of current technical developments indicates that the latter type may not be practicable for some time to come. Accordingly, it is considered more realistic to approach the problem in increments, establishing initially the characteristics for a purely assault conveyance, and it is with that kind of craft that this paper will be concerned."[9]

The Marine officers who drew up this report did not seem optimistic about the prospects of such large craft as the 42-place prototype XH-16. But from this historical distance it is evident that they were setting their sights too high in their idea of a small helicopter. Such a machine, the report continued, "should provide seating space for a minimum of fifteen (15) and a maximum of twenty (20) infantrymen suitably armed and equipped to initiate combat.

"This personnel requirement is established in the interest of maintaining tactical integrity in the basic infantry combat units. The lower figure, considered to be a practical minimum, will permit the transportation, as a unit, of the basic rifle squad plus two additional individuals from platoon or company headquarters. The maximum figure, considered to be far more desirable, will permit the transportation as a unit of the basic rifle squad, plus a skeletonized machine gun squad or 60mm mortar squad, along with several individuals from platoon or company headquarters."

The ideal payload of an assault helicopter, according to this report, should not be less than 3,500 pounds, and 5,000 pounds was considered "a desirable optimum." A range of 200 to 300 miles was prescribed, since it was considered that "the landing craft should be prepared to commence the ship-to-shore movement at a point between fifty (50) and one hundred (100) miles from the landing area." Speed was thought to be less important, though a cruising speed of 100 knots was mentioned as a minimum. And while armor was believed to be impracticable, self-sealing fuel tanks were recommended.[10]

Considering the rose-tinted claims of helicopter public relations men in 1947, the Marine committee was bleakly conservative in its expectations. Nevertheless, the time was far distant when a 15-place craft would become an aeronautical reality, and then it would not be regarded as "relatively small."

As for the year 1947, the Marine Corps would not be able to get delivery on a helicopter of any sort. In spite of this lack, the last month of the year found HMX-1 (Marine Helicopter Experimental Squadron One) doing business on a basis of hope, faith, and enthusiasm.

HELICOPTERS AT QUANTICO

Eight officers and a single enlisted man made up the original roster. None had ever flown a helicopter. Most of them, in fact, had never been aloft in one.

Colonel Dyer became commanding officer when HMX-1 was commissioned on the first day of December after receipt of orders from the Chief of Naval Operations.[11] Thanks to Colonel Clayton C. Jerome, the new unit was not exactly starting from scratch. As commanding officer of the Marine Corps Air Station at Quantico, he had already seen to it that

Marine Corps Photo

oneer Marine Aircraft Above, the OP-1 autogiro which saw test service in icaragua in 1932; and, below, the first two helicopters of HMX-1 at Quantico.

Marine Corps Photo

Marine Corps Photo

The Military Campus A Flying Banana in front of the HMX-1 headquarters at Quantico in 1948, and in the background

Marine Corps Photo

One of the First An HO3S-1 prepares to land on the strip in front of the squadron headquarters building.

An Early Demonstration Combat troops rush out of a Piasecki Flying Banana of HMX-1 in field tests of the helicopter

Land, Sea, and Air A landing craft, a tank, and a Flying Banana during a simulated "triphibious" assault at Marine Corps Schools.

CREW CHF. PFC. BURROW

A New Kind of Decal Two crew chiefs of VMO-6 paint crosses on a helicopter
for live-saving instead of death-dealing missions.

Pickup at Sea A downed pilot slips into the helicopter rescue sling and gives the
pilot the signal to hoist away.

Marine Corps Photo

Taking on a Casualty A Marine helicopter in Korea lands on the square marked by ground panels and takes aboard a wounded

Flying Ambulance   An HO5S loaded with stretcher patients.

Islands of Mercy The destination of Marine helicopter rescue flights, hospital ships lying off the coast of Korea. Above, the flight deck of the USS *Haven*. Below, a helicopter of HMR-161 at rest on the deck of the USS *Repose*.

Marine Corps Photo

Grasshoppers on the Flight Deck Marine helicopters with their rotors folded get a final checking aboard the USS *Valley Forge* before taking off on a landing exercise.

At the Reservoir Helicopters of VMO-6 hover above troops of the First Marine Division breaking camp at Koto-ri before the withdrawal to the sea in Chosin Reservoir campaign of December 1950.

Marine Corps Photo

Flying in Formation Four HRS helicopters en route to land troops behind enemy lines during a simulated vertical envelopment.

Vertical Envelopment Above, combat-equipped Marines enter an assault heli copter on the flight deck of an aircraft carrier. Below, loaded with troops and equipment, the helicopters take off for the beachhead.

Simulated Operation Above, battle-ready Marines en route via helicopter from aircraft carrier to assault beach. Below, the last stage of the assault is reached as a helicopter lands troops directly on the enemy shore.

An Enemy's Eye View   Troop-carrying Marine assault helicopters as seen by the
defenders of Tok-chok-to in OPERATIONS MARLEX (1952).

Dyer had his pick of personnel and the best facilities of the Station.[12]

A Kansan who graduated from the Naval Academy in 1922, Jerome had trained at Pensacola two years later as a student aviator. In World War II he was three times awarded the Legion of Merit. And after directing Marine air support of group operations on all fronts during the battle of Luzon, he was appointed to the command at Quantico.

Although Jerome had won the Distinguished Flying Cross, he was better remembered for an exploit in 1930. While flying acrobatics over San Diego, his "stick" broke off at the socket. Instead of parachuting while his plane crashed in a thickly populated area, he managed to right the machine by maneuvering the socket with his hand. Then, lashing the stick to the socket with his trousers belt, handkerchief, and necktie, he made a safe landing.

All of the first officers and enlisted men of HMX-1 were volunteers recommended by Jerome and chosen by Dyer for their spirit. The squadron was under the operational and administrative control of the Commandant of the Marine Corps, who assigned two general missions on December 3, 1947:

"Develop techniques and tactics in connection with the movement of assault troops by helicopter in amphibious operations;

"Evaluate a small helicopter as a replacement for the present OY type aircraft to be used for gunfire spotting, observation, and liaison missions in connection with amphibious operations."[13]

The very idea of an earthbound helicopter squadron was repugnant, and Dyer arranged for his officers to have flight training while waiting for the delivery of aircraft. This was not easy, since the Naval experimental helicopter squadron, VX-3, had only a few qualified pilots at this early date. Among them was an attached Marine officer, Major Armond H. DeLalio, who is recognized as the pioneer helicopter pilot of the Marine Corps. He had taken part from the beginning in the Navy's helicopter program; and as operations officer of VX-3 in 1947, he provided training for Dyer's officers in Navy helicopters at the Naval Air Station, Lakehurst, N. J.

DeLalio was born in Farmingdale, N. Y., and became an aviation cadet in the Marine Corps Reserve in 1940 at the age of 23. After training at Pensacola and Miami, he was badly injured the following year at San Diego when his plane crashed into the sea, due to engine failure. On June 5, 1942, the Marine captain won the Navy Cross for heroism in the battle of Midway. As pilot of a scout bomber, diving in at an altitude of 400 feet to release his bomb, he was severely wounded.

After recovering, he was assigned to duty in the Bureau of Aeronautics at Washington. There he became interested in helicopters and took pilot training in 1944 under the U.S. Coast Guard at Floyd Bennett Field, Brooklyn, N. Y. Two years later, when the Navy organized its experimental squadron, Major DeLalio became operations officer.* He had personal charge of training the first Marines from Quantico, and at Dyer's urgent request he was reassigned early in 1947 to begin a tour of duty as operations officer of HMX-1.[14]

February 9, 1948, was a memorable date for HMX-1. Two HO3S-1 helicopters were flown to Quantico that day from the Naval Air Station at Lakehurst, so that the squadron was no longer earthbound.[15]

These Sikorsky utility machines were something of a come-

* Lieutenant Colonel Marion E. Carl, World War II ace who brought down 18 Japanese planes, was another Marine pioneer in the rotary-wing field. While testing planes at the Navy's Patuxent field in 1946, he learned how to fly a helicopter with his usual facility but returned to the jets. In September, 1953, he set a new altitude record of 83,235 feet in a Douglas-built Skyrocket.

down, of course, after the large prototype and theoretical helicopters discussed in doctrinal writings. For the HO3S-1, though listed as a four-place craft, could actually lift only two combat-equipped men in addition to the pilot, or two casualties on external litters. It had a 450-horsepower Wasp engine, a VHF (Very High Frequency) radio, a main rotor with a small torque-compensating tail rotor, and a payload of 500 pounds.

The maximum load (gas, pilot, and passengers or cargo) was 1,180 pounds; the operating radius, 80 miles; and the maximum speed at sea level, 103 miles per hour. Cargo space (with seat for passengers removed) was 35½ inches long, 56 inches wide, and 46 inches high, giving a total of 53 cubic feet. The luggage compartment held 145 pounds, but this weight must be subtracted from the load in the cargo space, and the design did not allow for underslung cargo.[16]

Both Sikorsky and Piasecki expected to have ten-place transport helicopters in production within the next year or two. Dyer and Twining, in fact, may be credited with having done much to acquaint both manufacturers with military needs. But a small utility machine was obviously better suited to training purposes; and pilot instruction now went on full blast at Quantico for officers who had been given only the rudiments at Lakehurst. Some of them thought the helicopter difficult as compared to conventional aircraft, but Dyer did not include this word in the vocabulary of HMX-1.

"Not difficult," he maintained. "Just different."[17]

At any rate, the difference was so pronounced that former fixed-wing pilots had to start all over again as novices. They soon discovered that a helicopter could never be trusted to "fly itself." There were too many things to watch in a ship that could move in any one of 360 directions, or not move at all—such things as the stick which controlled the pitch of the rotor blades, or the foot pedals which made a rudder out of the vertical, torque-neutralizing tail rotor by changing the thrust of its blades.

It took a delicate touch on the stick and the motorcycle-grip-type throttle operated by a twist of the wrist. Beginners grumbled sometimes that two hands and as many feet weren't enough. They said that a helicopter compared with a conventional plane like a half-broken broncho with a well-trained saddle horse. You never could tell what the broncho might do, and some of the early experimental machines reacted to a pilot's mistake by virtually committing suicide—diving sidewise to the earth and beating themselves to pieces with wildly flailing rotor blades.

The conventional plane gets its lift from the forward motion, creating a flow of air over the surfaces of wings scientifically designed for maximum effect. The helicopter utilizes the same principle by means of rotor blades—small wings controlled so as to increase or decrease their bite on the air. Lateral flight in a helicopter is much more complicated than vertical, depending as it does upon the "cyclical pitch" of the rotor blades in response to the pilot's stick.

Instead of rotating in a perfect circle, the flexible blades actually describe a figure which has been likened to a whirling dancer's skirts. When the stick is pulled back, the pitch of the blades is decreased in that direction, then increased throughout the other 180 degrees of its circle. In other words, the "disk" of the rotor is tilted up in front and down in back. This causes the hovering helicopter to go into reverse, since there is more lift at the front half of the circle than the rear 180 degrees. Indeed, Sikorsky found it harder during his experimental days to utilize pitch for forward motion; and it was suggested that he solve the problem quite simply by turning the pilot's seat toward the rear.

Eventually he found a way, and when the stick is pushed

forward, tilting the "disk" of the rotor in that direction, the hovering helicopter moves forward because of the added lift on the blades throughout the rear 180 degrees of rotation. Moving the stick to one side or another will bank the ship to the right or left.

Any such explanation, needless to add, would be regarded by an aeronautical engineer as approaching the kindergarten level. It would take several books of this length to tell what makes a helicopter fly, and these pages can only pretend to offer a few hints as to how it is done.

Centrifugal force keeps the flexible blades from folding up from the pressure of the lift. And as compensation for being more complicated than a conventional plane, the helicopter has the safety feature of functioning as its own parachute. For if the engine fails, the whirlybird can land by means of "auto-rotation" with the force of gravity supplying enough lift to the rotor blades so that they let the entire machine down gently.[18]

When the engine turns the rotor, the air flow is downward through the blades. But when autorotation takes over, the air flows upward. This was the distinguishing principle of the autogiro, and it has saved the necks of a good many helicopter pilots.

OPERATION PACKARD II

It has been said that the helicopter of 1948, as compared to the automobile, had reached "the acetylene lamp stage of development."[19] But it was both newsworthy and photogenic, so that too much was expected of it by newspaper readers nourished on a rich diet of publicity.

All manner of stunts had been conceived by helicopter public relations men—settling down upon the roof of an office building, directing traffic over a busy street intersection, lowering a basket of eggs without breaking a shell. Frank Piasecki once landed his first model at a gasoline station in a Washington suburb and murmured to the astonished attendant, "Fill her up!" After his windshield was wiped, the 23-year-old manufacturer took off nonchalantly, as befitted the first American to be granted a flying license without ever qualifying as the pilot of a conventional plane. But he was not to be the last, and some helicopter pilots maintain that it is an advantage for the novice not to have had previous fixed-wing experience. Then he has "nothing to *un*-learn."[20]

In spite of the stunts pictured in Sunday newspapers, the Marines of HMX-1 could have testified that rotary-wing aircraft had a long way to go aeronautically. For if the helicopter led the conventional plane in versatility, it was far behind when it came to stability.

The first mission of HMX-1, other than training, was the prosaic task of determining the best route for a salvage party sent to extricate a mired-down amphibian vehicle. This was one of the few departures from the daily practice sessions conducted by Major DeLalio to improve pilot techniques.

Three new HO3S-1's were flown directly from the Sikorsky plant late in February, bringing the total up to five. More Marine volunteers were accepted by Colonel Dyer, so that the squadron had 12 officers and 32 enlisted men on duty by May 1, in addition to four officers and eight men taking pilot and mechanical training at Lakehurst.[21]

It is a tribute to the training progress of HMX-1 that the squadron was ready to participate that month in Operation PACKARD II. This was the second amphibious command post exercise held jointly by Navy and Marine forces to simulate a ship-to-shore assault landing against an enemy defending the beaches. The following objectives were assigned to HMX-1:

"To take a positive step forward in the development program by making an actual landing of troops by carrier-based helicopters;

"To gain experience in operating helicopters on board an

aircraft carrier and experience in helicopter landing operations upon which a sound doctrine for these operations could be written;

"To gain individual and collective experience for pilots, aircraft crews and other squadron personnel so that more extensive operations could be undertaken in the future;

"To determine probable military requirements for landing force helicopters of the future."[22]

The second of these objectives calls attention to the fact that the helicopter doctrinal writings of the Marine Corps Schools had kept pace with the progress of HMX-1. Pages of material were already in mimeographed form, awaiting the findings of Operation PACKARD II before being finally revised.[23] Planning for the operation was meanwhile conducted by the Schools with a view to putting doctrine to the test.

Training for HMX-1 pilots in carrier operations began in April at Quantico. Flights were made under maximum load conditions, and instruction given in starting and stopping rotors in high winds. Daily lectures were devoted to carrier deck procedures, weight and balance techniques, and rescue missions.

The problem, as outlined by the official Marine report, "contemplated the landing of an amphibious corps in the New River [N. C.] area as part of a major counter-offensive against an enemy which had previously overrun the southeastern United States. Two divisions were to land abreast on Onslow Beach at H-hour, cross the island waterway and advance inland. One regimental combat team, borne by helicopters, was to be landed on order to seize the Sneads Ferry area on the Corps left flank."[24]

HMX-1 had orders to report to Captain R. E. Dixon, USN, commanding the CVE (escort aircraft carrier) *Palau*. He in turn operated under the immediate control of Rear Admiral E. H. Von Heimburg, USN, commander of Amphibious

Group Two, in his capacity as the naval task force commander.

Such statistical items as "a landing force organized into an amphibious corps of three divisions" were not intended to be taken literally. Nor would it have been possible for HMX-1, with its five small craft, to have landed a whole regiment. RCT-9 was to embark in the *Palau* under the operational control of the commanding general, 3d Marine Division, who in turn answered to the Corps and Landing Force Commander. But this regimental combat team was of simulated strength; for the Marine report admitted that "a number of artificialities were accepted, but not to such an extent that the instructive value of the operation was reduced."[25]

It must be remembered that annual exercises of this sort, including many simulated units and conditions, did much to prepare the Navy and Marine Corps during the 1930's for the amphibious operations of World War II. Twelve officers and 31 enlisted men represented HMX-1 in PACKARD II. The five helicopters, landed on board the *Palau* on May 19, were scheduled to take part in a rehearsal the next day off Little Creek, Va. But helicopters were such unfamiliar aircraft on board a carrier that some confusion resulted. That night Dixon and Dyer put their heads together and worked out a system for the co-operation of bluejackets and Marines on the flight deck. And on the 20th the rehearsal went off smoothly as a result.[26]

The *Palau* sailed that night and anchored off New River the next day. But the operation had to be postponed until the 23d on account of bad weather.

On the new D-day the sea was calm, with ceiling and visibility unlimited. The *Palau* was anchored about 6,000 yards southeast of New River Inlet (see accompanying map) when the five HMX-1 craft took off at 0935, rendezvoused over the carrier and flew in formation to the landing zone, where the first troops were put ashore 25 minutes later. It was followed by continuous flights until the last men were landed at 1500. All aircraft used the same route; but shore-bound helicopters proceeded at less than 300 feet, while those returning to the *Palau* flew above 300 and below 500 feet. Control operations were satisfactory except at times when air-ground communications suffered because the helicopters dropped below the VHF line of sight.

After the troop landings, logistical flights were made to simulate the putting ashore of cargo. Altogether, 66 passengers and much equipment were landed; and the squadron logged 103 carrier landings and take-offs in a total of 28.6 flying hours. Aircraft availability was maintained at 100 per cent throughout the day.

"The operation was entirely successful," concluded the HMX-1 report, "in that its limited objectives were reached. No attempt, however, was made to exploit the capabilities of rotary-wing aircraft. Much remains to be done in the future and these operations must continue to be thought of as experimental and developmental."[27]

This summary takes no account of the fact that Operation PACKARD II was a landmark in moral respects. Marines who took part in the New River exercises could not doubt that the ugly duckling of military aviation had proved itself worthy of the affectionate nicknames bestowed upon it. The whirlybird had arrived. The flying windmill was here to stay. The egg beater had shown what it could do, and the United States Marine Corps was all the more firmly committed to new techniques of amphibious warfare.

CHAPTER VI

The Training of HMX-1

On a June afternoon in 1948, an absent-minded osprey flew straight into the main rotor of a Marine helicopter just off the North Carolina coast. The HMX-1 pilot reported afterward that he heard a loud report and felt a jolt. Then he was surrounded by a swirling explosion of feathers.

No fishhawk ever made a worthier contribution to aeronautical science, for its sacrifice provided HMX-1 with the first evidence as to how much punishment the rotor could take. It had long been a disputed question, and the squadron was naturally loath to experiment. Pessimists croaked that a forced landing would result if anything hit the flexible blades, but this first experience was reassuring. Although the pilot was far from any landing area, he found his controls working adequately and made his way back to the base without trouble. There he discovered that the rotor had functioned in spite of a large dent in one blade.[1]

Of course, it was still a conjecture as to what effect hostile bullets might have. But HMX-1 pilots felt certain that soon enough they would have firsthand knowledge if the Marine Corps continued to live up to its tradition as the nation's force in readiness.

The squadron spent more than a month, following Operation PACKARD II, in demonstrating the capabilities of the HO3S-1 to Marine ground force units. By this time HMX-1 pilots had learned that providing aerial transportation for VIP's, both military and civilian, was to be one of their most persistent missions, regardless of other duties.[2] Very Important Persons had learned in their turn that there is nothing like a helicopter to set the passenger down at the very doorstep of his destination. Besides, the helicopter was still enough of a novelty in 1948 that it flattered even a VIP to be taken for a flight.

It was also noted in HMX-1 reports of this period that "the many civilian requests, along with the assigned military demonstrations, kept the small squadron very busy."[3] This was a polite way of referring to a wide variety of morale-building stunts designed to satisfy military as well as public curiosity. Already it could be foreseen that Marine helicopters would be virtually a necessity for Fourth of July celebrations; and no Christmas at Quantico was to be complete without Santa Claus arriving by helicopter instead of driving the traditional reindeer. But perhaps the oddest of these missions resulted when a crucial baseball game between Marine teams at Quantico was about to be postponed because of wet grounds. Someone thought of the flying windmills, and an HMX-1 ship hovered low so that the minor tornado of its rotor wash would sweep the pools of water off the diamond and into the orbit of Marines wielding brooms.[4]

Such missions often had to be carried out in the "spare time" of pilots who put in full days at training during the summer and autumn of 1948. One of the experiments of this period was conducted to test the possibilities of an airborne public-address system for directing traffic, troop movements, or rescue work. Results were "highly satisfactory" up to 1,500 feet, using equipment weighing only 50 pounds.

Training in formation flying and fighter evasive tactics went on constantly. Pilots were taught to change altitude suddenly and use terrain for cover in the event of attack by enemy fighters. But HMX-1 "also recommended that heavy fighter cover be employed for any helicopter operations in enemy controlled air."[5]

High-speed wire laying was successfully tested in conjunction with the Marine Corps Equipment Board, which had been evaluating various dispensers under all climatic conditions.[6]

On August 9 the first Bell helicopter was flown to HMX-1 from Lakehurst. A three-place craft powered by a 178-horsepower motor, the HTL-2 was suitable for reconnaissance, artillery spotting or aerial photography. No familiarization syllabus was necessary, since HMX-1 pilots who trained at Lakehurst had been given their first 15 hours of flight instruction in this light machine adapted to Navy needs.[7]

The great event of the summer for HMX-1 came on August 15 with the delivery of the first HRP-1—a ten-place transport helicopter, designed by Piasecki. This manufacturer had shown a co-operative spirit in endeavoring to meet military requirements of the U. S. Air Force and Marine Corps, and the HRP-1 was the world's largest helicopter at the time. A 600-horsepower engine drove longitudinal twin rotors at opposite ends of such an elongated and curved configuration that the nickname "Flying Banana" was inevitable. As was customary in helicopter statistics, the ten-place capacity indicated that four to six combat-equipped troops could be lifted at sea level by a machine with a payload of 900 pounds in addition to full fuel capacity of 100 gallons. But this was double the payload of the HO3S-1, and the new transport helicopter could take aboard four casualties in litters.

The maximum speed at sea level was 100 miles per hour, and 75 miles per hour represented the cruising speed. Cargo space about 14 feet long and 5 feet wide and deep was available through a door 5 feet high and nearly as wide at the bottom. There was also a cargo hoist with 400 pounds capacity and a cable length of 100 feet.[8]

Four more HRP-1's were delivered to Quantico during the autumn months as flight indoctrination training continued both for pilots and crews. This preliminary stage was followed by an intensive program of testing tactics and techniques for landing assault troops in an amphibious operation.

PUBLICATION OF PHIB-31

The transport helicopters arrived just in time to be helpful in the final editing of the tentative manual of doctrine. Officers of the Marine Corps Schools took pride in the fact that it was the world's first publication of the sort, just as a former generation of Marines had brought out the first manual of landing operations. They were also proud of the many revisions the text had undergone in accordance with the results of HMX-1 operations. Some of the last changes, in fact, were suggested by tests of the new HRP-1 machines.[9]

A preliminary mimeographed edition came out earlier for limited circulation at Quantico. Then the 52-page booklet was published in November, 1948, by the Marine Corps Schools under the title, *Amphibious Operations—Employment of Helicopters (Tentative)*. As the thirty-first in a series of manuals on amphibious operations, the production was usually referred to as *Phib-31*.[10] Its purpose was outlined in the preface:

"The advent of the troop carrying helicopter and its establishment as standard equipment within the Marine Corps gives rise to a variety of questions related to the employment of such conveyances in the conduct of amphibious operations. It is the purpose of this pamphlet to explore the various aspects of helicopter employment, discerning the manner in which the characteristics of the vehicle can best be exploited to enhance the effectiveness of the amphibious attack, and providing thereby the basis for a body of doctrine governing helicopter landing operations."

It was admitted in the introduction that the helicopter had limitations "of the same nature as those which have been encountered during the development of other conveyances employed in the amphibious attack, being mainly technical in nature. They are, at present, reflected in sharp limitations on load carrying ability, and on range, speed and mechanical reliability. It is accepted that such shortcomings will be overcome, as in the past, by a process of gradual development. However, the evolution of a set of principles governing helicopter employment cannot await the perfection of the craft itself, but must proceed concurrently with that development. Certain of these principles are now apparent, and a concept of employment based thereon is presented in the sections to follow."[11]

Much of the spadework had already been done in amphibious manuals of pre-helicopter days. Thus in dealing with the intricate subject of command relationships, *Phib-31* could simply state that the basic principles governing the conventional amphibious attack were still generally applicable:

"Since the basic naval character of the operation is in no way modified or abridged, it follows that the naval commander of the amphibious task force should be responsible for landing the helicopter landing forces and for supporting them in their subsequent operations ashore. Such variations as will arise will be minor in nature, stemming from the fact that the helicopter formations will be landing force units."

Beginning with organization and command problems, the booklet took up every phase of the employment of helicopters —tactical considerations, embarkation, the ship-to-shore movement, fire support, logistics, and communications. Twelve diagrams were included as illustrations.

The limitations of rotary-wing aircraft having first been considered, *Phib-31* also took into account the potential advantages:

"The ability of the helicopter to rise and descend vertically, to hover, and to move rapidly at varying altitudes all qualify it admirably as a supplement or substitute for the slower, more inflexible craft now employed in the ship-to-shore movement. Furthermore, its ability to circumvent powerful beach defenses, and to land assault forces accurately and in any desired altitude, on tactical localities farther inland, endow helicopter operations with many of the desirable characteristics of the conventional airborne attack while avoiding the undesirable dispersal of forces which often accompanies such operations. The helicopter, furthermore, when transported to the scene of operations in aircraft carriers, makes operations possible at ranges which have not yet been achieved by the existing conventional troops carriers."[12]

Basic tactical principles remain constant even when weapons change, and there is no better yardstick than the calendar for measuring the merit of a doctrinal manual. An outstanding example may be found in the manual turned out in 1934 by the Marine Corps Schools. Not only was it composed prior to the employment of amphibian landing vehicles; it helped to inspire some of those developments. Yet it has worn remarkably well throughout the ensuing two decades. Many of the original solutions have been amended, but the foundation itself has stood up under the weight of the years. As a tribute to this record, the authors of *The U.S. Marines and Amphibious War* have commented:

"If . . . later publications by all the services during and after World War II can be considered the Holy Writ of modern amphibious warfare, then the *Tentative Manual for Landing Operations* published by the Marine Corps Schools in 1934 deserves to be thought of as a sort of combination of the Pentateuch and the Four Gospels."[13]

It remains to be seen whether *Phib-31* will hold up as well, particularly since there has never been a demonstration of Marine helicopter tactics in an actual amphibious operation. At least, the booklet has weathered its first six years, including the test of combat in Korea. Later publications on helicopter tactics have been put out by the Marine Corps Schools, but the basic principles of *Phib-31* are still accepted as doctrine.

Credit for the editing is due to the Academic Board of the Marine Corps Schools. And though the authors are nameless, as is the custom with such publications, there can be no doubt as to the officer who had most to do with molding the original helicopter concept into tactical form. That it was largely the contribution of Colonel Merrill B. Twining is the general opinion of officers on duty with the Marine Corps Schools at that time.

COLD WEATHER OPERATIONS

Several new missions were assigned to HMX-1 by the Commandant during the autumn of 1948. An HO3S and the HTL were detached from the squadron in September to spend the next two months at Camp Lejeune, N.C., and familiarize infantry units with the helicopter while developing new practical uses. And in November an HO3S with its pilot and crew participated in the cold weather operations of the Second Task Fleet off the coast of Newfoundland.

The mission of this aircraft, attached to the *Palau*, was one of observation, liaison, and personnel transport ashore with the landing force. It is not often that Newfoundland weather disappoints in November by being too clement, but this was the exception. Never once did the temperature drop below freezing, and the expedition proved to be a failure as a cold weather exercise.[14]

Another and more promising test of this sort took place the following month when CNO directed that helicopters and crews be sent on board the CVL (small aircraft carrier) Saipan to assist the Air Force in rescuing 13 men who had been stranded on the icecap in Greenland. Three HRP-1 helicopters with their pilots and crews boarded the carrier at Norfolk on Christmas Eve and sailed the following morning. Two Piasecki utility helicopters had been sent from the Naval Air Training Center at Patuxent, Md., as well as three TBM (torpedo bomber) planes from the Naval Air Station at Quonset Point, R.I.

The Marines made all possible preparations for testing equipment, gear, and clothing in sub-zero temperatures. There was some doubt as to the ability of loaded helicopters to hover safely at an altitude of 7,700 feet, but the expected temperature of −30° F. would result in an atmospheric density equivalent to that found at about 3,500 feet. It was agreed, therefore, that the HMX-1 aircraft were not to make any rescue attempts at a higher temperature or in winds of more than 30 knots.

Daily conferences were held on the Saipan to work out the details of the rescue plan. But at noon on December 28, when the carrier was less than 600 miles and 22 hours from the proposed launching site, a commercial broadcast brought the news that the Air Force had rescued the stranded men with a ski-equipped Douglas R4D. On the return trip the HMX-1 machines flew from the Saipan to Argentia, Newfoundland, but again the weather was too mild for a cold weather test.[15]

At the other extreme, a test under tropical conditions was scheduled early in 1949. HMX-1 had grown by that time to a strength of 16 officers and 64 enlisted men. Six officers and 26 men were detached with four HO3S's and a Bell helicopter to take part in the Atlantic Fleet Exercises (FLEX-49) off the coast of Puerto Rico. The HTL-2 was assigned in the operations plan as a command helicopter, and the Sikorsky craft were to be used for search and rescue work plus such special missions during the operation as observation, reconnaissance, artillery spotting, personnel transport, aerial photography, and evaluation of naval gunfire damage.

The 2d Marine Division had operational control of the HMX-1 detachment which depended for administrative and logistical support upon the 2d Marine Aircraft Wing. All assigned missions were executed competently by the helicopters, but the pilots were disappointed because they had not been given a larger part in the amphibious landings. Hence the squadron report concluded that "the helicopter's extensive capabilities were not fully exploited."[16]

The same doleful comment might have been made at this time on the other side of the earth by an HMX-1 pilot on detached duty. Captain Wallace D. Blatt had trained at Lakehurst among the first group sent from Quantico. Late in 1948 he volunteered along with other HMX-1 officers after hearing a rumor that Marine helicopter pilots were wanted for active service in China. Blatt was accepted and set off on three days' notice.

When he reached Tsingtao, early in January, he was assigned a U.S. Navy HO3S-1 helicopter and a Navy maintenance crew. Another machine of the same type, flown by a Navy lieutenant, had orders to operate from a carrier.

Blatt's helicopter was attached to Headquarters Squadron, Air, Fleet Marine Force, Western Pacific, commanded by Lieutenant Colonel George W. Nevils. This organization had requested the assignment of a helicopter as a rescue aircraft for pilots making forced landings in hostile territory or in water too shallow for crash boats.[17] Officially the United States was on good terms with various Chinese factions at this time; but actually, as the Marines at Tsingtao well knew, the Chinese Communists could not be considered neutrals if a pilot fell into their hands.

As it happened, there were no such incidents during Blatt's few weeks at Tsingtao. The squadron was preparing to evacuate the area, so that he had no opportunity to use the helicopter for anything except mail runs and other such routine chores. The only danger was that the machine might be damaged by the curious crowds of Chinese which engulfed it at every landing.

A week before the evacuation date of February 6, 1949, Blatt's helicopter was taken aboard the carrier *Boxer*. The squadron was disbanded after reaching the United States, and Blatt reported to Aircraft Engineering Squadron 46 at the Marine air station at Cherry Point, N.C. There he flew a HO3S-1 recently assigned to this unit.[18]

OPERATION PACKARD III

Helicopter training at Quantico was speeded up during the spring of 1949 in preparation not only for Operation PACKARD III but also a demonstration before members of the Eighty-first Congress. The purpose was to show the advances made in techniques and weapons of amphibious warfare since World War II.

High-level officers of the Navy and Marine Corps were on hand as well as legislators when the demonstration took place on May 9 at Quantico. HMX-1 now had nine Piasecki transport helicopters, and the show began with eight of them lifting 56 combat-equipped Marines from a simulated carrier deck painted on the airstrip. The machines flew past the Congressmen in formation, and next the visitors were shown a simulated assault landing. Fighter planes strafed and laid smoke screens to provide cover for helicopters which required only 25 seconds in which to land, discharge their troops, and become airborne again.

Just five minutes later, four helicopters returned to land two sections of artillery with 75mm pack howitzers. It took the gunners another three minutes to fire on the target. Meanwhile the helicopters were laying wire, spotting for the artillery, and evacuating casualties.[19]

A few days later the squadron departed in three groups from Quantico to take part in Operation PACKARD III, the Marine Corps Schools' Amphibious Command Post exercise. The main echelon, consisting of eight Piasecki aircraft, was based on the *Palau* and represented a helicopter unit for the landing of an RCT. A land-based group of three HO3S's acted as a search and rescue unit, while an HTL-2 based on an LST had a mission of aerial observation and naval gunfire spotting.

After a rehearsal at Little Creek, Va., the fleet moved into position on May 20 off the coast of North Carolina. There a two-day assault landing was held with the landing boats hitting Onslow Beach while the Flying Bananas transported troops inland to a point about five miles up the New River.

High winds and rough seas throughout the operation made it an instructive comparison between old and new amphibious techniques. Many of the landing boats were swamped by the waves, and others were delayed on their return when attempting to tie up to the AKA's. Yet the effectiveness of the helicopters, each carrying six fully equipped combat troops, was little impaired as they shuttled back and forth from the carrier to the objective area. They landed troops at a strategic road junction to prevent the defenders from reinforcing the beach area. Cover was provided meanwhile by fighter planes simulating smoke and strafing attacks.

This was the most ambitious attempt so far to demonstrate the contribution which the helicopter could make to an amphibious assault. And though only eight aircraft were available, they demonstrated the possibility of lifting an RCT for a vertical envelopment in the rear of a beach area.

It was also proved that a small helicopter such as the HTL-2 could operate successfully from an LST for observation and naval gunfire spotting. Fortunately, there were no missions to be performed by the three search and rescue HO3S's based on land, and they were used for message drops or transportation of personnel from ship to shore.[20]

On June 30, 1949, the squadron had ten HRP-1 aircraft, two HTL-2's, and three HO3S-1's. The shrinkage in the Sikorsky machines had been due to the only two major accidents in 19 months of training, neither of which resulted in personnel deaths or serious injuries. The synopsis of flight operations for the first six months of the year was as follows:

PURPOSE	NUMBER OF FLIGHTS	NUMBER OF HOURS
Administration	6	2.7
Demonstrations	286	117.9
Flight Training	102	124.9
Familiarization	230	140.1
Ferrying	8	11.2
Navigation	2	3.1
Observation	40	34.9
Photography	27	12.9
Reconnaissance	94	83.9
Tactics	13	8.8
Tests	188	77.4
Pilot Training	65	46.6
Transportation	225	127.9
Utility	58	40.2
Totals	1,344	832.2[21]

By this time the squadron had gone far toward completing its second major mission, the evaluation of the helicopter as a replacement for OY aircraft. These light fixed-wing planes had been used by Marine observation squadrons for such missions as reconnaissance, liaison, and artillery spotting. The question as to whether helicopters could replace them was decided affirmatively by two Marine Observation Squadron One (VMO-1) officers, Captain Robert B. Luckey and Captain William L. Dick, after a demonstration of Bell helicopters at Quantico on April 15, 1948.

These officers recommended that VMO-1 be equipped with two-place Bell helicopters in place of OY aircraft "at the earliest practicable moment." It was further urged that the squadron be expanded from eight OY's to 14 HTL-2's—six for spotting, six for infantry liaison, and the remaining two for headquarters liaison.[22]

Colonel Dyer's report to the Commandant on November 22, 1948, was based on 304.2 hours flown by five HO3S-1's and an HTL-2 in completing missions ordinarily performed by OY aircraft. The helicopter impressed him as being equal or better for observation and artillery spotting; and he found it "superior" for reconnaissance, wire laying, and limited supply and evacuation. Dyer concluded, therefore, that the helicopter could carry out observation and liaison missions in support of ground forces more efficiently than current fixed-wing observation aircraft.

His recommendation was that helicopters of the Bell type be used as interim aircraft to replace "not over 50 per cent of the present operational OY aircraft." In the lack of "a light helicopter specifically designed for military observation," Dyer urged that development of jet observation helicopters be encouraged, "due to their indicated simplicity and ease of maintenance."[23]

The Division of Plans and Policies, USMC, concurred in a memorandum to the Director of Marine Corps Aviation. The 50 per cent ratio was considered ideal "in view of the respective and complementary capabilities of the two types of aircraft." It was recommended that helicopters be procured for the purpose, but the project struck a snag when the Bureau of Aeronautics replied that new machines of the desired type were not available.[24]

CAREY IN COMMAND

Colonel Dyer was relieved on June 30, 1949, after completing 19 months as commanding officer. This does not take into account the fact that he had devoted most of his time to the Marine helicopter program since the summer of 1946. His contributions in administrative and aeronautical respects during these three years can only be compared to Twining's work in the field of helicopter tactics.

Major DeLalio, the pioneer Marine helicopter pilot and trainer of pilots, had already left HMX-1 for reassignment to the Naval Air Station at Lakehurst. There the Navy's experimental helicopter squadron, VX-3, had expanded until it formed the nucleus of two new units, designated HU-1 and HU-2.[25]

Dyer was relieved by Lieutenant Colonel John F. Carey, a graduate of Macalester College in Minnesota who entered the Marine Corps in 1937 as an aviation cadet and trained at Pensacola. He became a flight leader in 1942 during the defense of Midway, and was credited with shooting down the Japanese group leader. Awarded the Navy Cross, after being twice wounded in an ensuing air battle, he served in an air mission in Peru until the end of the war.

Carey took command of HMX-1 at a time when the Marine helicopter development program had lost momentum. Despite an urgent shortage of trained pilots and maintenance crews, it was impossible to plan intelligently for the future without having a long-range decision on the helicopter itself.

Was it advisable to plan for the next few years on the basis of present ten-place helicopters such as the HRP-1? Or should the Marine Corps of 1949 take its chances on the prototype Air Force XH-16 reaching the stage of actual production in 1952 or 1953?

A bird in the hand, or two speculative fowls in the bush? This was essentially the question put up to a Marine committee with the impressive title of the Board to Study and Submit Recommendations on a Transport Helicopter Program for the Marine Corps. The six members deliberated throughout the summer months "to determine the type transport helicopter procurable in 1952-53 which most nearly meets Marine Corps requirements." Representatives of HMX-1, BuAer, and CNO were heard as the Board studied the characteristics of existing helicopters.

On October 14, 1949, the verdict was that "none of the current models will be a sufficient improvement over the Piasecki HRP-1 to justify procurement; nor do they sufficiently approximate the assumed Marine Corps requirements for an assault transport helicopter."

As for the Piasecki XH-16, the Board decided that "because of the time that may be required to fully perfect such a large helicopter, and because of its doubtful ability to operate in numbers from a small aircraft carrier, it appears advantageous to proceed with a project for the procurement of a smaller helicopter which will meet our minimum requirements, . . . which will be suitable for carrier operations, and will be available in 1952-53."

It was recommended that the Commandant establish these minimum helicopter requirements for future development:

RANGE: 250 nautical miles
PAYLOAD: 3,000-3,500 pounds
CAPACITY: 13-15 combat troops, 2 pilots
STOWAGE: To fit the elevator of escort class aircraft carrier and be capable of being stowed and moved about the hangar deck.

As a final recommendation, it was urged that the Commandant direct the commanding officer of HMX-1 "to prepare and submit to this headquarters a tentative Table of Organization for an Assault Transport Helicopter Squadron."

This report to the Commandant, which reads like prophecy in the light of later events, was signed by Lieutenant Colonel George S. Bowman, Jr., as senior member, and Lieutenant Colonel James B. Moore, Lieutenant Colonel Paul E. Becker, Major Charles J. Bailey, Major Jack R. Moore, and Major Russell R. Riley.[26]

Only an optimist could have supposed in the autumn of 1949 that the Marine helicopter transport squadron would become a reality in 1951, or that a helicopter bettering the minimum requirements would be airborne in 1954. At any rate, the Commandant's acceptance of the Board report cleared the way for intelligent planning, and HMX-1 stiffened its training program.

Just at that time, unfortunately, one of the Sikorsky helicopters developed engine trouble while giving a demonstration at the Cleveland Air Races. And on October 7, CNO grounded all HO3S-1's until the 26th for a major service change on the mid-transmission oil pumps.[27]

Interruptions of this sort were to be expected at intervals, for CNO and BuAer took drastic action to correct any mechanical defect. On such occasions the helicopter plants co-operated with all their resources.

Late in November it was the turn of Piasecki transport machines to be grounded. A Navy HRP-1 crashed at the Naval Air Station, Key West, Fla.; and subsequent examination cast suspicion on the mid-transmission oil pump shaft. Meanwhile the HO3S's were grounded again in November because the near crash of a U.S. Air Force machine had resulted from a defective flywheel sprocket. No fault could be found with Marine HO3S's, and they were declared operative again in three days.

Training in night flying was undertaken for the first time by HMX-1 that winter. Helicopter instruments were primitive as compared to those of conventional aircraft, so that it was necessary for pilots to "have a horizon." In other words, they had to depend on their own vision, and training exercises were limited to nights when the silhouettes of hills and trees could be seen. Marine pilots were given practice in landing in an area of 100 by 200 feet which was marked by flare pots. But the need for the development of better landing lights and instruments was so urgent that the squadron made it the subject of a recommendation to BuAer.

"These items," concluded the HMX-1 report, "are considered to be absolutely essential before any large-scale night operation can be undertaken."[28]

Only a limited training program could be carried out that winter, since the HRP-1's were not given a clean bill of mechanical health until late in March, after being grounded more than four months. Then the squadron had barely time to practice and rehearse for a series of operations and demonstrations.

Pilots, crews, and aircraft participated in the sixth Joint Civilian Orientation Conference on April 19 at Quantico. Next came Operation CROSSOVER, the maneuvers of the 2d Marine Division held at Camp Lejeune, N.C., during the last three days of the month. And on May 27 the helicopters of HMX-1 flew troops from the carrier *Mindoro* to beaches along the North Carolina coast in Operation PACKARD IV. Both of these operations afforded good training, though no new techniques were exhibited.[29]

On June 15 a demonstration was given at Quantico for President Harry S. Truman. After the presentation of a simulated amphibious assault, such techniques as wire laying, evacuations of casualties, and "flying crane" lifts of 75mm pack howitzers were shown.

The next day HMX-1 had a part in a parade and review staged in honor of Lieutenant General Lemuel C. Shepherd, Jr. During the "fly-by" the jets and Corsairs were followed by six HRP-1's, six HO3S's, and an HTL-3. This was believed to be the largest group of rotary-wing aircraft ever to fly in formation anywhere at one time.[30]

THE INCIDENT IN KOREA

Lieutenant Colonel Keith B. McCutcheon relieved Carey on July 9, 1950, as commanding officer of HMX-1. Born in East Liverpool, Ohio, where he still resided, he had graduated from the Carnegie Institute of Technology in 1937. That same year he was commissioned a Marine lieutenant at the age of 22. After flight training at Pensacola in 1940, he won the Silver Star medal and Distinguished Flying Cross in World War II. Altogether, McCutcheon flew 40 missions as a dive-bomber pilot in the Pacific, and after the war he headed the Experimental Pilotless Aircraft Branch of the Navy's Bureau of Aeronautics.

Lieutenant Colonel George W. Herring, who had recently completed the helicopter pilot's training course at Lakehurst, was named executive officer of HMX-1. Major William P. Mitchell became the new operations officer.[31]

The new officers inherited an experiment to determine whether a bazooka could be fired from the skid of a Bell helicopter. Early in May, a special rocket-launcher mount, controlled from the cockpit, had been designed and installed at the Naval Air Development Center, Johnsville, Pa. HMX-1 officers then held conferences with the Electronics and Armament Test Sections of the Naval Air Station at Patuxent, Md., to plan the actual firing tests.[32]

It was established that the bazooka blast would clear all parts of the aircraft, but ammunition could not be obtained until late in the summer. Then, on August 29, a 3.5" rocket was successfully fired from the right skid of the little utility helicopter.[33]

A special bombing experiment, planned by HMX-1 that summer and carried out on October 6, 1950, added another to the mounting list of Marine Corps "firsts" in testing helicopter combat techniques. As a preliminary, brackets were improvised at Quantico and installed after landing the HRP-1 on three stake trucks.

Herring and Mitchell flew the Piasecki transport craft to Edgewood Arsenal, Md. Landing on a specially constructed stand, ten feet high, they took off after the bomb was attached horizontally. In the air it was suspended by cables in a vertical position and dropped from an altitude of 8,000 feet.[34]

The rocket-firing and bombing experiments might have aroused more widespread interest in military circles if they had not been overshadowed by events in the Far East. Headlines announcing that civil war had broken out in Korea on June 25, 1950, probably meant less to a great majority of Marines on that Sunday morning than the pennant chances of the Dodgers. Even when the United Nations ordered military sanctions three days later against the North Korean (NK) invaders of the Republic of Korea, the incident seemed only of minor concern. President Truman ordered the Seventh Fleet into action; and on the 30th it was assigned by the Joint Chiefs of Staff (JCS) to the operational control of General of the Army Douglas MacArthur, soon to be named supreme commander of United Nations (UN) forces.

The first American shots of the war were fired by Navy warships and Air Force bombers. Then MacArthur urged that U.S. Army troops be flown from Japan early in July to the aid of the retreating Republic of Korea (ROK) forces. And on July 2, 1950, he requested that a Marine RCT be sent to Korea with its own air support. CNO concurred that same day, and on the 7th the 1st Provisional Marine Brigade was activated in southern California under the command of Brigadier General Edward A. Craig.

This organization was made up of a reinforced infantry regiment, the 5th Marines, and Marine Aircraft Group (MAG) 33 of the 1st Marine Aircraft Wing—a total of 6,534 officers and men. The air component, commanded by Brigadier General Thomas J. Cushman, consisted of three fighter squadrons and an observation squadron.[35]

It took the Brigade only a week to prepare for embarkation, and the last units sailed from San Diego on July 14, 1950. By that time it had become painfully evident that the Korean incident amounted to more than a "police action." Communism had challenged Democracy to a test of strength, and an Asiatic peninsula threatened to become the Spain of a third world war. Soviet Russia had supplied the arms and Red China the instructors for a tough, well-led NK army, equipped with tanks and planes, which rolled back the lightly armed ROK forces with ease. When the first outweighed U.S. Army contingents reached the front, they too had little choice but to fall back while fighting delaying actions.

The Marine officers of HMX-1 took a professional as well as patriotic interest in the conflict. For on July 7, the day of the Brigade's activation, HMX-1 was directed by Headquarters USMC to send eight officers and 30 men to the Marine Corps Air Station at El Toro, Calif., for reassignment to the Far East. These pilots were ordered to depart the following day for California:

Captains Victor A. Armstrong, George B. Farish, and Eugene J. Pope; Lieutenants Arthur Bancroft, Floyd J. Englehardt, Robert A. Longstaff, Gustave F. Lueddeke, and Max N. Nebergall.[36]

Thus the Marine helicopter program had been overtaken by war after a total of only 31 months in which to evaluate the capabilities of a new type of aircraft. In Korea a good deal would depend on the training of HMX-1 and the doctrinal conclusions of the Marine Corps Schools, since it was a truism of history that no new weapon is any better than the doctrines and techniques behind it. Among the object lessons of past wars was France's failure in 1870 to derive any advantage from Europe's first practical machine gun. Napoleon III and his generals, insisting upon secrecy, kept the *mitrailleuse* under wraps to such an extent that its capabilities were never well evaluated. Because it was mounted on wheels and drawn by horses, the weapon was supposed to be a legitimate member of the artillery family. When the test came, the French gunners fired at ranges too long to do much harm to the Prussian infantry. And the Franco-Prussian War was lost in a few weeks by an army which had never learned how to use the key to victory.[37]

By the same token, now that the helicopter was going into combat for the first time, novelty alone was not enough. The military value of the new type of aircraft would depend to a large extent on how well the Marine Corps had worked out combat doctrines and techniques where none had existed before.

CHAPTER VII

VMO-6 in Korea

The Marines had been in Korea less than 24 hours when the helicopters got into action. On August 2, 1950, the 1st Provisional Marine Brigade landed at Pusan. And early the next morning General Craig made a reconnaissance in an HO3S-1 of the observation squadron, VMO-6.[1]

This flight marked the dawn of a new era in command and liaison. Thanks to the helicopter, a general and his staff could now maintain a direct physical contact with operations at the front such as never had been possible before. Not only was vertical flight an aid to reconnaissance, but it also enabled a commander to keep in personal touch with his forward units, since the helicopter could land virtually anywhere without asking favors of the terrain. Thus the brain of the military body was given a more precise and immediate degree of control over the muscles and sinews.

VMO-6 had sailed from San Diego on the CVE *Badoeng Strait* under the operational control of the Brigade and the administrative and logistical control of the 1st Marine Aircraft Wing. The rotary wing group, consisting of seven officers, 30 enlisted men, and four HO3S-1 aircraft, had a good claim to being the first helicopter unit of history to be organized and trained for combat duty. Major Vincent J. Gottschalk was the commanding officer of an observation squadron completed by a fixed-wing group of eight officers, 43 enlisted men, and eight OY-2 planes.[2]

A native of Michigan and engineering graduate of the University of Michigan, Gottschalk had been commissioned in the Marine Corps in 1941 at the age of 22. Most of his World War II service had been on board the USS *Langley*,* and afterward he took flight training at Corpus Christi and Pensacola.

It could never have been said that life was dull for this Marine officer early in July, 1950. After assuming command of VMO-6 on the 3d, he was alerted on the 7th for immediate shipment overseas. On the 11th he had his squadron ready to go, including the helicopter group which arrived from Quantico on the 9th.

Marines often have to be resourceful to uphold their tradition of a force-in-readiness, and there were not enough OY's in good condition for VMO-6. Gottschalk solved the problem by taking four planes which he considered fairly "flyable" and four more to be cannibalized for spare parts when the need arose.[3]

His outfit shared space on the carrier with two Marine fighter squadrons, VMF-214 and VMF-323. A small area on the flight deck was left clear for the helicopters, which flew daily mail runs and liaison missions between the ships of the fleet. The Brigade had originally been ordered to land in Japan for training; but during the voyage the military situation in Korea deteriorated so alarmingly that General MacArthur directed the ground forces to proceed to Pusan.

The *Badoeng Strait* docked at Kobe, Japan, on the evening of July 31. Officers and men of VMO-6 were busy all night unloading their gear. Early the next morning, the helicopters took off from a vacant lot while four OY's used a city street

---

* The original USS *Langley* went down in the battle of the Java Sea in 1942, and a light aircraft carrier was later given the name.

for a runway, even though the wing tips had precious little clearance between telephone posts. This forward echelon flew to the Itami Air Force Base, and thence across the inland sea to Pusan on August 2, just as the ground forces were disembarking. Meanwhile the rear echelon of VMO-6 came on four days later from Kobe in an LST.[4]

Some of the original personnel having been left behind in California or Japan for later arrival, the squadron was now down to a fighting strength of eleven officers (six OY and five helicopter pilots), 65 enlisted men, eight OY planes, and four helicopters.[5] The HO3S-1's had their work cut out for them immediately, since General Craig was already a convert to the advantages of rotary-wing aircraft.

A veteran of 33 years' service in the Marine Corps, he was born in Connecticut and educated at the St. Johns Military Academy, Delafield, Wis. In 1917 he was commissioned a second lieutenant, and his foreign shore duty during the next decade took him to Haiti, the Dominican Republic, the Philippines, China, and Nicaragua. Craig was both student and instructor at the Marine Corps Schools during the 1930's. In World War II he commanded the 9th Marine Regiment on Guam. As operations officer of the Fifth Amphibious Corps, he participated in the planning and assault on Iwo Jima. In 1949, commanding the 1st Provisional Marine Brigade on Guam, he was introduced to his first helicopter—a Navy aircraft "loaned" to him by a carrier. He needed no further recommendation, and after the Marine landing at Pusan he made the helicopter his principal vehicle.

Both Craig and his G-3 (operations) officer, Lieutenant Colonel Joseph L. Stewart, were airborne most of the first day. The Brigade commander's initial flight took him from Pusan about 30 miles to the Changwon area (see accompanying map). On the way he landed to give instructions to the commanding officer of the Marine battalion leading the route march to the assembly area selected by Stewart on a basis of helicopter reconnaissance.

Craig's pilot, Lieutenant Gustave F. Lueddeke, set the HO3S-1 down in a yard between three native huts, and took off vertically a few minutes later. Next, the general selected a site for his forward CP and landed again to deposit his personal gear. Then he flew to Masan to confer with Lieutenant General Walton H. Walker, USA, commanding the Eighth U.S. Army in Korea (EUSAK), and Major General William B. Kean, USA, the commander of the Army 25th Infantry Division. On his return trip, Craig landed three more times to speak to Marine battalion or company commanders.[6]

Only the helicopter could have made this itinerary possible in a period of a few hours. A fixed-wing plane could not have landed in such unlikely spots, and a jeep could not have covered the same route before nightfall over narrow, twisting roads choked with Army and Marine vehicles.

The mission of VMO squadrons had been officially stated in 1949 as the conduct of "tactical air reconnaissance, artillery spotting, and other flight operations within the capabilities of assigned aircraft in support of ground units."[7] As for the personnel situation, Major Gottschalk commented that VMO squadrons had been "considered in the past as of something of a stepchild of aviation. Fortunately, due to the career management program in aviation, several well-qualified fighter pilots had been recently assigned to VMO-6, flying the OY's."[8]

The helicopter group consisted of picked men, so that VMO-6 had both the personnel and opportunity to set standards for future VMO squadrons. Gottschalk, an OY pilot himself, operated from the outset on the principle that practically any flying task, no matter how difficult, came within the capabilities of assigned aircraft in support of ground units.

This left plenty of room for both helicopters and OY's to show what they could do under combat conditions.[9]

THE MARINE COUNTERATTACK

Up to this time the Korean Reds had not suffered a reverse worth mentioning while overrunning most of the Republic of Korea. Late in July the recently committed Eighth Army included the 24th and 25th Infantry Divisions and 1st Cavalry (infantry) Division. These early U.S. arrivals, consisting largely of occupation troops from Japan, shared with five battered, understrength ROK divisions a struggle against material odds. Necessity imposed a strategy of trading space for time, and the UN forces sold ground as dearly as possible. But their left flank was "up in the air," for lack of numbers, and an end run took the enemy all the way to the southwest tip of the peninsula. Then, wheeling eastward, the NK forces drove past Chinju to a point within 20 miles of Pusan.

This was the situation when the Marines landed, just the day after the debarkation of the Army 2d Infantry Division and 5th RCT. Stateside radio listeners, depressed by the outlook, did not yet suspect that the Korean "police action" would become the fourth largest military effort of U.S. history before the end of the year. But Moscow had not erred in military calculations, and the NK army was actually a capable military instrument. The well-trained infantry divisions were at their best in camouflage, infiltration, and night attacks. North Korean generalship was by no means contemptible, and supply problems were largely solved by living on the invaded country.

Until the first two days of August, when reinforcements arrived, General Walker lacked the weight to strike back. On the 4th, however, the Plans Section of EUSAK completed a study of plans, quickly approved, for a counterattack along the Masan-Chinju axis. August 6 dated the organization of Task Force Kean, named after the commanding general of the 25th Infantry Division, with a mission of counterattacking toward Chinju. The primary object was to defend the vital UN supply port of Pusan, and it was further desired to relieve the pressure on the secondary port of Masan.[10]

Task Force Kean had as its main components the 25th Division, the 1st Provisional Marine Brigade, and the Army 5th RCT. The Marine ground forces, after spending three days in EUSAK reserve at Changwon, moved into position near Chindong-ni on the 6th in preparation for the jump-off the next morning.

In 1947 a committee of the Marine Corps Schools had reported no less than 46 possible military uses for helicopters. Although this would appear to be a comprehensive list, the committee had never supposed that a helicopter could become a substitute for a map. Yet this was what happened during the first week of August, 1950, according to General Craig.

"Maps were poor," he recalled, "and no one in the Brigade had personal knowledge of the terrain over which we were to fight. Helicopters were a life saver in this connection, as they provided the means for even commanders of small units to get into the air quickly from almost any point and identify roads, villages and key points prior to moving their troops.[11]

Ever since the first day, the aircraft of VMO-6 had been on call from dawn to dark. While the helicopters flew staff and command missions, the OY's provided convoy escort for the Brigade or went out on observation and reconnaissance missions. Both types were used to search the surrounding mountains for evidences of infiltrating North Koreans.[12]

Seldom in military history has a new weapon been the means of saving lives, but the helicopters made a start on August 4 with their first casualty evacuation. Five seriously wounded Marines were brought out the next day, three of them from hillsides too steep for a jeep. On the return trips from Pusan, the helicopters delivered blood plasma to a field hospital.

The HO3S-1 had not been designed as a flying ambulance, but Marine resourcefulness prevailed when the aircraft were modified by removing the right window and installing straps in the cabin on the opposite side to hold a stretcher securely. Even so, the patient's feet protruded about 20 inches outside the window.[13]

Staff and command missions kept the helicopters occupied on the 6th. General Craig flew to Masan to receive orders and verbal instructions for commitment of the Marines. And the following morning, the eighth anniversary of the Marine landing on Guadalcanal, the Brigade jumped off to initiate the first sustained counterattack of UN forces in Korea.

Craig and Stewart learned at an early hour that a helicopter makes an inviting target. After landing in a dry stream bed under NK observation, they found enemy artillery and mortar shells registering too intimately for comfort. The Marine officers ordered the helicopter to take off in haste as they continued their tour on foot.[14]

The counterattack ran into heavy opposition at the road junction west of Chindong-ni, and at 1120 Craig was directed by the task force commander to assume control of all Army as well as Marine troops in the area—a responsibility which he held until the afternoon of the 9th.[15] During this critical period he relied largely upon helicopters for command and staff missions. And though he could not actually be in two places at once, the Brigade commander gave that illusion with his frequent landings at Army or Marine battalion CP's.

Such occasions had a historic significance. For the helicopter promised to bring back a personal element to command that has largely been lost in modern times. Obviously it is no longer possible or even desirable for a general to lead the advance in the eighteenth-century manner. But it could be argued that the pendulum has swung too far in the other direction when a present-day division commander and his staff sometimes become remote figures to junior line officers. Craig's helicopter did a good deal to restore the balance by bridging the gap between staff and line. The slender, energetic Marine general became a familiar sight to company and even platoon commanders as he landed to give oral instructions, and his leadership had much to do with the smashing of NK resistance at the Chindong-ni road junction.

THE FIRST UN VICTORY

By the morning of the 10th the enemy was in full retreat. The Marines pounded in pursuit along the southern route to Chinju while the Army 5th RCT took the northern road. Just beyond Kosong the Marines caught up with the NK transport, and the Corsairs had a "turkey shoot."[16] About 20 vehicles were destroyed and an equal number of Russian-made trucks or jeeps abandoned in good condition.[17]

The advance continued for two more days. As the first UN victory of the war, it was heartening after weeks of retreat. Then, with the final objective in sight, both Marine and Army units were pulled back. The reason, as the disgruntled troops learned later, was because of preparations for a new EUSAK counterattack in the Naktong Bulge area, where enemy advances threatened the UN lifeline from Pusan to Taegu.

As a preliminary, Craig received orders from the task force commander at noon on the 12th to rush a reinforced battalion about 25 miles to the rear in the Chindong-ni area. Infiltrating Korean Reds had overrun an Army artillery battalion and threatened to cut the MSR.[18]

Only the helicopter could have enabled the Marine general

to execute in a single afternoon a maneuver calling for the 25-mile road lift of a reinforced battalion with its munitions, and an assault in the opposite direction. After taking off from his CP at Kosong, he made two landings to give orders to his regimental and battalion commanders. Next, he spotted two columns of Marine trucks from the air and landed twice more to direct them to dump their loads and provide transportation for the troops. His G-3 and the battalion commander had meanwhile been sent ahead by helicopter to reconnoiter the objective area and plan for the Marines to deploy and attack upon arrival. Owing to these preparations, the assault troops seized part of the enemy position before darkness.[19]

From his helicopter Craig saw the attack launched at sunset while flying to Masan for a conference with Kean. There he was informed of General Walker's orders for a withdrawal at daybreak. He returned to Kosong and Lueddeke landed successfully at the CP in the early darkness.

"This was just another instance of the value of the helicopter," said Craig. "It enabled me to attend a personal conference with the over-all commander in the area at a critical time, and to return to my command without delay. The late hour and number of other units involved did not permit General Kean to issue a complicated written order and distribute it through channels prior to darkness, nor would I have had time to commence the withdrawal."[20]

Breaking off an action, as any platoon leader knows, can be harder than starting one. At first light on August 13, Craig had the problem of directing two Marine attacks, 25 miles apart, in opposite directions. Helicopters were used by the Brigade command and staff to maintain positive control over the heavily engaged rearguard battalion as it broke off contact with the enemy east of Chinju, while the other battalion was taking the remainder of the NK position near Chindong-ni.

One of the helicopters "dodged" enemy 20mm fire to make drops to Marine infantry on a 1,600-foot ridgeline, and another helicopter had rifle grenades lobbed at it after landing in a forward area. VMO-6 helicopter and OY flights that day totaled 45, adding up to 53.9 hours in the air.[21]

Terrific heat and choking dust had created the need for frequent air drops of water to Marine ground forces during the seven days of this operation. Helicopter evacuations of seriously wounded men were of almost hourly occurrence, and August 8 dated the first night evacuation of history. The patient, a wounded regimental surgeon, was safely landed by Captain Victor A. Armstrong in an area marked by flares.[22]

Rescue missions were added to the duties of the helicopters two days later when Lieutenant Doyle Cole's F4U was shot down by antiaircraft fire while flying close support. As it glided into the sea not far offshore, General Craig was a witness while making a command flight in Gus Lueddeke's helicopter. And the Brigade commander supplied the muscle to hoist Cole from his raft into the machine as it hovered a few feet over the water.

Later that same afternoon Lueddeke rescued a second Corsair pilot, Captain Vivian Moses of VMF-323, who had crash-landed behind the enemy lines. Unfortunately, Moses was shot down again three days later, and the unconscious pilot drowned in a rice paddy before Captain Eugene J. Pope could rescue him in a VMO-6 helicopter.[23]

Major Gottschalk did not overestimate the value of such operations when he asserted that "the availability of the helicopters to pick up wounded from units that were cut off some distance from the main body improved the morale of the men in the lines." He added that VMO-6 rescue missions also "helped the morale of the fighter pilots in support of the Marine brigade."[24]

THE MARINES AS FIREMEN

The Marine ground-air team, as the "firemen" of the Pusan Perimeter, launched two more counterattacks in rapid succession. Eighth Army strategy was primarily defensive at this stage, aiming above all to hold the Pusan Perimeter—that irregular semicircle of thinly manned positions stretching from the secondary port of Pohang on the east coast to Taegu and the Naktong Bulge, then dipping southward to the vicinity of Masan.

Enemy pressure in the Naktong Bulge area had become menacing before the Sachon-Chinju operation ended. This threat to the Taegu-Pusan supply route resulted in Eighth Army orders placing the Marine brigade under the operational control of the 24th Infantry Division for a new counterattack. On August 17 the Marine infantry and tanks went up against Obong-ni Ridge, sometimes known as No Name Ridge, while Army units attacked on the right. Twice the assault troops fought their way to the crest, only to find the position untenable. A third desperate attempt won a foothold for two depleted companies. There they clung all night, fighting off repeated enemy attacks in the darkness. It was nip and tuck until daybreak, when Marine air support and artillery fires helped to restore the lines. Enemy resistance suddenly collapsed at noon on the 18th, and the Corsairs took a frightful toll of routed NK troops swimming the Naktong in their efforts to escape.[25]

After a week in an assembly area at Changwon, the Marines were back in this same area for a new counterattack, this time under the operational control of the 2d Infantry Division. On September 1 the Red Koreans had mounted their supreme effort. Realizing that time was fighting against them as the Eighth Army gained strength, they struck in the Naktong

Bulge area with a total of 13 divisions, including many green troops hastily raised for the attempt. Again they crossed the Naktong in force, pushing seven miles beyond Obong-ni Ridge and threatening the Taegu-Pusan route.

The Marines jumped off at daybreak on September 3, 1950. Attacking toward Obong-ni Ridge, they drove about 3,000 yards the first day against heavy opposition as 2d Division units advanced on the right. Two more days of steady slugging took General Craig's men to their assigned objectives, where they were relieved on the 6th by 2d Division elements. The last NK offensive had been stopped cold and the enemy was now on the defensive.[26]

Altogether, the 1st Provisional Marine Brigade had been employed three times in a month by the Eighth Army as a hard-hitting mobile reserve. The firemen of the Pusan Perimeter had fought three difficult offensive operations and traveled a total of 380 miles.[27] Brilliant close air support was provided throughout by the two carrier-borne fighter squadrons, VMF-214 and VMF-323, as well as elements of Japan-based VMF(N)-513. Often their results owed to the reconnaissance missions of VMO-6 aircraft, and there was no better morale factor than the knowledge that the helicopters would attempt a rescue if a fighter pilot crashed in enemy territory.

VMO-6 aircraft carried out their usual command, staff, liaison, artillery spotting, rescue, and casualty evacuation flights in the two Naktong Bulge operations. And on September 3 the helicopters claimed a new "first" with a successful wire-laying operation mission in combat. The squadron reported 898 flights for a total of 805 hours in August—580 flights and 348 hours being logged by the helicopters, and 318 flights and 457 hours by the OY's.[28]

This was a heavy schedule in view of the primitive development of helicopter instruments. Makeshifts had to be devised continually by pilots who flew with their heads outside the windows for vision in rainstorms, and moved sandbags or rocks about the cabin to maintain the balance so essential to safety with this delicately poised type of aircraft.

On the other hand, these operations offered fresh evidence that the egg beaters were not as vulnerable as had sometimes been supposed. Both the rotor blades and cockpits took hits from enemy small-arms fire without a machine being brought down, and some spine-jarring landings were made in rough country without serious damage.

Lieutenant Colonel Raymond L. Murray, commanding officer of the 5th Marines, could testify as to the ability of the helicopter to "dodge" enemy bullets. While making a reconnaissance flight in the Chindong-ni area, his helicopter became the target of automatic and small-arms fire at uncomfortably close range from NK troops hidden along both slopes of a narrow valley. But Pilot Gene Pope maneuvered the ship so skilfully, changing speed and altitude and taking every advantage of the terrain, that no harm resulted.

By the middle of August it had become apparent that four helicopters could not meet all the Brigade demands. An appeal was made on the 15th to the 1st Marine Aircraft Wing, which sent two more HO3S-'s from Japan with two pilots and five mechanics.[29]

Throughout the Brigade operations the helicopter had been, as General Craig put it, the "emergency weapon" of the command and staff. Early in August he sent a message to General Shepherd, now commanding FMFPac, requesting that machines of troop-carrying capacity be attached to the Brigade.[30] But such equipment was not available at the time, and helicopter troop lifts in Korea had to wait until the following year.

In his final report of Brigade operations, dated September 11, 1950, Craig summed up the case for the helicopter:

"The mountainous terrain of Korea presents a difficult problem for security of flanks and rear, and of bivouac areas. The troop carrier type of aircraft (helicopter) would be ideal for use in Korea to post patrols and outguards on high, dominating terrain which would take hours to climb. There are many missions, both combatant and noncombatant, which these helicopters could perform. It is believed that their use would materially contribute to the effectiveness and security of our operations and insure the earlier defeat of the enemy. They should be made available for use at the earliest possible date."[31]

The helicopter had not made its excellent showing at the expense of the OY plane. One of the primary missions of HMX-1, it will be recalled, was evaluating the two types of aircraft for the purposes of an observation squadron. Some enthusiasts were in favor of an all-helicopter VMO squadron, but Colonel Dyer favored a fairly even balance. His judgment was upheld by a recommendation of VMO-6 on the basis of combat experience in the Pusan Perimeter:

"A composite squadron composed of light OY type liaison aircraft and liaison type helicopters is considered both desirable and necessary."

It was further recommended that a VMO squadron be made up of 25 officers and 100 enlisted men, including three ground officers specializing in engineering, matériel, and intelligence. Equipment was to consist of ten OY type aircraft combined with eight liaison and two transport helicopters.[32]

THE INCHON LANDING

Early in July, before the Brigade sailed, General Shepherd had flown to Tokyo to confer with General MacArthur. The UN commander had already determined to strike a decisive blow with an amphibious operation, and on July 25 he was granted his third request for a Marine division in Korea.

At this time the 1st Marine Division was a mere skeleton organization at Camp Pendleton. In order to reach a wartime strength of about 22,000 men, it would be necessary to call up the reserves—"the Minute Men of 1950"—and absorb the units of the Brigade.[33]

It took a miracle of organization for the main body of the division to sail from California on August 18, minus one infantry regiment as well as the Brigade troops. Major General Oliver P. Smith, the commanding general, flew to Tokyo just ahead of 23 officers and enlisted men who constituted a Marine planning group for the proposed amphibious operation. In the Japanese capital he was to encounter General Shepherd and General Harris, the other two members of the Special Board of 1946 which launched the Marine helicopter development program. But the new amphibious operation would have to be carried out in the old manner—there were not enough helicopters on earth to lift the assault troops.

The supreme commander had never swerved from his insistence upon a landing at Inchon as a prelude to striking inland and seizing Seoul, the enemy's chief communications center. He visioned the peninsula as a sack in which the NK forces were burrowing toward the bottom, and he proposed to pull the drawstring. Adverse tides, mud flats, and other hydrographical obstacles made the operation one of the most hazardous the Navy-Marine team had ever attempted, but the planning went ahead while the Brigade was fighting in Korea. A new Army organization, designated as X Corps, was set up by MacArthur as a landing force and placed under the command of Major General Edward M. Almond, USA. The 1st Marine Division, the Army 7th Infantry Division, and the Army 187th Airborne RCT were to be the main components, though the last two could not arrive in time for D-day on September 15, 1950.

The main body of the 1st Marine Division landed at Kobe,

Japan, on August 31. Three days later a typhoon named JANE provided a boisterous welcome with winds of 110 miles per hour. This meant a serious loss of time at the task of unloading mixed-type cargo and combat-loading it into assault-type shipping. But the cargo ships managed to sail for the objective area on September 10, and the troopships two days later. A second typhoon, bearing the romantic name of KEZIA, threatened to have the last word at Inchon. The carrier *Boxer*, nearing Japan from the U.S. with 96 planes on deck, actually did have to contend with 90-mile winds. But the skirts of the hussy KEZIA merely brushed the amphibious armada, and by the 12th the planners could put this worry out of mind.[34]

That day the 5th Marines and other Brigade troops embarked at Pusan for the objective area, having reassumed their old designations in the division. The 7th Marines could not arrive until the 21st, so that the assault troops would consist of only two Marine infantry regiments, the 1st and 5th, to seize a seaport of 250,000 prewar population (see accompanying map). X Corps G-2 estimates did not credit the enemy with more than 2,500 troops, but even a few well-directed battalions could make another Tarawa out of Inchon.

Surprise was out of the question, since only a few days in the middle of the month had high enough tides for the LST's. The inner harbor was guarded by a fortified island, Wolmi-do, which must be neutralized during the morning tide so that an assault could be mounted on the mainland during the last 90 minutes of daylight. Thus the defenders would be given most of D-day for last-minute preparations.

Only a fraction of the time ordinarily allotted to planning had been available. Nevertheless, the preliminary bombardments and air strikes of Joint Task Force 7 took place according to schedule; and at 0631 on the morning of D-day the first wave of a battalion of the 5th Marines hit GREEN Beach

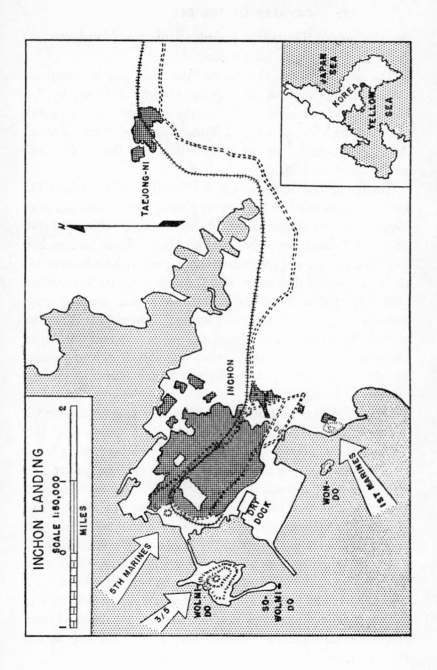

on Wolmi-do. Thirty-one minutes later the island was secured at a cost of 17 men wounded.[35]

The assault troops ran up an American flag in token of victory. It was seen on the flagship *Mount McKinley* by the three topmost leaders in the chain of command—General MacArthur, Vice Admiral C. Turner Joy, and Vice Admiral Arthur D. Struble. In celebration they left the bridge and went below for coffee.

The great test still awaited for Read Admiral James H. Doyle, commander of the attack force, Task Force 90, and General Smith, commander of the landing force, the 1st Marine Division. As H-hour approached, planes and rocket ships joined in the 45-minute barrage poured into Inchon by the cruisers and destroyers giving direct support. The target area was hidden by smoke and flame as the landing craft churned the water of the inner harbor. Rain squalls added to already low visibility, so that some confusion resulted when the assault waves hit the beaches at 1730. But Marine amphibious experience paid off after veteran company officers and NCO's took charge.

Enemy mortar and automatic weapons fire was scattered and poorly directed as Ray Murray's 5th Marines (less the Wolmi-do battalion) scrambled over the sea wall rising from the narrow strip of urban waterfront. Not enough scaling ladders had been provided, but the Marines surmounted the barrier as best they could and re-formed for the drive to the objective line, about 1,000 yards distant. The critical moment approached as the six infantry companies plunged through the premature dusk into the narrow streets and alleys of a strange Oriental city. But company officers had been well briefed as to directions, and the defenders were disorganized by the barrage. Speed was the best resource of attackers who reached their objectives within three hours and dug in for the night.

Another calculated risk of the Inchon landing was vindicated when eight LST's wallowed toward the 1,000-foot strip of RED Beach in the wake of the assault waves. The planners had decided to beach these Navy workhorses at H-plus-30 minutes with high priority supplies, even though they would be targets for such enemy shore guns as had not yet been silenced. This bold gambit succeeded, even though a few enemy mortar rounds registered on hulls containing gasoline and napalm. But fortune as usual blessed the bold, and no serious damage resulted before the shore guns were silenced.[36]

During the BLUE Beach landings, the leading waves of Colonel Lewis B. "Chesty" Puller's 1st Marines also had their troubles with delay, confusion, and intermingling of units. But enemy resistance was light in this sparsely settled factory district south of the city, and the assault troops pushed ahead through the darkness without much regard for flanks. After crossing a bottomland of rice paddies, they reached the high ground of the objective line within four hours and dug in for the night.[37]

At 0630 the next morning the attack was resumed. The two battalions of the 5th Marines moved out in column through the principal east-west streets, rejoined by the Wolmi-do battalion. Marine artillery had also crossed over from that island, but the assault troops had little need of such support. For the 5th Marines met only scattered resistance, and the 1st Marines found the terrain more of a handicap than the enemy during the 7,000 yard advance to seal off the base of the Inchon peninsula. Mopping up pockets of bypassed resistance was left to the Korean Marine Corps (KMC) troops as the two Marine regiments made contact at 1000 on September 16 and combined for a drive to the eastern outskirts of the city.*

---

* This was the baptism of fire for Korean Marines who were given a brief period of training by U.S. Marine instructors. They developed a high *esprit de corps* and were taken into the 1st Marine Division as a fourth infantry regiment in the spring of 1951.

The landing phase ended at 1730, exactly 24 hours after hitting the beaches, when General Smith set up his CP near the force beachhead line just east of Inchon. Marine casualties so far were 21 killed and 186 wounded. Enemy losses amounted to nearly 300 prisoners and an estimated 1,350 killed and wounded.[38]

Navy and Marine teamwork had succeeded brilliantly in spite of the enemy's foreknowledge that a landing would be attempted. It was a victory in logistical as well as tactical respects, for Marine engineers announced that the harbor facilities could soon be made operative without major repairs.

THE ADVANCE ON SEOUL

On D-day the pilots and crewmen of VMO-6 had been spectators. The next morning, however, an LST-based helicopter of the squadron rescued a Navy F4U pilot who had ditched in Inchon harbor. Such operations had become so commonplace by this time that the squadron report did not bother to mention the name of either the rescuer or the rescued.[39]

Both JTF-7 and X Corps had organic air support during the landing. JTF-7 depended on a Naval fast carrier task force, TF-77, for deep support and interdiction strikes. Tactical air command, X Corps, was a provisional 1st Marine Aircraft Wing organization under the operational control of General Almond and tactical direction of General Cushman. Three fighter squadrons, based on the *Sicily* and *Badoeng Strait*, had the responsibility of close air support. After the securing of Kimpo Airfield, they were to be based there along with VMO-6 and the command and ground echelons flown in from Japan.[40]

On the 17th the observation squadron moved to the eastern outskirts of Inchon near General Smith's CP. There a road served as a strip for the OY's, and the helicopters needed only a vacant lot.[41]

That morning the two infantry regiments began the 20-mile advance on Seoul, a capital of a million and a half population before the war. On the 16th the Eighth Army had launched a combined offensive in the Pusan Perimeter with the object of driving northward and making contact with X Corps.

The two Marine infantry regiments took parallel routes toward Seoul (see accompanying map). They depended on air strikes and naval gunfire for flank protection at first. Then elements of the 7th Infantry Division landed and moved up on the right, while the 187th Airborne RCT took a position on the left after its arrival.[42]

On the afternoon of the 17th the hard-driving 5th Marines seized Kimpo Airfield, the largest in Korea. A VMO-6 helicopter was the first U.S. aircraft to land. Enemy resistance in the area had not been fully put down when Vic Armstrong set his HO3S down upon the runway with General Shepherd and Colonel Krulak as passengers.[43]

VMO-6 combat missions on September 19 resulted in the carrying out of two directed air strikes, 14 utility and liaison missions, eight artillery fire missions, seven evacuation flights, and seven tactical air reconnaissance missions. Utility missions included such routine jobs as wire laying, resupply, and transporting passengers.[44]

After moving to Kimpo Airfield the next day, Gottschalk and his men went on a dawn-to-dark schedule. Enemy resistance was stiffening as the 5th Marines fought its way across the river Han and attacked the northwest approaches to the former ROK capital. Meanwhile the 1st Marines, slugging ahead on the southern route, had a hard fight to take Yongdungpo, an industrial suburb of Seoul. In this area an OY plane was so badly riddled by enemy fire that it had to be abandoned by a pilot and observer who parachuted to safety.

That same day a Marine fighter pilot was shot down in NK territory, and Lieutenant Arthur R. Bancroft flew to the rescue in a VMO-6 helicopter. Enemy fire destroyed his aircraft on the ground after he landed, but Bancroft and the fighter pilot were unhurt. They were rescued a few minutes later by Lieutenant Robert Longstaff, who made a daring landing in his HO3S and picked up both stranded airmen under fire.[45]

As the grinding advance on Seoul continued, the aircraft of VMO-6 had their job cut out for them. Operating over a large area, they were daily exposed to enemy small-arms, automatic, and antiaircraft fire.

"It was found," reported Gottschalk, "that OY's and helicopters could and did sustain considerable small-arms fire and still return to base to fly again. However, with the intense small-arms fire and automatic fire of 50-caliber, 20mm, and 40mm automatic weapons, the pilots had to make every use of the terrain, the sun, and other factors that could possibly aid the flight."[46]

Even so, VMO-6 pilots sometimes took serious risks. When a Navy F4U pilot was shot down north of the 39th Parallel, nearly a hundred miles inside the enemy lines, Vic Armstrong made a successful rescue on September 23 and landed at Kimpo Airfield after dark while the crewmen held flashlights.[47] The next day Bob Longstaff set a record for speed by completing in six minutes the rescue of a Marine pilot and crewman who crash-landed in a rice paddy five miles north of Kimpo.[48]

It was a fairly typical day's work on the 23d when VMO-6 flew ten reconnaissance, five artillery spot, one utility, six evacuation, and two rescue missions for a total of 30.2 hours. The results were five artillery registrations, four artillery fire missions, two directed air strikes, six casualty evacuations, and a successful rescue mission.[49]

The 7th Marines having landed two days before, the 1st Marine Division now had three infantry regiments closing in on Seoul—the 7th on the left and the 5th in the center to the north of the Han, and the 1st on the right to the south of the city and river. This scheme of maneuver resulted in a difficult command situation for General Smith, with his CP south of the Han at Kimpo. There was no bridge as yet, and crossing by amphibious tractor could be a slow process.

"In this situation," commented the general, "the helicopter was of inestimable value to the division commander and his staff in keeping personal contact with subordinate units with a minimum of in-transit time."[50]

Owing to the limited number of helicopters, it became standard procedure to divert such aircraft at a moment's notice from command and liaison flights to evacuation or rescue missions. Frequently, upon arrival at a command post, General Smith or his ADC, General Craig, released a helicopter for a casualty evacuation and continued by jeep.

The enemy put up a terrific fight at the northwest approaches of Seoul. But the 5th Marines fought its way to the outskirts while the 1st Marines crossed the river and sliced straight through the heart of the city. It took a two-day battle before Marine infantry, supported by tanks, artillery, and air strikes, reduced NK street barricades defended to the death. But on September 29 General MacArthur turned the city over to President Syngman Rhee of the Republic of Korea.

The liberation ceremonies were a bit premature. On that very day, VMO-6 had its heaviest losses so far in Korea. With the enemy retreating from Seoul, aircraft of the squadron were kept busy at directing strikes and artillery fires. While carrying out an observation mission, an OY was shot down five miles north of Seoul, resulting in the death of the observer, Captain Edwin E. Rives, and the capture of the pilot, Lieutenant Thomas D. Odenbaugh. An HO3S-1 flown by

Arthur Bancroft had been sent to the rescue, but it too was destroyed by antiaircraft fire with the death of the pilot.[51]

During the first week of October the 1st and 5th Marines set up defensive positions north of Seoul while Colonel Homer L. Litzenburg's 7th Regiment advanced to Uijongbu with a mission of blocking the main route leading to Pyongyang, the Red Korean capital. Eighth Army forces, thrusting northward, had made contact twenty miles south of Seoul on September 26 with Army units of X Corps. Thus the remnants of 13 enemy divisions were caught between the strategic hammer and anvil, and organized resistance was rapidly collapsing early in October.

VMO-6 pilots flew reconnaissance, command, liaison, and artillery spot missions in support of the 7th Marines during its advance. Lieutenant Floyd J. Englehart completed two successful rescues of downed fighter pilots, and his helicopter also provided transportation on October 4 when General Clifton B. Cates, Commandant of the Marine Corps, made a tour of inspection.[52]

At 1200 on October 7, 1950, the three-week Inchon-Seoul operation came to an end with the 1st Marine Division being relieved by Eighth Army elements driving northward in pursuit of a shattered enemy. The Leathernecks returned to the Inchon area by convoy, and three days later they were boarding the troopships for a new adventure on the other side of Korea.

CHAPTER VIII

Wings of Mercy

Planning for a new amphibious operation began before the old one ended. On September 29, 1950, the date of the official liberation of Seoul, the Marines and other major units of X Corps were warned that plans had been initiated for an assault landing at Wonsan, on the northeast coast of Korea.

Five days later a X Corps operational order designated the 1st Marine Division as landing force of TF-90 under the command of Admiral Doyle. After being relieved, the Marines crowded into LST's at Inchon on October 12 for the voyage around the peninsula. But the beaten NK forces were disintegrating so rapidly that Wonsan fell like a ripe plum to the ROK's on the 10th before the Marines could be outloaded.

High-level Army, Navy, and Marine Corps planners found themselves unable to catch up with a fluid situation. Next, they contemplated a X Corps administrative landing at Wonsan on October 20, followed by a drive across the rocky spinal column of the peninsula to link up with the Eighth Army for an attack on Pyongyang (see accompanying map). But the NK capital was taken on the 19th by Eighth Army forces advancing up the west coast.

The Marines were kept on shipboard an additional week while TF-90 minesweepers cleared Wonsan harbor of Russian-made influence-type mines. Bob Hope and Marilyn Max-

well had already hit the beach to put on a USO show for
Marine air units when the ground forces began their landing
on the 25th. It was probably the tamest of some 280 landings
in Marine Corps history.[1]

Two VMO-6 helicopter pilots, Captain Wallace D. Blatt
and Lieutenant Charles C. Ward, reached Wonsan two
days before the infantry landed. Newly arrived in Korea, they
had flown from Kimpo while the main body of the squadron
proceeded by LST.[2]

At Kimpo a flight echelon had been left behind under the
command of Captain Armstrong. Emergency requests were
received on October 22 from the Fifth Air Force for assistance
in evacuating casualties of the 187th Airborne RCT in the
Sukchon area. Captain Gene Morrison brought out eight
seriously wounded men in his HO3S to Pyongyang, and five
more were evacuated by OY planes.[3]

This was one of many mercy flights made by Marine helicopters to aid Army or Air Force units. Stateside critics who
viewed with alarm the supposed lack of unity in the U.S.
armed services might have been pleasantly disillusioned to see
the co-operation prevailing at the front.

Marine flying windmills were on call for rescue missions as
well as casualty evacuations. On October 24 Blatt and Ward
flew deep into enemy territory to Koto-ri, about 100 miles
north of Wonsan. There they rescued two downed U.S. Air
Force pilots, Lieutenant Edwin Thomas and Lieutenant
Thomas J. Pointeck.[4]

The Air Force had long been interested in rotary-wing aircraft for such purposes, and its 3d Air Rescue Squadron had
used helicopters prior to the conflict in Korea. The Marine
Corps led the way in all-around tactical employment, however, and it did not take long for the other services to become
converts. As early as August 26, 1950, General Craig noted in
a letter to the Assistant Commandant of the Marine Corps:

"The Army is enthusiastic over our ideas of employment of this type of aircraft and is going ahead with the idea of employing them on a large scale."[5]

Helicopter gospel spread during the Inchon-Seoul operation until VMO-6 aircraft completed nearly as many missions for the Army on some days as the Marine Corps. "The X Corps commander time and time again used the helicopters for his front line reconnaissance," reported Major Gottschalk. "On several occasions, VMO-6 aircraft were used to evacuate wounded from the 1st Cavalry Division and elements of the Eighth Army which had advanced so rapidly from the southern perimeter that their supporting medical facilities and ambulances were outdistanced. Again, later in the campaign, the helicopters and OY's were used to assist in evacuating wounded of the Eighth Army on the advance toward Pyongyang."[6]

Even at this early date, there could be no question that the helicopter had proved itself far superior to any other means of evacuating badly wounded men from mountainous or roadless country at the front. A single mission by a Marine helicopter usually sufficed to convince Army medical officers of the urgent need for this type of aircraft.

As for the 1st Marine Division, it is likely that General Shepherd expressed the prevailing opinion in a report of his visit to the front. The following excerpt was quoted in a joint memorandum sent on September 19, 1950, by Brigadier General Clayton C. Jerome to five U.S. Navy admirals:

"There are no superlatives adequate to describe the general reaction to the helicopter. Almost any individual questioned could offer some personal story to emphasize the valuable part played by the five HO3S planes available. Reconnaissance, liaison, visual flank security, movement of security patrols from one key locality to the next, posting and supply of security detachments, and many more. There is no doubt that the enthusiasm voiced by the Brigade is entirely warranted. Moreover, the usefulness of the helicopter is not by any means confined to a situation such as encountered in Korea. No effort should be spared to get helicopters—larger than the HO3S if possible—but helicopters in any form, to the theater at once, and on a priority higher than any other weapon . . . helicopters, more helicopters, and more helicopters in the Korean area!"[7]

This was the conviction of a Marine leader, destined to be the next commandant, who had been one of the founding fathers of the helicopter concept in 1946. Twelve months after he wrote these words, General Shepherd was to see Marine helicopter doctrine adopted to a large extent by other U.S. armed forces in Korea. The helicopter was on its way to becoming the foremost tactical development of the war.

WINGS OVER THE RESERVOIR

More HO3S-1 pilots, mechanics, and HO3S-1 aircraft reached Japan on the USS *Leyte* early in October and reported to Major Gottschalk at Kimpo just before the move to Wonsan. This brought the strength of VMO-6 up to 25 officers, 95 enlisted men, eight OY-2's, two L5G planes, and nine HO3S aircraft.[8]

Immediately after the 1st Marine Division landing, a battalion of infantry was sent to Kojo, about 30 miles south of Wonsan. Korean Red guerrillas attacked on the night of October 27, and the helicopters of VMO-6 evacuated Marine casualties after the enemy was repulsed. Blatt, Ward, Lueddeke, Englehardt, and Morrison brought out wounded men the next day, and Captain George B. Farish was kept busy with rescue missions. While flying low over the Kojo area, he saw the word HELP spelled out in rice straw near a small strawstack which set up a violent agitation. Out crawled PFC William Meister, who had hidden from the enemy after being cut off from his outfit during the confused fight in the darkness. Farish landed and took him aboard, and on his return trip he rescued two more beleaguered Marines, Corporal Donald Pluim and PFC Richard Graham. Next, he was directed by Marine fighter planes to a Corsair which had crashed in the hills west of Kojo. Farish hovered a few feet above the wreck and determined that the pilot was dead. He was unable to bring back the body but guided a ground patrol to the spot.[9]

Early in November the echelon left at Kimpo rejoined the squadron, which moved from Wonsan to the Yonpo Airfield near Hungnam. There VMO-6 came under the operational control of the 1st Marine Division and the administrative and logistical control of the 1st Marine Air Wing. General Harris took personal command of the fighter squadrons at Wonsan and Yonpo.

The new over-all plan of the supreme command called for UN forces to move up to the border of Manchuria. A three-pronged advance was envisioned by X Corps planners in northeast Korea—the 1st Marine Division on the left, the 7th Infantry Division in the center, I ROK Corps (3d and Capital Divisions) on the right, and the 3d Infantry Division in reserve.

These were now the main components of X Corps. The ROK divisions were already well on their unopposed way toward the Yalu, but the two Army divisions did not land until early in November. This left General Smith and his 1st Marine Division with the responsibility of a sector about 200 miles long and half as wide. While elements of the 1st Marines were at Kojo and Majon-ni, the 7th Marines advanced toward the Chosin Reservoir, 125 miles to the northward.

General Smith actually had two separate wars on his hands. While the 1st Marines was fighting Korean Reds, the 7th Marines had the first large-scale clash of the U.S. forces with the Chinese Communist forces secretly infiltrating down from the Yalu through the mountains to the aid of the beaten NK forces. Colonel Litzenburg's men fought a running battle south of Chinhung-ni from the 3d to the 7th of November with the 124th CCF Division, punishing it so severely that the remnants were pulled back into permanent reserve.[10]

The three Marine regimental CP's being so widely separated, VMO-6 tried a policy of assigning a helicopter to each on a daily basis for liaison, reconnaissance, and evacuation missions. During the battle of the 7th Marines with the Chinese Reds, however, all helicopters were sometimes on call for the evacuation of casualties.[11]

Rescue or evacuation flights continued to be made from time to time at the request of Army or Air Force units. Lieutenant Ward figured in one of these missions on November 5 when he flew 115 miles from Yonpo to Songjin and rescued an Air Force pilot, Lieutenant R. C. Opalenik, who had parachuted from his disabled T-6 plane.[12]

A strange and uneasy lull fell over northeast Korea after the defeat of the 124th CCF Division. The 7th Marines continued to Hagaru without further opposition, and along the west coast the Eighth Army was not disturbed in its advance to the border after a few minor brushes with the Chinese. Stateside newspapers called it "the race to the Yalu," but the command of the 1st Marine Division chose the role of tortoise both as to speed and protection. While the 7th Infantry Division actually reached the Yalu and the ROK's came within a day's march, the Marines were still 125 miles away at Hagaru.[13]

General Smith was preparing for trouble at a time when optimism prevailed in high state and military circles. He had begun to pull his scattered units together in the Chosin Reservoir area, and he made every effort to strengthen his tenuous line of communications from Hagaru to Hamhung.

The first 35 miles, from Hamhung to Chinhung-ni, were

a gradual ascent with a fair road and a narrow-gauge railway. Then the twisting mountain road climbed 2,400 feet in the next 10 miles over the hump to Koto-ri, and the next 11 miles to Hagaru were little better than a mountain trail.

This was the main supply route (MSR) on which the eyes of the world would soon be fixed. It became a scene of round-the-clock activity after November 15 as Marine engineers made it fit for tanks and began a C-47 airstrip at Hagaru. Supply dumps were established at Koto-ri and Hagaru at Smith's orders as he brought the 5th Marines to the Reservoir area and gave the 1st Marines the responsibility of protecting the MSR with a battalion at each of the three main positions, Chinhung-ni, Koto-ri, and Hagaru.[14]

While the Division CP remained at Hungnam, the commanding general and his ADC, General Craig, depended on helicopters to supervise preparations along the MSR. The division had no more than achieved a relative degree of concentration when X Corps orders called for the 5th and 7th Marines to move out in readiness for the combined offensive of the Eighth Army in the west and X Corps in the east.

The 7th Marines led the 14-mile advance from Hagaru to Yudam-ni, arriving on the 24th after leaving Fox Company behind to guard the critical Toktong Pass near Sinhung-ni. Meanwhile the 5th Marines completed a patrolling mission east of the Reservoir and set out for Yudam-ni.[15]

On November 24 a D-day message from General MacArthur announced to X Corps troops that the forthcoming "massive compression envelopment . . . if successful, should for all practicable purposes end the war." But the Chinese struck the ROK right flank of the Eighth Army next day and stopped the offensive cold. The recent lull was now revealed as a period in which the enemy had been secretly massing in the mountains for the counterstroke.

The Marines pushed ahead about 5,000 yards west of

Yudam-ni in response to X Corps orders of the 25th for an effort to relieve the pressure on the Eighth Army. General Smith made a 75-mile helicopter flight the next day from Hungnam to Yudam-ni. Upon reaching the CP of the 7th Marines, at an altitude of 4,000 feet, the pilot was hovering about 15 feet above the ground when the aircraft dropped like a stone.[16] No harm resulted to the machine or its passengers, but such accidents occurred so frequently in the Reservoir area as to be explained in the Division Air Section report:

"The helicopter descends vertically to a landing and hovers near the ground by building up a cushion of air which literally bounces into the ground from the downthrust of the rotor and rebounds, building up a compressed mass upon which the vehicle rests. At altitudes of 4,000 feet the atmosphere is rarefied to an extent that the present helicopter has a great deal of difficulty in hovering or accomplishing a vertical descent."[17]

The sub-zero cold of late November helped a good deal to overcome this effect, though it meant hardships for pilots and crewmen. Nevertheless, they were confronted with their heaviest responsibility so far in Korea after the great Chinese counteroffensive exploded in the X Corps area. Eighth Army forces were already in retreat on the other side of the peninsula when the 5th and 7th Marines came under attack west of Yudam-ni just before midnight on November 27, 1950.[18]

THE DIVISION ISOLATED

The 1st Marine Division was probably the best prepared major unit on the UN front, thanks to the farsighted decisions of its command. But the Marines needed every resource to fight off the eight Chinese divisions (two of them in reserve) attacking at various points along the MSR. Two helicopter pilots, Wallace Blatt and Gene Morrison, were first to report road blocks between Koto-ri and Hagaru, indicating that major units of the division had been separated from one another.[19]

CCF generals aimed to "fractionalize" an enemy and devour him piecemeal after reducing him to small enough morsels for tactical mastication. By November 29 the Chinese had the 1st Marine Division separated into five self-contained perimeters along the MSR from Chinhung-ni to Yudam-ni. These groups ranged in size from the single company surrounded at Taktong Pass to the two infantry regiments and supporting units cut off at Yudam-ni. But they all had one thing in common. All of them held firm and beat off repeated enemy attacks. Even Fox Company of the 7th Marines, guarding the 4,500-foot pass halfway between Hagaru and Yudam-ni —even Fox Company stuck it out for five days and nights in its 360° hilltop perimeter against the efforts of Chinese in estimated regimental strength.[20] Radio was the only means of communication, and twice the helicopters of VMO-6 flew perilous missions under fire to air-drop replenishment batteries.[21] Radio batteries had a short life in temperatures ranging from 15 to 25 below zero.

On one of these missions George Farish's helicopter was so riddled by enemy fire that he barely managed to make the return trip with a damaged main rotor transmission. Aircraft and crews of VMO-6 moved up to Hagaru on the 28th, even though repair and upkeep facilities were primitive as compared to Yonpo. But these brief November days were too short for the HO3S's to waste a minute—some desperately wounded Marine's life might ebb away meanwhile. And a total of 50 wounded men were evacuated to Hagaru that day, most of them such serious cases that their lives were saved as a result.[22]

Mercy flights were varied by missions dealing death to the enemy. Large groups of Chinese and 29 road blocks were located along the MSR. Seven air strikes and two artillery fire missions, directed by VMO-6 aircraft that day, resulted in an estimated 370 enemy killed. Altogether, the OY's and helicopters completed 68 flights for a total of 73.7 hours.[23]

Floyd Englehardt's HO3S was so badly damaged by enemy fire on the 29th that it had to be laid up for heavy repairs. But the aircraft of VMO-6 had another busy day, what with locating three enemy battalions and six other groups ranging in size up to 200 troops. Twelve air strikes and three artillery fire missions were directed, and 44 casualties evacuated.[24]

Helicopters now provided the only dependable means of physical contact between the five isolated groups of the 1st Marine Division. Whenever an HO3S flew to Yudam-ni for a casualty evacuation, a load of medical supplies was taken from Hagaru to that perimeter or air-dropped to Fox Company on the way.[25] Without these replenishments, Marine death casualties would have been much higher.

During the last three days of November the 1st Marine Division remained on the defensive, with all five groups denying the enemy a single penetration of any lasting consequence. These results demonstrated that Chinese armed with grenades, automatic weapons, and mortars could not make headway against the terrific firepower of a Marine perimeter supported by tactical air and supplied if necessary by air drop. Never was there more daring and effective close air support than that given by Marine Corsairs flying from the fields at Wonsan and Yonpo and from the *Badoeng Strait*. Originally, all units north of the 38th Parallel were under operational control of the Fifth Air Force, but on December 2 the responsibility for X Corps tactical air support passed to General Harris. Navy aircraft of TF-77 were also on station at times, and Air Force planes flew deep support missions beyond a bomb line about five miles on either side of the MSR.[26]

THE MARINE BREAKOUT

A X Corps order of November 30 placed General Smith in operational control of all Army as well as Marine forces in the Reservoir area. His main problem, of course, was reuniting a division split into five groups by enemy forces estimated as high as 80,000 troops. First, it would be necessary for the two Yudam-ni infantry regiments, burdened with hundreds of casualties, to cut their way to Hagaru. And upon them fell the responsibility of relieving Fox Company.

The Hagaru perimeter, defended by Lieutenant Colonel Thomas L. Ridge's 3d Battalion, 1st Marines, plus an assortment of cooks, clerks, and other armed service troops, must continue to hold out meanwhile against nightly CCF attacks in estimated division strength. There the Division CP was located as well as the field hospital and half-completed airstrip. Hagaru, in short, was the rallying point for the forthcoming breakout.[27]

The plan of the two regimental commanders at Yudam-ni having met General Smith's approval, the Marines seized the initiative on the first night of December and came out fighting. Maneuver was a rarity in mountain terrain with few roads, but the planners decided on the bold project of sending a reinforced battalion across the trackless mountaintops to the relief of Fox Company on a night when the temperature dropped to 24 below zero. Lieutenant Colonel Raymond G. Davis carried out this daring maneuver with the 1st Battalion of the 7th Marines. The enemy was so taken by surprise that the Leathernecks had only 21 men wounded by long-distance fire, though two deaths resulted from the terrible hardships.[28]

While Davis relieved Fox Company and secured the vital pass, the Marines at Yudam-ni began their breakout. These unshaven, parka-clad troops would doubtless have been astonished to know that they were making the headlines on state-side front pages. Following the defeat of the Eighth Army, it had appeared that the Marine division was doomed to encirclement and annihilation. But now that a glimmer of hope could be visioned, such terms as "miracle" and "deliverance" found their way into news accounts.

System and discipline would have been more appropriate words. Only badly wounded men and essential personnel rode the vehicles, and all engineers or artillerymen who could be spared were assigned to rifle companies thinned by losses. Even the walking wounded carried rifles and limped along beside the trucks.[29]

Progress was slow and methodical, averaging a quarter of a mile per hour. While the point battalion fought its way forward astride the mountain road, the two flanking battalions secured the high ground on either side until the vehicles passed, then plugged on ahead to repeat the process. If the ever-encroaching enemy could not be held off by these means, the long column halted to call in air and artillery support.[30]

It was in effect a mobile 360° perimeter, bristling with organic firepower and supported by air and artillery, which covered the 14 miles to Hagaru in 59 hours. There the Marine engineers, contending day and night with the frozen earth, had been able to complete only 2,900 of the 6,000 feet prescribed as "minimum" at this altitude. Yet the first C-47 landed without accident on December 1 and took off with 24 wounded Marines.[31]

Air evacuation of casualties continued after the arrival of the Yudam-ni troops until 4,675 were flown out from Hagaru and another improvised strip at Koto-ri. This total included more than a thousand casualties from three 7th Infantry Division battalions cut off east of the Reservoir and badly mauled. Lieutenant Colonel Olin L. Beall and other Marine volunteers crossed the Reservoir ice under fire to bring in helpless soldiers, and about 450 unhurt survivors were issued Marine equipment and formed into a provisional battalion.[32]

Ammunition and supplies were being air-dropped, meanwhile, to the Hagaru and Koto-ri perimeters by the C-119's of the Combat Cargo Command of the Fifth Air Force in Japan.

On December 6 the Marines initiated the next phase of the breakout, the attack from Hagaru to Koto-ri. The same methodical tactics of flank protection prevailed in this two-day operation. Then, with only the last 11 miles lying ahead, the Marine command learned that the enemy had blown a vital bridge on the mountain road between Koto-ri and Chin-hung-ni at a point which could not be bypassed by vehicles. Again the Flying Boxcars came to the rescue by dropping sections of a 24-ton Treadway bridge. The engineers installed it while the 1st Battalion of the 1st Marines fought a battle in a snowstorm to keep the enemy at bay. Thus on December 11 a great epic of American military history ended with the Marines safe in the warming tents at Hamhung.[33] Although a total of 7,350 casualties had been suffered, they included 3,655 in the non-battle category which consisted chiefly of frostbite cases soon restored to active duty. Enemy losses were estimated at 25,000 killed and 12,500 wounded, and it appeared certain that more thousands had perished from freezing and privations.[34]

VMO-6 aircraft were on call every day of the breakout, even though the altitude reduced payloads and the cold added to the difficulties of upkeep and repair. The most critically wounded of the marching column were evacuated by helicopter on the march. On one of these flights Bob Longstaff was killed near Toktong Pass when CCF fire brought down his HO3S on the way to an evacuation mission.[35]

From October 28 to December 15 the squadron made 1,544 flights for a total of 1,624.8 hours. The principal missions were as follows:

Reconnaissance—OY's, 393; helicopters, 64; *Transportation* —OY's, 130; helicopters, 421; *Evacuation*—OY's, 29; helicopters, 191; *Liaison*—OY's, 35; helicopters, 90; *Artillery Spot*— OY's, 39; helicopters, 0; *Utility*—OY's, 26; helicopters, 60; *Rescue*—OY's, 0; helicopters, 11.[36]

THE LONG GRIND

Events soon proved that the 1st Marine Division had done more than fight its way to the seacoast. It had rendered militarily ineffective the 9th CCF Army Group, numbering 12 divisions, which could have turned the retreat of the Eighth Army into a catastrophe if some of them had been shifted to west Korea. Finally, the Marines had made possible the redeployment of X Corps by sea without serious interference from the remnants of these CCF divisions.

The evacuation of five X Corps divisions from Hungnam, aptly called "an amphibious operation in reverse," was completed from December 10 to 24 by Admiral Doyle's TF-90. Navy and Marine officers planned the operation, and Marine shore party elements had charge of the outloading.[37] The enemy was kept at a respectful distance by naval gunfire and Navy, Marine, and Air Force aircraft, so that the Army ground forces had only a few minor clashes. Altogether, TF-90 evacuated about 100,000 troops, 90,000 Korean civilian refugees, 17,500 vehicles, and 350,000 measurement tons of cargo in two December weeks.[38]

The Marine division was the first major unit to embark. After landing at Pusan, the weary Leathernecks found themselves back in a bean patch near Masan which had been the first assembly area of the Brigade in Korea. During the ensuing five months they had completed some sort of a cycle by fighting their way entirely around the peninsula.

It was not, to be sure, an inspiring sort of conflict, this undeclared war in the Far East. American troops have never had to fight harder operations, yet there was little applause from a bewildered public at home. The war went on, nevertheless, and the Chinese were obviously preparing to launch a new blow when General Walker was killed in a jeep accident late in December. Lieutenant General Matthew B. Ridgway took command of the Eighth Army only a few days before a second CCF offensive began in the bitter cold of New Year's Eve.

This was one of the few large-scale fights of the American forces in which the Marines had no part. The 1st Marine Division, much depleted by losses, was recuperating in the Masan area while awaiting the first arrivals of 3,387 replacements. Then, on January 10, 1951, after passing from X Corps into Eighth Army reserve, the Marines were given the mission of neutralizing an NK guerrilla division, armed by the Chinese, which had infiltrated through UN lines into the Pohang-Andong area of southeast Korea. About 1,600 square miles of trouble were contained in a new sector which offered some knotty problems of transport and supply as well as reconnaissance. The OY's and helicopters of VMO-6 helped appreciably in the solution, and the Marines carried out their mission so effectively that General Smith reported on February 6 an estimated reduction of 60 per cent in the strength of an enemy division originally numbering 6,000 to 8,000 troops.[39]

These results owed largely to self-sufficient Marine "rice paddy patrols" which combed the wildly mountainous region on foot. "Helicopters were particularly valuable for command and liaison purposes," recalled General Smith, "not only for Division Headquarters but also for the regimental commanders whose units were widely dispersed."[40]

The Marine general had been summoned to Taegu on January 10 for a conference with the Eighth Army commander. All fixed-wing aircraft were grounded the entire day by fog, but he took off in an HO3S. Pilot Lueddeke flew at about 400 feet, following the dimly visible railroad tracks, and managed to surmount two tunnels without an accident. When the fog became too dense even for a helicopter, he sat his ship down in a dry rice paddy. The tall, scholarly, white-haired Marine general lit his pipe and chatted with Lueddeke for an hour while waiting until the telephone posts could be discerned again. Then he continued the flight, arriving in time for his appointment with Ridgway.[41]

The Eighth Army made a strategic withdrawal in January which could be mentioned without a skeptical smirk. General Ridgway won the confidence of the troops by the promptness with which he re-formed his lines and struck back at the enemy. The purpose of his limited offensives was not so much the gaining of ground as keeping the Chinese off balance in their preparations for a new offensive.

The HO3S aircraft of VMO-6, as they crashed or wore out, were gradually being replaced by HTL-4 machines. These Bell helicopters, improved according to Marine specifications, were particularly well adapted to evacuation missions with their built-in litters on both sides, sheltered from the weather by plexiglas hoods. Excellent pilot visibility was afforded by the round plexiglas cockpit which gave the effect at a distance of an airborne goldfish bowl.

It was one of the tired old HO3S's, however, that completed a perilous night flight on February 1. Despite the lack of instruments for safe flying after dark, Gene Morrison brought a desperately wounded Marine from the Division hospital near Pohang to the hospital ship *Consolation*, anchored off Pusan. The patient's life was saved by emergency surgery late in the night.[42]

Another HO3S figured in a hair-raising adventure when a delirious Marine patient became violent while being flown from the Division hospital to the *Consolation*. Captain Clarence W. Perkins, the pilot, had to land and bind the man to the stretcher with the aid of a Navy corpsman. Then the evacuation was successfully completed.[43]

In February the 1st Marine Division was placed under the operational control of IX Corps, commanded by Major General Bryant E. Moore, and alerted for the jump-off of Operation KILLER on the 21st. This was the most ambitious of Ridgway's limited offensives so far, and on February 16 he explained his strategy at a high-level command conference:

"We are fighting a numerically superior enemy. We must make up for it by good footwork, by maximum use of movement, combined with firepower."[44]

In past operations the Marine division had been in effect a self-sufficient army. All this was changed now. Henceforward, it would be a major unit of one of the largest and most cosmopolitan armies in which Leathernecks have ever served. For the UN establishment of February included small armed contingents from no less than twelve countries in addition to the United States and the Republic of Korea.

Only the helicopter could have enabled General Smith to solve his time and space problems prior to Operation KILLER. The division was required to move 150 miles by road and rail from Pohang to the objective area near Wonju in central Korea, with only one road being available for the last 30 miles. Traffic congestions delayed the Marine assault troops on the 20th, with H-hour scheduled for 1000 in the morning. Brigadier General Puller telephoned General Smith for instructions as to the minimum number of Marines warranting a jump-off at that time. The original plan had called for two full regiments, but the commanding general told his ADC that he would authorize the attack on schedule if a single battalion of the 5th Marines could arrive to take part with the 1st Regiment.[45]

That is precisely what happened after Smith flew by helicopter to the line of departure the next morning and supervised the final arrangements. "Here history repeated itself," commented the Marine general. "On July 18, 1918, the 5th Regiment had to double-time at Soissons in order to attack on schedule. And on February 21, 1951, the lone battalion of the 5th had to scramble out of trucks and double-time to reach the line of departure at H-hour."[46]

The Marines took all their assigned objectives in spite of being two battalions short. Three days later their commanding general was hurriedly summoned to the advance CP of X Corps. There he was informed that he had been placed in command of the Corps after General Moore's sudden death from a heart attack.

In his temporary new post Smith found that "at the Corps level the helicopter was even more essential for command purposes than at division level. I immediately appropriated a helicopter from the Division, as the Corps had none."[47]

He was relieved on March 5 by Major General William H. Hoge, USA. Just as Smith assumed his Marine command again, after relieving Puller, final orders were received for the new UN limited offensive to begin on the 7th. This was Operation RIPPER, and once again the Marines were to spearhead the advance of IX Corps on the east-central front.

END OF THE FIRST YEAR

As far as the troops were concerned, one operation was like another. One day you took Hill 662 and the next morning you went up against Hill 704. And even though gaining ground remained a secondary object, the 1st Marine Division seized Hongchon and Chunchon in March while driving toward the 38th Parallel.[48]

After the final objectives of Operation RIPPER had been secured, orders were received for further advances. General Ridgway was appointed UN commander-in-chief by President Truman on April 14 to succeed MacArthur, and Lieutenant General James A. Van Fleet assumed command of the Eighth Army. Another shift occurred a few days later when General Smith was relieved by Major General Gerald C. Thomas of the command of the 1st Marine Division.

The Marines had reached the Hwachon Reservoir on the east-central front when the long expected CCF offensive struck on the night of April 22. The retirement of a ROK division stripped the entire left flank of the Division, but the 1st Regiment faced west as well as north to beat off all attacks. A general Eighth Army withdrawal to long-prepared lines was ordered, and the 1st Marine Division methodically retired along with other IX Corps units. General Ridgway's primary object remained the destruction of enemy personnel, and his elastic defense strategy took a frightful toll before the CCF offensive came to a standstill at the end of the month.[49]

When the enemy made a second effort on May 16, the Marines helped to restore the situation after Chinese penetrations in an adjacent sector. The Eighth Army seized the initiative before the enemy could lick his wounds, and General Van Fleet's forces bagged more CCF prisoners during the last week in May than had been taken during the entire course of the war so far.

The 1st Marine Division, now under the operational control of X Corps in east Korea, participated in the general advance of June, 1951, as UN forces gave the battered enemy no rest. By this time the Chinese were sacrificing North Korean units in desperate defensive stands to cover their withdrawal north of the 38th Parallel. It was the conviction of General Van Fleet's troops that victory was in sight, even though much hard fighting lay ahead, when the enemy proposed peace talks with the United Nations early in July. The Chinese were not yet defeated, but there could be no doubt that they desperately needed a breathing spell. Communist tactical treatises frankly advocated the mending of a bad military situation by seeking a political respite on the pretext of discussing peace. For even if the stratagem failed, a refusal put the enemy in an unfavorable light for propaganda purposes.[50]

Thus the first year of the Marines in Korea ended with minor patrol actions and training exercises during the lull at the front while peace conferences went on at Kaesong. It was virtually a new 1st Marine Division, since replacements had largely taken over during the past few months from "rotated" veterans of the early operations.

VMO-6 also had a station list of new names. Major Gottschalk had been relieved by Captain Parkins late in March, and on April 5 Major David W. McFarland became the new commanding officer, with Parkins as his executive.[51] During the spring months the squadron was based at Wonju, Hongchon, and Chunchon in turn. It was at Wonju, on March 3, that the fortunes of war again brought together the three members of the Special Board of 1946—Generals Shepherd, Harris, and Smith. They learned that a total of 114 wounded Marines had been evacuated during the past two days by a squadron numbering 28 officers and 125 enlisted men with 9 OY-2 planes, 5 HO3S's and 6 HTL-4's.[52]

Rescue missions under fire or in enemy territory were regarded as routine. On March 24 two helicopters flown by Captain Norman G. Ewers and Lieutenant Robert A. Strong went to the aid of a crashed Air Force C-119. Landing beside the wreckage of the Flying Boxcar, they evacuated the three survivors and brought out the body of a dead airman.[53]

Some of the escapes of VMO-6 pilots would have provided material for adventure thrillers. On April 13, while flying to the rescue of a downed Air Force pilot 20 miles behind the enemy lines, Captain Valdemar Schmidt and Corporal Robert Sarvia had their HO3S shot so full of holes that they were forced to make a crash landing. The machine rolled over to its destruction, but the men received only minor injuries.

Fighter aircraft of VMF-214 orbited in a strafing attack to keep the enemy at a distance while another HO3S piloted by Captain Frank E. Wilson picked up the two Marines and the Air Force pilot, Major B. W. McIntyre. Darkness had fallen before Wilson could return, but jeeps, trucks, and flares lit up the field for a safe landing of the overloaded helicopter.[54]

A few days later an HTL-4 was shot down on the way to an evacuation mission. Lieutenant Robert E. Mathewson crash-landed without injury into a position held by infantry of the 1st Battalion, 1st Marines, which was completely encircled by the enemy. He asked for a rifle and gave a good account of himself while his new comrades fought their way out to a friendly area. Demolition charges completed the destruction of his helicopter.[55]

VMO-6 carried out an impressive number of reconnaissance, artillery spot, liaison, transportation, and command missions in the first half of 1951, when the 1st Marine Division was a unit of the Eighth Army. On a basis of evacuations alone the squadron could have justified its existence during this period. Following are the totals by months:

January, 80; February, 99; March, 370; April, 179; May, 269; June, 399.

Altogether, 1,396 wounded men were flown to hospitals in six months by VMO-6 wings of mercy. Most of them were serious cases, picked up in mountainous areas where other means of evacuation would have been long delayed. Thus it is a reasonable conjecture that Marine helicopters saved not far from a thousand American lives during this half year.[56]

Captain E. R. Hering, (MC) USN, surgeon of the 1st Ma-

rine Division who had charge of the aerial evacuation of casualties at Hagaru, has said that the saving of critically
wounded men often meant "whole blood in adequate
amounts, administered in time to obviate prolonged shock;
in time to bring the serious [casualties] back into condition
so that immediate surgery, if indicated, could be performed
at the most opportune time."[57]

Military surgeons use the term "golden period" to denote
the few hours after a man has been wounded in a vital part
of the body. Resuscitation and definitive care can still save his
life, but delay may be fatal. Despite this danger, definitive care
usually had to wait in the military past until a man could be
borne from the firing line on a jolting stretcher to the nearest
road for a prolonged journey by ambulance.[58]

Marine helicopters in Korea set a precedent that the other
branches of the armed service were not slow to follow. The
result was the co-operation of Army, Navy, Air Force, and
Marine Corps for the saving of American lives, according to
a report by Captain J. W. McElroy, USNR, commanding
officer of the famous hospital ship *Consolation,* to the Commander of Naval Forces, Far East.

Tests, asserted Captain McElroy, "proved conclusively the
superiority of the helicopter method of embarking and evacuating patients to and from the ship. There was less handling
in that patients were moved directly from airstrip to ship in
one short hop, thereby eliminating the sometimes long and
rough stages by boat and ambulance. Incidentally, 'copters
continued to operate when seas were too rough for boating
patients."[59]

A helicopter landing platform was installed on the *Consolation* in July, 1951, during an overhaul at the Long Beach
Naval Shipyard, Calif. Marines gave advice, and a Marine
helicopter pilot was invited aboard to instruct as to landing
procedures.

After returning to Korea and anchoring off Sokcho-ri, on the west coast, two helicopters of the 3d Air-Sea Rescue Squadron of the Air Force were first assigned to duty on the *Consolation*. Next to be attached were two aircraft from a new U.S. Army helicopter unit. "A few Naval helicopters from various sources made occasional landings," added Captain McElroy, "and USMC 'copters of the HRS type also carried in a number of patients.* The later HRS type helicopters appeared to be most useful for the purpose—flying by day or night seemingly without regard for the weather. In a typical night landing with seriously injured patient, the ship's log shows the pilot was cleared at 0011, discharged his litter patient and took off within 45 seconds."[60]

By the end of 1951, in short, evacuations of casualties by helicopter was no longer a Marine Corps speciality. It had become the American way.

* This new Marine helicopter will be discussed in the following chapter.

CHAPTER IX

HMR-161 at the Front

Marine helicopters had tackled a wide variety of jobs during their first year in combat. Yet nothing had been done so far about the mission most closely related to the basic helicopter concept—the mission of transporting troops and supplies in preparation for future amphibious landings of the Atomic Age. The first step toward filling this gap was taken on January 15, 1951, with the commissioning of Marine Transport Helicopter Squadron 161 (HMR-161) at El Toro, Calif., as a unit in Aircraft FMFPac.[1]

Lieutenant Colonel George W. Herring was designated the commanding officer. Born in Georgia, he graduated from the Naval Academy in 1940 and was commissioned in the Marine Corps. After participating in the first Guadalcanal landing in 1942, he saw combat service with the ground forces on New Georgia the following year. Joining HMX-1 as executive officer in 1949, he took helicopter flight training later at Lakehurst.

Herring's executive and administrative record made him the choice of HMX-1 for the command of the first Marine helicopter transport unit. Thus did the experimental organization at Quantico function as the parent squadron of the various new helicopter units planned by the Marine Corps for 1951 and 1952. HMX-1 trained the pilots and crews, tested the techniques, and had much to do with selecting the personnel of these units before they were commissioned.

The new transport squadron started with a strength of ten officers and 44 enlisted men. Nearly three months passed before the first three HRS-1's—Sikorsky transport helicopters—were flown from Quantico to California. These ten-place aircraft, developed to meet Marine specifications, were of the familiar Sikorsky configuration, with a single main rotor and a vertical tail rotor. About 62 feet long with the maximum extension of rotor blades, the HRS-1 was 11½ feet wide with the blades folded. With a gross weight at sea level of over 7,000 pounds, the machine had a maximum cruising speed of 90 knots.

A payload of 1,420 pounds at sea level was possible with a crew of two and a full load of gas and oil. Under field conditions in mountain country, the HRS-1 could lift four to six troops with combat equipment, or cargo ranging in weight from 700 to 1,500 pounds, or three to five casualties in litters. These capabilities varied according to such factors as altitude, heat, cold, fuel load, visibility, and pilot competence.[2]

Lieutenant Colonel William P. Mitchell, executive officer of HMR-161, shared with Herring the task of building the squadron up to a strength of 43 officers and 244 enlisted men with a full complement of 15 HRS aircraft during its seven-month training period. Mitchell was also a native son of Georgia. Educated at Springfield College, Springfield, Mass., he became a flight training cadet at Miami in 1941 at the age of 22. As a Marine dive-bomber pilot on Guadalcanal, he was credited with a direct hit on an enemy ship.

HMR-161 sailed from San Diego on August 15, 1951, and landed at Pusan on the last day of the month. That same day the 1st Marine Division launched an attack in east Korea. The Marines had been in Eighth Army reserve during the peace talks, but passed again under X Corps operational control when the front flamed up into renewed activity.

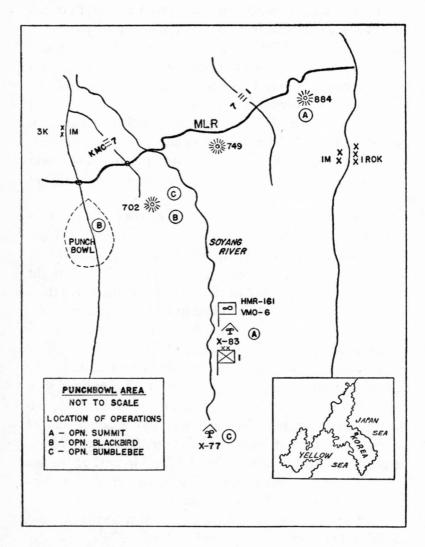

Conditions were realistic enough, therefore, when the new-comers moved up behind the front in the Punchbowl area—so-called because of the curious oval valley left by the crater of an extinct volcano. There the squadron shared Field X-83 near Chondo-ni with VMO-6, and pilots of the observation squadron briefed the transport pilots on wartime flying problems in Korea.[3]

It could never be said that HMR-161 let any moss grow under its rotors. On September 10, the move to X-83 was completed.* On the 11th, reconnaissance flights were made in search of landing sites. On the 12th, indoctrination in loading and landing techniques was given to picked personnel of the 1st Shore Party Battalion. And on the 13th, HMR-161 successfully carried out the first mass helicopter supply operation of history.

OPERATIONS WINDMILL I AND II

In anticipation of the squadron's arrival, planning conferences had been held by Colonel Krulak, chief of staff, with staff officers of the 1st Marine Division. The purpose was to prepare for the employment of transport helicopters in combat, since HMR-161 would be under the operational control of the Division. A tentative SOP (standing operating procedure) for the employment of helicopters was drawn up, with *Phib-31* serving as the principal source.[4]

When the squadron did arrive, the 1st Marine Division was heavily engaged in terrain of appalling difficulties. Mountains were no novelty in Korea, of course, but the Leathernecks had never encountered such a forbiddingly vertical area before. Narrow valleys seemed to exist only to make possible more cliffs and rocky heights covered with a meager growth of scrub trees twisted and distorted by the winds. Even Asiatic peasants found this region too barren for them. Although Koreans could scratch a living from a small patch of soil, only

---

* Airfields designated "X" in Korea were auxiliary strips, and those in the "K" category were major installations. Fields in proximity to U.S. Army installations had an "A" designation.

a few forlorn hut villages could be found all the way north from Inje to the Punchbowl. The river Soyang carved its way through the center of the Marine sector, and on either side rose mountains reached by few and poor roads—sometimes by no roads at all. Nevertheless, the Leathernecks were slugging their way forward even though supply and evacuation of casualties presented unusual problems. By September 12, indeed, it had become apparent that the attack of Colonel T. A. Wornham's 1st Marine Regiment would have to be supported by a supplementary logistical effort.

"Under other circumstances," continued the Division report, "it would have been necessary either to call for a parachute drop or to increase greatly the native bearer complement assigned to the Regiment. The situation represented a clear opportunity to exploit the mobility of the helicopter."[5]

It was a rugged assignment to throw at an outfit which had been at the front only a few days, but Herring, Mitchell, and Co. were equal to the job. They were informed by Colonel Krulak that the operation would involve the lift of a day's supply for the 2nd Battalion (reinforced) of the 1st Marines a distance of about seven miles from X-83. The infantry regiment was to select a suitable landing point; and the commanding officer of the Shore Party Battalion, Lieutenant Colonel Harry W. Edwards, was directed to provide a helicopter support team consisting of a landing point section and embarkation point section.[6]

This team, comprising a platoon with two officers, moved into bivouac at X-83 for two days of intensive training. The helicopter squadron gave instruction in such tasks as selection, clearing and marking of landing sites, loading and unloading techniques, maintenance of liaison, and control of traffic. Meanwhile an emergency dump of rations, water, ammunition, fortification material and signal and medical supplies was established at X-83.[7]

All morning on the 13th the embarkation point section kept busy at the task of separating the supplies into balanced loads. A weight limit of 800 pounds per machine was prescribed by Herring as loading commenced at 1520. Thirty minutes later, seven aircraft were ready to depart while four others carried the landing point section to the previously reconnoitered landing point. The seven-mile route followed a deep valley providing good concealment and reasonable security from enemy fire. As an additional security measure, a restrictive fire plan had been put into effect and smoke was laid by the artillery of the 11th Marines.[8]

The landing point was located about 600 feet from the valley floor on the reverse slope of a front-line hill. It had not been adequately prepared, according to the report, and the first helicopters were compelled to hover with only two wheels resting on the slope. The landing point section debarked and cleared an initial landing point 20 by 40 feet in dimensions and marked it with fluorescent panels. A man wearing a white shirt over his utility jacket guided aircraft in and out, and it was arranged that a red flag would warn of enemy fire falling on the landing point.[9]

At 1610 the first helicopter arrived with cargo nets suspended from a hook released by a manual control in the cabin. After landing its cargo, the HRS was loaded by Shore Party specialists with seven battle casualties—two litter cases and five walking wounded.[10]

The number of casualties taken aboard varied with each aircraft according to the amount of gasoline in the tanks. But HMR-161 felt that a record had been established when only 30 minutes elapsed between the time when one Marine was wounded and the time of his admission to a hospital facility 17 miles from the area where he received his wound.

Communications between aircraft in flight, HMR-161 headquarters, the landing point section, and the 1st Battalion CP were based upon an MHF helicopter support control net, while an alternative VHF net provided a secondary means. A direct telephone line also connected the embarkation point section with X-83. Hand signals and panel signals were used at the airfield as well as the landing point.[11]

Following are the statistics of Operation WINDMILL I:

Aircraft employed: Eleven for one hour, three for two hours, and one for two hours and 45 minutes. Total number of flights, 28.

Flight time: Total of 14.1 hours.

Weight lifted into landing area: 18,848 pounds, including 3,520 pounds of Shore Party personnel and gear.

Casualties evacuated: 74 flown to X-83.

Fuel carried: 70 gallons in the aft (self-sealing tank; aircraft refueled when gas level dropped to 20 gallons.

Altitude: 2,100 feet at landing point.[12]

On the morning of September 19 a similar logistical situation turned up in the zone of the 5th Marines. Supplies were urgently needed, with routes of approach exposed to enemy observation and fire. A request for helicopter support was submitted at 1100, and HMR-161 instructed the embarkation point team to assemble the supplies. After some delay in selecting a suitable landing point, Operation WINDMILL II proceeded smoothly. Ten aircraft lifted a total of 12,180 pounds in 16 flights amounting to a total flight time of 6.5 hours. Over-all time for the operation was exactly an hour.[13]

OPERATION SUMMIT

Two days later HMR-161 completed an operation which made front-page headlines all over the United States, giving the public its first knowledge of Marine helicopter combat lifts. This time the problem was tactical. With their three-week offensive successfully completed, the Marines were given a new mission of occupying and defending a zone of action enlarged by about 9,000 meters. The added area represented a sector previously held by the 8th ROK Division. After relieving the Korean troops, the Marines were to organize and construct defensive positions.

The new area to be taken over by the Marines included some of the wildest mountains of Korea, reported by G-2 to be under enemy observation and exposed to hostile fire and small unit incursions. On the extreme right flank, just behind the main line of resistance (MLR), Hill 884 rose from a region so remote as to be served by no roads at all (see accompanying sketch). Yet an ROK unit had to be relieved at this point, which could not be reached on foot in less than nine hours.[14] This assignment fell to the Division Reconnaissance Company, since the region must be promptly reconnoitered to determine its tactical possibilities. And Recon put in a request for a helicopter lift.[15]

There was nothing unusual about Hill 884 at a glance. It appeared to be another ridge in a tumbled area abounding in razorback ridges. But Hill 884 might well have been named Mount Helicopter, for it was to be the destination during coming weeks of airborne troop movements which made tactical history.

Air reconnaissance disclosed only two partially suitable landing sites. About 100 yards apart, and some 300 feet below the crest, they could be cleared sufficiently for the landing of one aircraft. Each site was about 50 feet square, with a sheer drop on two sides. Planning called for an assault squad of Recon Company to land first and provide security for the trained Shore Party personnel who would follow with pick and spade to clear the sites. These specialists were given intensive training in disembarking from hovering aircraft by means of 30-foot knotted ropes. And in the event that communication with the squadron CP at X-83 should fail, a helicopter was to remain in the vicinity and relay the signal that the landing sites were ready to receive aircraft.[16]

Performance came up to plan, even though H-hour was delayed 30 minutes by fog. Just an hour after the landings of the assault squad and Shore Party group, the first troop landing site was ready for business. Flying time from X-83 averaged eight minutes, and it took about 90 seconds for four men with full equipment to land by rope.

The second landing point was opened 20 minutes after the first, and five men were carried in each HRS afterwards to scramble out on the ground in an average of 20 seconds. Troops continued to pour in steadily until the completion of Operation SUMMIT in 65 flights amounting to 31.2 hours flying time and four hours over-all time. As a final flourish, eight miles of wire were laid in 15 minutes to the CP of the 1st Marines.

The radio communication net did not function too satisfactorily. Voice contact was possible between orbiting aircraft and the landing point at H-plus-15, but there was no contact between the landing point team and X-83. Although a primary MHF was employed, with a secondary VHF available, a helicopter had to be kept on station to alert X-83 when the landing point was ready to receive aircraft.[17]

Altogether, 224 fully equipped troops and 17,772 pounds of cargo were landed in addition to supplies carried by the men. General Shepherd congratulated HMR-161 on "a bright new chapter in the employment of helicopters by Marines." Major General Clovis Byers, commanding general of X Corps, also congratulated "those organic and attached units of the 1st Marine Division that participated in the first relief of units on the battle position. Your imaginative experiment with this kind of transport is certain to be of lasting value to all the services." And this message was received from General Thomas, commanding the 1st Marine Division:

"Operation SUMMIT, the first helicopter-borne landing of a combat unit in history, was an outstanding success. To all who took part, well done!"[18]

Even the official report shed some of the customary reticence and allowed a discreet note of enthusiasm to lurk in the starched military English reserved for such documents: "These initial efforts have demonstrated strikingly the great contribution to tactical and logistical flexibility that the assault helicopter offers." Next, the report guardedly ventured to predict that "helicopter functions will be progressively enlarged as time passes, and that the aircraft type must be recognized as a requisite component of a balanced military force."[19]

OPERATION BLACKBIRD

An assigned frontage of 20,000 meters made it a problem for the 1st Marine Division to defend its roomy sector and still maintain an adequate reserve. The left flank being the most threatened area, a five-mile lift of a reinforced rifle company from the Division Reserve bivouac was contemplated in case of sudden necessity. And since such an emergency was most likely to arise at night, planning began for a lift under cover of darkness. A date of September 27 was set for Operation BLACKBIRD, and Division orders called for a full-dress daylight rehearsal that morning. Meanwhile the helicopter pilots made night indoctrination flights and memorized terrain features.[20]

The daylight rehearsal, simulating night conditions as closely as possible, began at 1000 on D-day. Lieutenant Colonel F. B. Nihart, commanding officer of the 2d Battalion, 1st Marines, and his operations officer, Major Carl E. Walker, rode in the first flights as six helicopters lifted 200 men of Easy Company in over-all time of two hours and ten minutes. It had been planned for the troops to land in the Punchbowl and proceed a mile on foot to the final objective. But there had not been time for a thorough reconnaissance of an area recently seized from the enemy, and a man of the landing force was wounded by a Chinese antipersonnel mine shortly after exiting from the helicopter. Lieutenant Colonel Nihart had a narrow escape when he discovered another mine just ahead, and it soon became apparent that the route to the objective was blocked by an entire mine field left by the enemy. Plans were revised, therefore, to call off the march, though the landing site remained the same.[21]

The HRS was the first Marine helicopter with a few instruments for night flying, but facilities were still primitive as compared to those of conventional planes. Thus it is understandable that some confusion resulted after the operation got under way at 1930 on a dark night without benefit of moonlight. Five fully equipped troops were carried by each helicopter as a shuttle system was set up for the 13-mile round trip. Three-minute intervals were established as a safeguard against mid-air collisions, with different altitudes being assigned to outgoing and incoming aircraft. Running lights were used only two minutes before entering or leaving the embarkation zone.[22]

Shore Party specialists landed in the first aircraft with the lighting and radio communication gear. After they prepared a landing area measuring 50 by 100 feet, the 233 men of Easy Company, 1st Marines, were transported in over-all time of two hours and 20 minutes as compared to the nine hours required for a march over mountain trails.[23]

Still, it could scarcely be said that Operation BLACKBIRD was an unqualified success. The flare pots illuminating the embarkation area were frequently blown out by rotor wash, and meanwhile they blinded the pilots temporarily by creating a glare on plexiglas windshields. The battery-powered beach lanterns in the landing area were inadequate, and artillery flashes added to the visibility troubles of pilots taking off from a dry river bed and threading their way through three mountain passes to reach the objective. Although efforts had been made in rehearsal to memorize terrain features, difficulty was experienced in locating the landing area. Good radio communications were maintained, however, between X-83, embarkation zone, landing zone, and aircraft in flight.[24]

It is perhaps significant that down to the end of the war, Operation BLACKBIRD remained the only large-scale helicopter combat lift to be attempted in the darkness. The Marine report of the operation concluded that "night troop lifts in mountainous terrain are feasible provided a daylight reconnaissance of the landing zone together with the avenues of approach and retirement can be effected. Present equipment indicates that under present conditions in Korea these night lifts should be limited to movements within friendly territory.[25]

OPERATION BUMBLEBEE

Two weeks later, HMR-161 completed a new operation on a scale surpassing anything up to this time—the lift of an entire battalion and its equipment.

General Thomas and his chief of staff, Colonel Krulak, had figured in the Marine helicopter development program ever since the pioneer days when doctrines were being discussed at the Marine Corps Schools for the preparation of *Phib-31*. Both had taken a keen interest in the planning of HMR-161 lifts, and at the end of September they determined on the movement of a battalion as the next practical step.

The first opportunity that could be foreseen was October 11, when the 3d Battalion of 7th Marines was due to relieve a battalion of the 5th Marines on the MLR. The primary purpose was to acquire planning experience in the determination of time factors involved in a tactical movement of this size. A secondary purpose was the speeding up of the relief and the reduction of demands on motor transportation.[26]

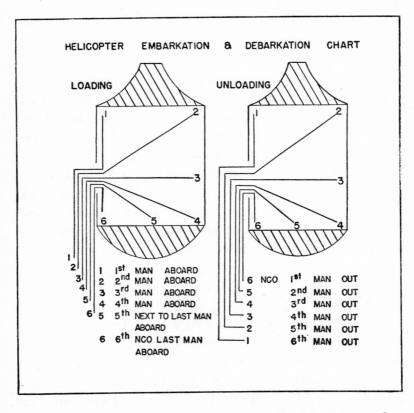

HELICOPTER   EMBARKATION   &   DEBARKATION   CHART

LOADING   UNLOADING

1	1st MAN ABOARD	6 NCO	1st MAN OUT
2	2nd MAN ABOARD	5	2nd MAN OUT
3	3rd MAN ABOARD	4	3rd MAN OUT
4	4th MAN ABOARD	3	4th MAN OUT
5	5th NEXT TO LAST MAN ABOARD	2	5th MAN OUT
6	6th NCO LAST MAN ABOARD	1	6th MAN OUT

Oral warning orders were issued on the 8th. Liaison between the helicopter squadron and the designated battalion being established, they conducted a joint reconnaissance of the assigned assembly area just behind the MLR and northeast of Hill 702. The new commanding officer of the battalion was Lieutenant Colonel Edwards, who had acquired knowhow as the recent commander of the Shore Party battalion.

He had a part along with Krulak, Herring, and Mitchell in working out practical details of the forthcoming lift. Planning was conducted as if for an amphibious operation, with the assignment and loading table for the HRS's being modeled after that of a landing boat assignment table. Each man was to have his assigned place in the cabin of the helicopter, so that loading and unloading could be completed with a minimum of delay and confusion (see accompanying chart).[27]

By October 10 the planning had reached the final stage, and arrangements were made for a trial loading and unloading. All officers and NCO's of 3/7 (3d Battalion, 7th Marines) attended a familiarization class conducted at airfield X-77 by the battalion operations officer in conjunction with Herring, Mitchell, and other HMR-161 officers. Trial helicopter teams of enlisted men were loaded, and 15 seconds appeared to be an average time for six men without heavy equipment.[28]

Operation BUMBLEBEE began at 1000 the next morning when the first helicopter took off from Field X-77 with trained Shore Party specialists to prepare the landing area. The flight path of 15 miles, though longer than necessary, took advantage of the concealment from enemy observation provided by valleys and defiladed areas. Ten to twelve minutes were required to cover the distance.

The dispatchers at the two loading zones, designated RED and WHITE, had a check-off and flight list containing the names of each six-man team to be loaded. The men went first to the standby box to await their turn at the ready box (see accompanying chart). And in the event that a team was found short, a replacement could be called immediately from a casual pool made up of extra troops from Headquarters Company.

As the helicopters landed at intervals of a minute, the troops were briskly assisted to the ground by the Shore Party men who had cleared the two landing sites. A six-man team could exit in 17 seconds, and new arrivals were hustled by guides to their own company assembly areas.[29]

Following are the statistics of the operation:

Number of helicopters used: 12.
Number of flights: 156.
Total flight-time: 65.9 hours.

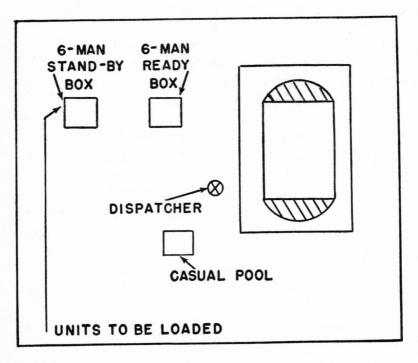

Over-all time: 5 hours, 50 minutes.
Average fuel consumption of each aircraft: 44 gallons per hour.
Average time for refueling one aircraft with one refueler: 7 minutes.
Average time for refueling 12 aircraft, using three refuelers: 30 minutes.
Number of troops lifted: 958.
Average weight per man: 240 pounds.
Total weight transported: 229,920 pounds.

Altitude of loading zones: 630 feet.

Altitude of landing sites: 1,440 feet.[30]

Newspaper correspondents were quick to sense that tactical history had again been created, and the wires hummed with stories about Operation BUMBLEBEE. Gratifying as such acclaim was, Marine planners had three less spectacular but equally instructive helicopter operations scheduled for October, 1951.

AID GIVEN TO ARMY UNIT

Before these operations could be carried out, HMR-161 distinguished itself in a king-size rescue, resupply, and evacuation mission on short notice. An ROK unit had been completely surrounded in the IX Corps sector to the west, and Army officers requested helicopter support from the 1st Marine Division.[31] Operation WEDGE, as the effort was called, took place on October 15, 1951. Lieutenant Colonel William P. Mitchell led the six Marine helicopters which flew in 19,000 pounds of ammunition. The squadron's own surgeon, Lieutenant Donald L. Hillian of the Navy Medical Corps, landed to offer emergency aid. Twenty-four wounded men were evacuated, some of whom would otherwise have died. Captain James T. Cotton and Captain Albert A. Black made four flights each into the beleaguered area.[32]

HMR-161 pilots were congratulated in person by Major General Claude F. Ferenbaugh, commanding IX Corps. Colonel Richard F. Dugan, of IX Corps, told newspaper correspondents: "We had no way to resupply the unit until the 'copters showed. They did one hell of a fine job."[33]

The next operation was planned as a solution to the problem of sniping and other enemy guerrilla activities behind the Marine MLR. A patrol program was the obvious tactical antidote, and it seemed logical to employ helicopters for speed and surprise in reaching remote hiding places.

The plan of Operation BUSHBEATER called for teams of Able and Baker companies of the 1st Marines to be landed at ten points along the Division east flank. They were to sweep westward toward the Soyang river while 60 troops of Recon Company were being landed on the west boundary to deploy and patrol from the opposite direction. All officers and men were to be indoctrinated in climbing down knotted ropes, and landing sites 100 feet square would be alternately designated RED and WHITE zones.[34]

Rain and fog caused a day's postponement, and adverse weather still handicapped the ten participating aircraft on October 22. Two helicopters lost power and crashed while hovering, both being badly wrecked, and another machine was damaged. It seemed a miracle that only one man was injured in the first serious accident to result from these pioneer helicopter transport operations. But the squadron took great pride in a subsequent salvage operation, using "flying crane" techniques, which recovered and flew out enough parts so that the two machines were rebuilt and flown again. Major Edwin E. Shifflett, the HMR-161 engineering officer, was assisted by Captain James T. Cotton and CWO Pat L. Summers. Men from the Shore Party and Engineers also lent a hand as Technical Sergeant Thomas M. McAuliffe of HMR-161 and his crew dismantled the two "completely destroyed" aircraft into components which could be moved by means of block and tackle, muscle, and Marine profanity to the nearest feasible landing site. Lieutenant Colonel Mitchell flew out an entire fuselage, stripped down to a weight of about 1,000 pounds and attached to the cargo hook by ropes secured to all four corners.[35]

In spite of its mishaps, Operation BUSHBEATER proved that helicopter-borne teams could perform many of the reconnaissance and security patrol missions formerly carried out on foot. Forty flights were made to the east boundary and 210 troops landed in over-all time of two hours, 21 minutes. The 60 men of Recon Company were carried to the west flank in an hour's total time.[36]

It was decided that three loading zones would have served more efficiently on the east flank than ten. As a lesson of the crashes, HMR-161 concluded that extreme caution was necessary when hovering at altitudes above 2,000 feet, and that debarking from knotted ropes should be reserved for emergencies.[37]

Experiments in working out anti-guerrilla techniques were continued during the next few days in Operation RABBIT-HUNT as the 1st Marine Division used helicopters for systematic patrolling of the vast area behind the MLR. An interested spectator was General Cates, the Commandant, whose party included General Thomas and General Jerome.[38]

Operation HOUSEBURNER I was planned to deprive the guerrillas of shelter before winter. Two helicopters were employed on October 26, each carrying a four-man destruction team with such incendiary equipment as satchel charges, flame throwers, and incendiary grenades. While one ship orbited over a hut to provide cover, the other machine hovered so that the team could spray unignited flame-thrower mixture over the roof and drop incendiary grenades to set it off. But this method was not found as satisfactory as having both helicopters land teams to do the job on foot.[39]

Four helicopters were committed to the work instead of two when HOUSEBURNER II took place on the last day of October. Altogether, 113 dwellings were destroyed by 36 troops in 20 flights amounting to 21.8 flight hours.[40]

Two BARmen were included in each destruction team, but the planners had not anticipated the air-ground fire flight which took place after several NK guerrillas were flushed out by a team that had just landed. The helicopter aloft, upon being notified by radio, opened small-arms fire on an enemy who returned the compliment. No harm resulted on either side.[41]

RELIEF OF FRONT-LINE BATTALION

Troop lifts had become an old story by this time, but HMR-161 and the Division staff planned an operation for November 11 that put all past performances in the shade— the relief of a front-line battalion, involving the lift of nearly 2,000 troops.

The 2d Battalion, 5th Marines, was to be airborne from X-83 to Hill 884 and take over the responsibilities of the 2d Battalion, 1st Marines, which would be returned to the airfield.

Three reconnaissance and liaison flights were made to Hill 884 during the first week of November. Shore Party troops were meanwhile improving the landing sites and arranging for radio communications. Telephone connections were also to be made available between loading zones and landing sites; and both air and artillery support would be provided throughout the operation.[42]

Operation SWITCH began at 0635 on D-day when the first three aircraft took off from X-83 with Shore Party specialists whose duty it was to signal aircraft into landing sites, and to take charge of the loading and unloading of troops. On the return trip the 12 helicopters were to debark five men each at RED and YELLOW landing sites on X-83, which had been marked by panels.

The weather was favorable except for a light morning fog at X-83. Refueling and flight operations continued smoothly for an hour. The only hitch came when the pool of troops was exhausted at the forward loading zones, so that aircraft had to return empty. This meant additional trips later in the day which prolonged the operation to an over-all total of ten hours,

Marine Corps Photo

The Old Eyes the New A Primitive "A" frame on his back, an aged South Korean porter gazes in wonder at an aerial workhorse of HMR-161.

Anything Goes Loading an ammunition cart into a helicopter of HMR-162, aboard the USS *Valley Forge.*

Marine Corps Photo

Flying Pickup Marines of the Air Delivery Platoon prepare to hook on another cargo net of supplies to be taken to the front in OPERATION HAYLIFT I.

Marine Corps Ph

Hazardous Hauls All in a day's work during OPERATONS HAYLIFT. Above, a Marin helicopter heads toward a Korean mountain outpost swinging beneath it rolls o communication wire; and, below, a truck stands by as a helicopter comes for landing with drums of gasoline.

Marine Corps Ph

Marine Corps Photo

On the Land and in the Air A "Mighty Mite," versatile variation of the famous Jeep, climbs a grade at the Marine Corps Schools proving grounds, while another is borne aloft by a helicopter of HMX-1.

Marine Corps Photo

Artillery from the Air   A helicopter prepares to set down a 75 mm pack howitzer brought up from the rear.

eadying for a Ripple   Above, a helicopter of HMR-161 sets down a 4.5 rocket
uncher. Below, crewmen of the rocket battery watch and wait as helicopters
bring in ammunition slung underneath in special baskets.

Marine Corps Photo

Landing at Sea A Marine helicopter returning to the deck of the carrier *Sicily* off the coast of Korea.

Evacuation Under Fire Two litter patients, one on each side, are brought out from combat areas by VMO-6 pilots standing by from dawn to dusk.

Awaiting Transportation As a Marine transport helicopter brings in a load of battle-weary Marines, more troops await the signal to load up and replace the men on the MLR.

Front-Line Traffic Director A member of a helicopter landing point team guides incoming troops to their assembly area.

Wind sock on the Battlefield An innovation of the Atomic Age, a wind directional indi-
cator set up at the front to guide helicopters shuttling troops and supplies.

omic Assault Marine helicopters leapfrog U. S. Marines around the atomic
st during maneuvers at the Nevada Proving Grounds during OPERATION
DESERT ROCK V.

The Shape of Things to Come Front and side views in flight of the Marin Corps' largest helicopter, the Sikorsky XHR28, unveiled in January 1954.

Payloads Above, two combat-equipped Marine squads enter a XHR2S. Below, from the open cargo doors emerges one of the three "Mighty Mites" which the helicopter can carry.

Formation for the Future

though the lift of the relieving battalion was completed in seven and a half hours.

All told, 950 men with combat equipment were transported to the front line, and 952 brought back to the rear. The 12 aircraft made 262 flights in 95.6 hours of flight time.[43]

WORKHORSES OF THE DIVISION

As the year drew to an end, HMR-161 had a strength of 42 officers and 244 enlisted men with 13 aircraft. It was an old saying that the capabilities of the versatile helicopter included "anything a horse can do," and this boast seemed to be taken literally by the 1st Marine Division in the last month of 1951. Flights totaled 621 and missions 390 during December. Total aircraft time amounted to 591.3 hours, of which 379.3 were combat time. The number of personnel lifted was 2,022, and the weight of cargo 149,477 pounds.[44]

When tons of men or material had to be moved somewhere in a hurry, the 'copters became the workhorses of the Division. Six thousand pounds of rations, 9,000 pounds of fuel oil in drums, 15,000 pounds of fortification material, 15,000 pounds of cold-weather clothing and other supplies—these were some of the cargoes flown up to front-line units from time to time.[45] Anti-guerrilla patrols with four-man teams of Recon Company were of frequent occurrence, as well as interludes when visiting VIP's went aloft for a tour of the front. Any gaps in the time of HMR-161 pilots were filled with such routine chores as reconnaissance, evacuation, or administrative flights.

Hill 884 again proved its right to be known as Mount Helicopter when it became the scene of three more large-scale operations. The 1st Battalion, 5th Marines, was transported from an assembly area to the front lines on December 19 and 20 for the relief of 2/5 in Operation FAREWELL. It was the last flight in Korea for George Herring, who had distinguished himself as the squadron's first commanding officer. He was being relieved by Colonel Keith B. McCutcheon, making his first combat flight in this operation.[46]

"I think it was about the roughest ride I ever had," he recalled two years later. "Replacement pilots had to learn by doing. The cold weather and wind velocity assisted performance; the altitude worked against it slightly. Few pilots had experienced such conditions prior to Korea."[47]

It was not mere coincidence that Herring returned to Quantico, after being relieved, to assume the command of HMX-1 which McCutcheon had just left. (The position had been temporarily filled by Lieutenant Colonel John H. King, Jr.) On the contrary, the parent squadron made an effort to bring back men with Korean combat experience as instructors and administrators. "HMX-1 accomplished more than formulating early tactics," said William P. Mitchell, who was associated with both Herring and McCutcheon as executive officer. "HMX-1 was also foremost in establishing the requirements for new helicopters for military use. . . . The success of the Marine Corps in the helicopter field can be attributed to its setting up in HMX-1 of a single source for its development work and using this source to expand the program."[48]

On December 14, 1951, the loading zone and landing site duties formerly performed by a Shore Party platoon were taken over by the 1st Air Delivery Platoon, Service Command, FMFPac. The basic mission of this organization had been "to prepare and deliver supplies by air, whether by parachute, air freight, or helicopter." An officer and 35 enlisted men made up the roster as the unit began its new duties with the 1st Marine Division.[49]

The Air Delivery Platoon was on the job during the first seven days of the new year when HMR-161 had the mission of completely resupplying by air the 1st Battalion of the 5th Marines on Hill 884. Cargo transported from supply dumps to the front lines in Operation MULETRAIN consisted largely of rations, wire, rope, tent stoves, and ammunition. Nearly all items, with the exception of such fragile cargo as "A" rations, were carried in nets or pallets. And since the five landing sites on Hill 884 had an average altitude of 2,300 feet, the maximum payload was reduced to 850 pounds.

The "flying crane" techniques owed a great deal to improvements suggested by Major Charles E. Cornwell of HMR-161. He adapted the underslung nets, manually controlled from the cabin, which replaced the pallet, or portable platform, for most types of cargo.[50]

An average of four aircraft a day were employed in Operation MULETRAIN. During that week they replaced about 580 hired Korean laborers who had been used to transport supplies from the battalion dump over mountain trails to troops in the line. Even so, there was difficulty at times because the helicopters brought in cargo faster than it could be handled by the unloading teams at the landing sites. Following are the principal statistics of the seven days:

Pounds lifted: 159,730.
Hours of flight time: 91.7.
Loads lifted: 219.
Average of miles flown: 9.6.
Average climb (feet) to landing site: 800.[51]

The next large-scale tactical lift, Operation CHANGIE-CHANGIE* on January 10, differed from Operation FAREWELL in that sites on the company instead of battalion level were employed both for loading and landing. Units involved were the 2d Battalion, 7th Marines, relieving the 1st Battalion of

---

* The expression "changie-changie" meant "swap" in the pidgin English used by Marines and Koreans, and hence the relief of one military unit by another.

the 5th Marines. Again the helicopters flew in defilade throughout the entire approach, landing, and retirement. Thanks to this concealment as well as artillery and air support, the troops were taken within 200 yards of their frontline positions.[52]

Operation MOUSETRAP, from January 14 to 17, consisted of a series of lifts designed to test the ability of both aircraft and troops to carry out an anti-guerrilla attack in rough country on short notice. At 0100 on the 14th the planners and HMR-161 officers had their first telephone conversation in regard to a two-company lift scheduled for 1000 that morning. Nevertheless, about 500 troops of the 2d Battalion, 5th Marines, were transported to the objective area without a hitch after the Air Delivery Platoon cleared a landing site. Three similar troop movements were completed successfully during the next three days, with supplies being dropped by helicopter.

"Operation MOUSETRAP," concluded the HMR-161 report, "illustrated that a relatively large number of troops can be moved by helicopter on very short notice. . . . With a minimum of planning and briefing, necessitated by the lack of time, the entire operation was completed with only minor difficulties."[53]

Hill 884 had its fifth operation on February 24, when nine aircraft of HMR-161 flew the 1st Battalion, 7th Marines, to the familiar landing sites for the relief of the 2d Battalion. Operation ROTATE was completed so smoothly that it added little tactical information to that acquired in previous battalion lifts.[54]

During the past six months the aircraft of the squadron had shown few mechanical defects, considering the heavy demands made upon them. But on February 24, while returning to X-83 from the Seoul area, Captain John R. Irwin felt a jolt followed by alarming vibrations. After landing by autorotation, he discovered that broken remnants of the tail pylon assembly had dropped about 12 feet behind the machine.

Only four days later, while flying a load of logs on March 1, Captain Calvin G. Alston's helicopter was so shaken by jolts and vibrations that he thought it had taken a fragment from enemy artillery. He made a forced landing in the snow, and again it became evident that a structural fault of the tail pylon assembly was the cause.

Three new aircraft had been received that day, but HRS's of the squadron were immediately grounded until the "bug" could be discovered and eliminated. And not until March 14, when 15 modified tail pylons were flown to Korea by BuAer, did HMR-161 take to the air again.[55]

CHAPTER X

The Test of Combat

Six hundred trucks shuttled back and forth across the peninsula, transferring nearly 6,000 loads of gear. It was the middle of March, 1952, and the 1st Marine Division, now commanded by Major General John T. Selden, was making a 180-mile move to west Korea. In the new sector, under the operational control of I Corps, the Division would be the western anchor of the Eighth Army front, squarely in the path of the enemy's invasion route to Seoul.

It is not likely that there were many regrets at leaving the vast old sector which the Marines had been defending since September. The Punchbowl area was not an alluring piece of real estate, even by Korean standards, but it had been the laboratory of some tremendous advances in helicopter combat techniques. Never, in fact, since the development of the first practicable American helicopter for military purposes in 1942 had there been such a fruitful period of rotary-wing experiment as the combat operations carried out by Marine fliers during these seven months.

While the HMR-161 transport aircraft conducted tactical and logistical lifts on the battalion level, the smaller helicopters of VMO-6 had also been setting records. Evacuations during the last six months of 1951 totaled 1,096. A total of 920 wounded were flown out during the first half of 1952, when 1st Marine Division casualties declined as the result of a prolonged defensive mission.[1] It was during this period that VMO-6 set itself a twofold program which has been summed up by Major William G. MacLean:

"Putting the evacuation of front-line casualties on a 24-hour basis;

"Cutting down the time required to evacuate a casualty from the front to the medical companies."[2]

The results began to show in the statistics for the first six months of 1952. Out of the total of 920 evacuations, 74 were completed at night. And during the last half of the year, the HTL-4's and HO5S-1's of the observation squadron flew 287 night evacuations out of a total of 1,752.[3] This accomplishment can be better appreciated by anyone who has ridden in the darkness beside a helicopter pilot flying "on the seat of his pants" while depending on a combination of skill, intuition, nerve, and eyesight.

There were days of heavy infantry action when VMO-6 pilots rode the air continuously from dawn until long after dark. One of the most memorable was September 16, 1951, as the ground forces drove toward the Punchbowl. No less than 85 evacuations from the battle lines were completed that day, with Lieutenant Joseph C. Gardiner figuring in 17 of them. The month's total of 541 evacuations remained the highest for such a period down to the cease-fire in Korea.[4]

Although evacuations were not a primary mission of HMR-161, a total of 293 wounded men were flown to hospitals by the transport aircraft from September, 1951, to February, 1952. During this same period, the HRS's made 3,809 flights, flew 3,375.6 hours, lifted 14,072 personnel, and transported cargo weighing 1,659,239 pounds.[5]

Nor were rescue flights a frequent mission of HMR-161 pilots, yet Lieutenant Colonel Mitchell and Captain Robert F. Warren made an attempt 40 miles behind the enemy lines on February 8, 1952. Word had been received from the 1st

Marine Division that a fighter pilot was downed, and that a rescue effort by a Navy helicopter had proved unsuccessful because of enemy fire. Mitchell and Warren landed first on the deck of the USS *Rochester* for briefing. Then, accompanied by an HMR-161 doctor, Lieutenant Burt C. Johnson (MC) USNR, and the helicopter crew chief, Technical Sergeant Walter F. Mortimer, they flew to the scene. Seven fighter planes provided cover as the Marine pilots made a tight orbit of the area. Sergeant Mortimer thought he saw several Chinese lurking near the wreckage and opened fire with a Thompson sub-machine gun. After the fighter planes had thoroughly strafed the area, Mitchell and Warren landed.[6]

"The wreckage was observed carefully as well as houses in the immediate vicinity," said the squadron report. "No activity or recognition was observed." The Marine helicopter was escorted by fighters to the *Rochester* for refueling, and made the return trip to X-83 without incident.[7]

It was not the business of helicopter pilots to take risks when they could be avoided. But risks did have to be taken daily, and it remained a matter for congratulation in the spring of 1952 that HMR-161 had not lost a man as yet. Unfortunately, the Marine Corps as a whole had lost two of its foremost helicopter pilots this past winter. The first of all Marine helicopter pilots crashed accidentally to his death on January 5, 1952, while flying a helicopter as a Navy test pilot at the Patuxent field. Lieutenant Colonel Armond H. DeLalio had made his start in 1944 when he trained with the Coast Guard fliers at Floyd Bennett Field. As operations officer of HMX-1, he instructed some of the first Marine pilots at Quantico in 1948. And it was one of his most promising pupils, Captain Gustave Lueddeke, who died suddenly of poliomyelitis after surviving the early operations of VMO-6 and returning to HMX-1 as an instructor.

At least the record of 3,375 helicopter flight hours without a fatality set by HMR-161 during its first six months in combat should have disposed of the pre-Korea legend of excessive vulnerability. "Certainly the helicopter is vulnerable," commented McCutcheon. "So are troops, tanks, ships and other aircraft. It is up to us to develop tactics and techniques to minimize this vulnerability. And that is what HMX-1 and the various VMO and transport squadrons have done."[8]

Major James R. Dyer, operations officer and later executive officer of HMR-161 in Korea, deserves much of the credit for this development. Born in Alabama in 1919, he became a Marine second lieutenant in 1942 and later took flight training. During World War II, he participated in Marine air operations in the Solomons, and returned to qualify as a helicopter pilot in 1951.

Both Dyer and McCutcheon paid tribute to Staff Sergeant Lewis S. Kelley, Master Sergeant Wesley M. Fussell, Master Sergeant McAuliffe, and the other NCO's who did so much to keep the helicopters flying. "Engine changes and other major repairs in the field became all too frequent but were always consummated," recalled McCutcheon. "Actually, the whole gang worked like the devil and they should all be given credit."[9]

OPERATION PRONTO

In the new sector a forward echelon of HMR-161 was located near Field A-17, with VMO-6 only a short distance to the south. The rear echelon of the transport squadron, consisting of Headquarters Company and the machine shops, was at Field A-33 near Ascom City.[10]

Operation PRONTO on April 5 combined the shortest notice and longest distance of any large-scale helicopter troop movement up to that time. The tactical situation involved MLR units on one side of a river and reserve troops on the other.

With only one dependable bridge at a time when flash floods threatened, these maneuvers had a special significance in determining time and space factors for reinforcing the front line in case of penetration.[11]

At 0210 on the morning of the 5th, McCutcheon received a telephone call from the 1st Marine Division, directing him to air-lift 622 fully equipped troops of 2/7 and 10,000 pounds of rations, beginning at 0545 that same morning. Because of the necessity for steering clear of the neutrality zone in the vicinity of Munsan, round-trip flights would average about 57 miles.

The first aircraft took off promptly with Air Delivery Platoon specialists for unloading missions at the two landing sites. Nine helicopters were employed, seven of them being competently flown by new pilots just arrived from the States. Each round trip took about an hour, which brought the overall time for the operation up to 14 hours and flight time to 115.9 hours—another new record for the squadron.[12]

The 99 flights during the day were of these types: troop lift, 81; cargo lift, 10; administrative, 8. Squadron experience paid off in smoothness of execution, so that the official report could conclude:

"This air lift, more than any other in which HMR-161 has participated, proved that a Marine transport helicopter squadron can successfully operate intact as an 'on call' tactical tool. . . . Longer notice before an operation would be beneficial but not absolutely necessary. Lack of time for liaison between HMR-161 and the 2d Battalion, 7th Marines, necessitated both organizations concerned to enter the operation without so much as a telephone call."[13]

The next big troop lift, Operation LEAPFROG on April 18 and 19, brought up two new problems—transporting combat units a short distance over water, and coping with a language barrier in the execution. There were also time and space factors, since the distance by road was excessive because of winding entirely around Seoul to reach the Kumpo Peninsula. A helicopter lift, therefore, was planned for the movement of the 5th Battalion, Korean Marine Corps (KMC) Regiment, across the river Han for the relief of the 3d Battalion which would be brought back the following day.* Pilots and copilots would wear lifejackets and be briefed on procedures of ditching aircraft in the water; and the cargo doors were to be left open for the troops as DUKW's (amphibious trucks) stood by on each bank to await rescue calls. As a final precaution, a Korean translation was painted beneath the NO SMOKING signs in the cabins of the helicopters.[14]

The distance averaged six miles to the four landing sites, so that each flight took about ten minutes. Interpreters managed to keep language difficulties at a minimum, and Operation LEAPFROG was completed according to plan.[15] Following were the statistics:

Total number of flights: 281.
Number of troops lifted (first phase): 893.
Number of troops lifted (second phase): 809.
Total number of troops lifted: 1,702.
Hours of flight time (first phase): 34.8.
Hours of flight time (second phase): 30.0.
Hours of over-all time (first phase): 1.8.
Hours of over-all time (second phase): 1.63.

Operation CIRCUS, the last troop lift of April, also involved a river crossing. The problem was to transport the 1st Battalion, 7th Marines (plus Headquarters and Supply Company) across the Imjin, so that the force could move into a blocking position on the MLR.

Rivers were potentially dangerous in this area with 35,000 meters of front divided by the Han, Sachon, and Imjin, all of

---

* In Korea the number four is considered unlucky, since the ancient written symbol also denoted death. In the four-battalion KMC Regiment, therefore, there were the 1st, 2d, 3d and 5th Battalions.

which were capable of working a great deal of mischief in floodtime. Four loading zones and five landing sites had been prepared when the first helicopter took off at 0830 on the 23rd. The nearest of the landing sites was 850 meters away on a straight line, and the farthest about 1,600. Thus the average trip took about three and a half minutes, and the shorter hops required alert flying to maintain safe distances between aircraft. HMR-161 pilots proving equal to three-ring demands, the 1,185 troops of Operation CIRCUS were transported by 11 helicopters in 246 flights. Over-all time of an hour and a half was logged, and flight time of 14.40 hours. Again, as in the previous operation, there were no rescue calls for the DUKW's.[16]

AIRCRAFT GROUNDED

An enforced vacation for pilots began three days later when a CNO dispatch, received on the 26th, grounded all HRS and HO4S aircraft until the receipt of new parts for the tail rotor driveshaft. The possibility of a structural fault had been suspected after a stateside accident, so that HMR-161 machines were idle for the second time that spring. Not until May 17 did the arrival of the new driveshaft assemblies make the HRS's operational once more.[17]

Early in June the squadron began planning for a series of exercises which was to continue throughout 1952 and overlap into the following year. At last the basic mission of Marine helicopters was to be realistically tested by the transport squadron. For the announced purpose of Operation MARLEX I on the 10th and 11th was "to gain experience for HMR-161 personnel and 'I' Company (3d Battalion, 5th Marines) personnel in vertical envelopment combined with an amphibious operation."[18]

Since a carrier was not available, the island of Sung Bong-do, about 40 miles southwest of Inchon, was selected

for loading zones (see preceding map). A nearby island,
Tokchok-to, offered two broad and sandy beaches for troop
landings. About five miles long and half as wide, the terrain
rose sharply from the seashore to heavily wooded ridges in the
interior. Sung Bong-do was located about six miles to the
southeast.

Shore Party and Air Delivery Platoon personnel took charge
of the unloading after descending to the beaches on rope
ladders. Seven aircraft lifted 236 fully equipped troops in 59
flights the first day, and 239 troops in 59 flights the second
day. Aircraft time totaled 46.3 hours for the two days, and
over-all time was nine hours and four minutes for both
landings.

The report of HMR-161 was anything but complacent.
Ground to air communications were declared to be "completely unsatisfactory," and it was recommended that some
more effective type of radio be used. It was further urged that
an island nearer to the beaches be selected as a simulated
carrier.

"The primary reason for recommending that the distance
be reduced in these Marlex exercises," explained Colonel
McCutcheon, "was the shortage of helicopters. One of the
aims of the Marine Corps concept of using helicopters is to
increase the distance over water for combat troop landings.
And if HMR-161 had had more aircraft available; the distance would have been lengthened."[19]

As it was, the squadron report had no praise whatever for
MARLEX I. "The time to land troops by helicopter," it concluded, "was too great in comparison to the time needed to
land troops . . . by boat."[20]

Toward the end of the month HMR-1 tried again, and
Operation MARLEX II showed some improvement. The island
of Soya-do, two miles from the landing beaches, was used as
the simulated carrier.

This time 235 troops of George Company, 5th Marines, made a tactical landing on June 24 and an administrative landing the next day. They were flown two miles over the water from the simulated carrier on Soya-do to Landing Zone

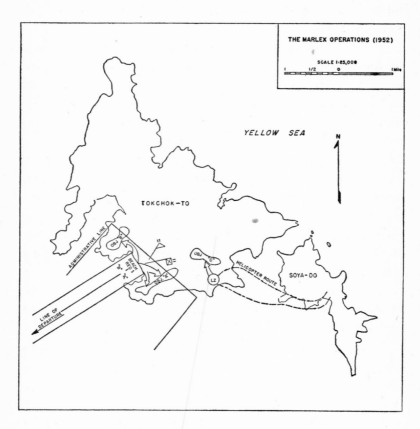

ABLE on Tokchok-to. Starting at 0555 on D-day, the four aircraft completed the tactical operation in 56 flights with an over-all time of an hour and 17 minutes as compared to 59 flights and an hour and 50 minutes for the administrative lift. Ground to air communications were better, noted the report, and air to air communications "excellent."[21]

Sandwiched in between the MARLEX operations in June were two others. BUTTERFLY involved another battalion relief across the Han River, and EVEREADY was planned to test the ability of HMR-161 to carry out a troop lift on a few hours' notice. Both operations were successfully completed.[22]

Next came two more MARLEX operations, designed III and IV. The purpose was to give training in helicopter assault landings to as many infantry units as possible on the company level.[23] The same two islands were used for further exercises, with a single exception, down to Operation MARLEX XII in December.

SPREAD OF HELICOPTER GOSPEL

There could be no doubt that Marine generals were helicopter-minded. General Shepherd, the new Commandant; Lieutenant General Franklin A. Hart, now commanding FMFPac; Major General Christian F. Schilt, and Brigadier General Clayton C. Jerome of the 1st Marine Aircraft Wing —these names appear frequently in HMR-161 records of visitors making a helicopter tour of the front. Command flights by General Selden are mentioned almost daily in squadron reports.

In the summer of 1952, however, it could no longer be assumed that the helicopter overhead was probably a Marine ship or just possibly a Navy aircraft. Both the Army and Air Force were bringing as many rotary-wing machines to Korea as their expanded pilot-training programs would permit. Even so, their helicopters were still limited in numbers, and it fell to HMR-161 on July 30, 1952, to evacuate 650 Army and Air Force troops as well as 150 Korean civilians to Airfield K-47 from a flooded island in the river Pukkan.

Six Marine helicopters formed the regular traffic pattern, with a 15-second interval between aircraft, while flying out troops from the 40th Division Headquarters Company, 34th Ordnance Depot Company, 443d Quartermaster Battalion, 223d Tank Company and other Army or Air Force units.

"An average load was five men and gear," said the HMR-161 report. "Later on, as we started lifting Korean civilians, as many as nine (9) small children complete with dogs and chickens were lifted in one trip, also several women of pleasure and/or ill repute were evacuated from the general area. The lift took about three (3) hours to complete and in that time our six (6) helicopters transported over eight hundred (800) people. Upon completion of the operation two (2) helicopters were committed to remain at K-47 during the night in the event that the personnel left for security purposes could be evacuated, should the whole island become flooded. Our efforts were well received by the Army and Air Force, who marveled at the expeditious way our helicopters carried out the operation."[24]

The entire evacuation was completed without operations orders, pre-briefing or scheduling, and with only a minimum amount of advance information. A total of 182 flights were made by the squadron that day in 39.8 flight hours.[25]

The increase of Army and Air Force helicopter evacuations had resulted in the hospital ships *Haven* and *Repose* constructing landing platforms modeled after that of the *Consolation*, which was designed by Major Stanley V. Titterud of HMR-161.[26] There were not many bright spots in this dreary conflict, but one of them was the care taken of battle casualties. Never before in history, not even in World War II, did a wounded man have the odds so much in his favor.

Night flights were now routine with both VMO-6 and HMR-161. "Although flying helicopters that represented no great strides in improved instrumentation," commented Major Lynn E. Midkiff, "Marine pilots in Korea not only proved the feasibility of night evacuation missions under even the most adverse circumstances, but pointed up the necessity for rotary-wing aircraft that are capable of round-the-clock operation."[27]

Army and Air Force as well as Marine pilots found their missions increased as the front had one of its sudden upswings of activity in the summer of 1952. It was an odd and distasteful war from the professional viewpoint of Marines who took pride in a long tradition of the offensive. As the conflict entered its third year, both sides dug in like the trench-bound military moles of World War I. The peace talks and ensuing lull had given the enemy the opportunity to create defenses in great depth and strength. By April of 1952 he was equal and sometimes superior to the UN forces in artillery. As a result the Marines, like the rest of the Eighth Army, took to the shelter of the earth in bunkers, trenches and outposts.

Not even a no man's land was lacking to complete the similarity to the Western Front of 1917. Pitted by shells, bristling with minefields and barbed-wire entanglements, this strip of scarred terrain was the battleground, usually at night, of assaults launched by one side or another against an opposing outpost.[28]

The Marine front erupted into violent activity during the summer nights of 1952 as the Chinese attacked Bunker Hill, Siberia, and other outposts. These efforts were accompanied by terrific concentrations of artillery, so that losses mounted. VMO-6 evacuations were nearly tripled as compared to the spring months. The helicopters brought out 332 wounded men in July, and 343 in August. Night evacuations totaled 94 for the two months.[29]

In spite of the added demands, both Marine squadrons kept up their usual routine missions. Colonel McCutcheon was relieved in August by Lieutenant Colonel John F. Carey, another former commanding officer of HMX-1.[30] He arrived just in time for an operation, originally conceived and tested by HMX-1, that was to become front-page news in the States. The purpose was "to evaluate under combat conditions the feasibility of transporting by helicopter, rocket launchers, crews and ammunition to firing zones, especially those inaccessible by roads, and to reduce the time required by standard methods of moving launchers, crews and ammunition from one zone to another."[31]

This official description does not make clear that the need for such a test was created by the rearward blast of the rockets sending up pillars of dust and smoke which quickly revealed the position to enemy observation. There was an urgent demand for some means of whisking both launchers and crews to another location, conducive to better health, before the enemy mortars or artillery registered.

Direct liaison with the Rocket Company of the 11th Marines was established by HMR-161 during the planning phase. Four launchers, three crews, and 66 rockets and fuses were to be lifted from the loading zone to each of two firing zones (see accompanying map). Advance tests had established that an HRS could lift one rocket launcher, or one crew plus an additional man, or 22 rockets and fuses. Two "ripples" were to be fired, each from a different zone and each consisting of 66 rockets.[32] Following are the distances in meters, direct and routed, between zones selected for the operation:

DISTANCE (Meters)	DIRECT	ROUTED
(a) HMR-161 Base to Loading Zone	14,300	15,550
(b) Loading Zone to Firing Zone #1	8,400	12,100
(c) Firing Zone #1 to Firing Zone #2	12,050	16,000
(d) Firing Zone #2 to Loading Zone	3,650	4,000
(e) Loading Zone to HMR-161 Base	14,300	15,550
(f) Total in meters	52,700	63,200

Two rehearsals were held to familiarize the rocket launcher

crews with helicopters, and the pilots with problems of transporting the loads. Operation RIPPLE began on August 19 and led up to this sequence of events:

EVENT	TIME
(1) Take-off from HMR-161 Base	1800
(2) First HRS-1 arrives at Loading Zone	1812
(3) Last HRS-1 departs Loading Zone	1831
(4) First HRS-1 arrives at Firing Zone #1	1819
(5) Last HRS-1 arrives at Firing Zone #1	1838
(6) Rockets commence firing on targets	1840
(7) Last HRS-1 departs Firing Zone #1	1843
(8) First HRS-1 arrives at Firing Zone #2	1851
(9) Last HRS-1 arrives Firing Zone #2	1854
(10) Rockets commence firing on targets	1900
(11) Last HRS-1 departs Firing Zone #2	1904

There was some delay due to sling-hoist hooking difficulties at Firing Zone #1, and several rocket launcher crews took too much time entering and leaving aircraft. But on the whole Operation RIPPLE was a great success, and the squadron recommended "that the helicopter be utilized in forthcoming rocket transporting missions."[33]

LANDING FROM CARRIER

Operation MARLEX VII on September 1 and 2, 1952, differed from the others in being conducted from the carrier *Sicily* (CVE-118), though Tokchok Island provided the landing beaches as usual. Twelve aircraft (with availability later reduced to ten) lifted 964 troops of the 1st Battalion, 7th Marines. Following are the statistics:

EVENT	TIME
(1) First aircraft off CVE-118 (1 Sept)	1305
(2) First aircraft on BLUE Beach	1329
(3) Last aircraft off BLUE Beach	1540
(4) Last aircraft on CVE-118	1546
(5) First aircraft off CVE-118 (2 Sept)	1344

EVENT	TIME
(6) First aircraft on BLUE Beach	1400
(7) Last aircraft off BLUE Beach	1506
(8) Last aircraft on CVE-118	1512
(9) Aircraft time in hours (1 Sept)	26.40
(10) Aircraft time in hours (2 Sept)	19.02
(11) Total time in hours (1 Sept)	
Carrier to carrier	2.41
On beach—off beach	2.11
(12) Total time in hours (2 Sept)	
Carrier to carrier	2.02
On beach—off beach	1.28[34]

Operation SILENT REDLINE I, on September 11, aimed "to effect the relief of a unit on the MLR and return the relieved unit to a rear area as expeditiously as possible." The 1st Battalion of the 1st KMC Regiment was to be flown across the Han to relieve the 5th Battalion, which would then be transported back to the loading area.

It was estimated by G-2 that the enemy had about "72 infantry battalions in position to affect the military picture in our sector, only 15 of which are believed to be on the line. In direct support of the infantry units the enemy has 16 artillery battalions and one armored regiment." The G-2 summary identified the enemy confronting the KMC Regiment as elements of two regiments of one CCF Army with six battalions in line and three in reserve.[35]

Air attack, artillery or mortar fire were mentioned as possibilities of enemy interference with the helicopter lift.

Squadron instructions for aircraft encountering CCF opposition were to "seek landing spots in defilade, maintain communication if possible, await further instructions. Ground personnel will seek natural protective defense positions and await further instructions. Protective measures for equipment and material will be taken if possible."

As it proved, Operation SILENT REDLINE I was completed

without enemy interference from 0900 to 1531 on D-day. Ten aircraft (with availability later reduced to eight) made 277 flights, carrying six men each, or five men and a crew-served weapon. Altogether, 1,618 troops were transported in 61 hours aircraft time, or six and a half hours over-all time.[34]

Two more RIPPLE operations, staged in August and September, demonstrated anew that helicopter lifts could add greatly to the effectiveness of rocket firing while reducing casualties among the launcher crews.

Further MARLEX operations took place from time to time on the two islands. And five more SILENT REDLINE operations were successfully completed between October and February, each representing the relief of an infantry battalion on the MLR.

Operation NEBRASKA on October 13 was planned "to effect a tactical move by helicopter of a unit from positions on one phase line to positions on another phase line."[36] HMR-161 had the mission of transporting by helicopter the second battalion, 1st Marines, and a platoon of the 4.2" Mortar Company to landing sites near prepared positions on the designated phase line. Ten helicopters were utilized in a shuttle system, with loading zones and landing sites being located in defilade for concealment. Only two and a half hours of over-all time were needed for the lift of 820 troops in 169 flights.[37]

VIP'S BY THE POUND

These tactical lifts were dwarfed by two mammoth logistical operations carried out by HMR-161 during the autumn and winter. The first, Operation HAYLIFT I, set a new record by transporting all supplies for five days to a regiment at the front. Even VIP's were counted by the pound among the cargo delivered.

It was estimated that about 77,000 pounds must be lifted

to the 7th Marines each day from September 22 to 26. The round-trip distance from the two loading zones to the four landing points averaged about 20 miles. Rations, water, ammunition, fortification material, and 55-gallon drums of fuel were among the supplies to be transported both by cargo net and wire basket.

The possibility of enemy interference was not discounted. It was estimated by G-2 that 4,200 troops of one CCF infantry regiment confronted the 7th Marines. There was a possibility that three battalions of another regiment of the same division were in local reserve, bringing the total up to 7,200. Enemy artillery pieces capable of firing on the 7th Marines positions were placed at 124, and all of the landing points lay within range. HMR-161 aircraft were instructed to fly in defilade and maintain a strict radio discipline.

The 1st Service Battalion had the responsibility of moving supplies to Loading Zone ABLE, while the 1st Ordnance Battalion was given a similar mission at Loading Zone BAKER. Air Delivery Platoon personnel were to supervise the loading, and to dispatch aircraft under the control of HMR-161 Operations Officer. Shore Party personnel had the duty of moving cargo from the trucks to the nets.

Performance came up to plan so successfully during the five-day execution phase that the squadron report summed it up in a sentence, "No unusual problems were encountered and the operation progressed smoothly and continuously throughout." Despite such weather conditions as the morning fog on the 23d and the rain on the 25th, the HRS's carried out their assignments.

Only 40 per cent of the total effort of the squadron, in fact, was required to supply the 7th Marines, and routine flights continued as usual on all five days. In most cases the maximum payload of 1,000 pounds was not utilized because the cargo was not flexible enough to be readily adjusted.

Altogether, 351,171 pounds were lifted by the ten aircraft employed. "Total weight," added the squadron report, "includes cargo (8,770 pounds) brought back from the 7th Marines on return trips; also includes 68 troops at 12,240 pounds . . . and seven VIP's at 1,260 pounds."[38]

OPERATION HAYLIFT II

This operation nearly tripled the results of MULETRAIN during the first days of 1952, when HMR-161 supplied a battalion at the front. But the records set by HAYLIFT I were not to last long. For in February, 1953, the squadron lifted five times as much cargo while supplying two regiments at the front over a period of five days.

Two tactical operations, RIPPLE V and SILENT REDLINE V, had been successfully completed earlier in the month when planning began for the big cargo lift. The purpose was "(a) to evaluate under combat conditions the feasibility of logistically supporting both MLR regiments" . . . and "(b) to determine the planning factors involved in a mission of this nature, such as number of aircraft required, maintenance load, time factor, and tonnage lifting capabilities of a transport helicopter squadron operating independently under combat conditions. To ascertain the feasibility of rendering such support should the actual need arise due to normal supply channels being rendered inoperative because of rain, snow, or impassable bridges."[39]

Cargo was to be transported from eight sites at the two loading zones, ABLE and BAKER. Again, as in HAYLIFT I, the 1st Service Battalion and 1st Ordnance Battalion were to move supplies at these zones. Personnel of the 1st Air Delivery Platoon would designate the load and dispatch aircraft under the supervision of HMR-161 Operations Duty Officer, and Shore Party personnel would move cargo from trucks to the nets and baskets, and assist in loading aircraft. A thousand pounds was set as the maximum payload.

The assistant Chief of Staff, G-4, 1st Marine Division, was to be the over-all co-ordinator of the lift, with his control headquarters at Loading Zone ABLE.

"Confronting the 1st Marine Division," said the G-2 estimate, "the enemy has seventy-two (72) infantry battalions in position to affect the military picture in our sector, only sixteen (16) of which are believed to be on the line. In direct support of the infantry units the enemy has sixteen (16) artillery battalions and one (1) armored regiment."[40]

Once more the helicopters were instructed to fly in defilade wherever possible and maintain radio discipline at all times. Clear weather was predicted for D-day on February 23, with light surface winds from the northwest, and minimum temperatures of 10 to 15 degrees Fahrenheit.

At 0655 on the morning of D-day, eight aircraft reported to Zone ABLE and four to BAKER. Some 260 loads were made available during the day. All were slung underneath in nets or wire baskets with the exception of fragile or perishable items, which were carried internally. Return trips were utilized to bring back empty fuel drums and high priority items or personnel, as determined by the operations officer of the two regiments.

The distance was 8.06 nautical miles from Zone ABLE (one way) and 7.81 from BAKER. At the end of the first day, the results were no longer counted in terms of pounds. About 160 tons of supplies had been moved, as compared to the original estimate of 130 tons.[41]

This gain was better appreciated the next day, when the 5th Marines put in a request for a large amount of additional ammunition. As many as nine aircraft had to be used for this purpose alone. As a consequence, some 65 tons of regular supplies could not be moved and were left at the loading zones.

Operations started at first light on the 25th in order to wipe out this deficit. But added requests for ammunition were received, and casualties now entered the equation as a consequence of a brisk action between a battalion of the 5th Marines and the enemy. Arrangements were made with VMO-6 to fly all possible evacuation missions, and that day the squadron transported 200 tons up to the MLR—"the greatest tonnage of cargo," according to the report, *"ever* lifted by a helicopter squadron in a single day."[42]

The fourth day was uneventful. So far the weather had been favorable, but fog slowed up operations for a few hours on the morning of the 27th. Nevertheless, the twelve aircraft finished moving the remaining supplies by 1700 that afternoon.

All refueling and light maintenance was conducted at the A-18 airstrip near Loading Zone ABLE. Major maintenance had to be accomplished at the squadron's rear echelon, near Ascom City, where adequate shops and equipment were available. Such repairs could usually be done at night, so that the helicopter would be on the job again in the morning. But one aircraft which required an engine change early in the day was back in the operation only three hours later.

About 95 per cent of the total capability of the squadron was devoted to supplying the two regiments. This was largely owing to the fact that a third of the tonnage consisted of drums of diesel fuel, which were awkward to handle and cut down on payloads. Following are the statistics:

Pounds lifted from Zone ABLE	1,185,348
Pounds lifted from Zone BAKER	300,060
Pounds of mail to regiments	8,648
Pounds of mail from regiments	4,393

Pounds of cargo returned to Zone ABLE   113,857
Total pounds lifted   1,612,306
Average pounds lifted per day   322,461
Total loads lifted   1,633
Average loads per day   326.6
Total hours of flying time   583.4
Average hours of flying time per day   116.8
Average number of aircraft available   12.4
Pounds lifted per hour   31,589

There were also a total of 65 passengers, and the helicopters brought out the bodies of five Marines killed in action.[48]

After this demonstration there could be no doubt that the helicopter was destined to work a revolutionary change in logistics of the future. Every aircraft in Operation HAYLIFT II had completed an average of about 27 round trips of some 15 miles each between dawn and dusk, transporting nearly 11 tons of supplies. It would have taken a tremendous fleet of trucks to haul 160 tons a day over Korean roads at a fourth of that speed. These trail-bound vehicles would have been more vulnerable both to weather and enemy fire than the helicopters. The trucks could not have chosen their own route, taking every protective advantage of the terrain. They could not have loaded at the most convenient spot, nor could they have dumped their supplies practically in the laps of the infantry at the front.

CHAPTER XI

Armistice in Korea

•

There was more to the Marine helicopter picture of 1953 than met the eye in Korea. Not only was the parent squadron at Quantico still going strong, but since organizing HMR-161 it had set up eight more transport helicopter units in this country plus the subsidiary and maintenance outfits to support them.* Thanks to these efforts, the Marine Corps undoubtedly had more trained helicopter pilots, crewmen, and aircraft, in proportion to total numbers, than any other military organization in the world when the fighting ceased in Korea.

Nearly all the operations carried out in Korea, for that matter, were first conceived and tested by HMX-1 at Quantico. Improvements in aircraft, according to Colonel H. R. Paige, were largely due to "the continuous liaison with manufacturers maintained by the Marine Corps Development Center, which is continually planning to improve the helicopter, to devise means to increase its usefulness, and to discover the many still unthought-of means to which this valuable aircraft may be put."[1]

Doctrinal studies had not only kept pace with tests and operations; they usually were a step or two in advance. Thus

---

* See Appendix B for a list of all Marine helicopter squadrons and their supporting units to the cease-fire in Korea, with dates of organization and names of commanding officers.

on January 5, 1951, before the Marine Corps had a single helicopter transport squadron, the Landing Force Tactics and Techniques Board of the Marine Corps Schools brought out a long mimeographed report entitled "Employment of the Assault Transport Helicopter."[2] A revised edition of this study appeared the following October.

On March 8 the same Board put out a booklet for the purpose of providing "a comprehensive concept for the employment of currently authorized HMR squadrons in amphibious operations."[3] And on the 30th, the Committee on Atomic Warfare of the Marine Corps Schools made its secret interim report on atomic weapons.[4]

The Landing Force Tactics and Techniques Board's next publication, on April 14, was a "Study to Determine the Requirements of the Marine Corps for a Flying Crane Type Helicopter."[5] After surveying all existing and prototype models of helicopters with a large payload, the Board considered the other extreme in its "Study of a Marine Corps Requirement for a One-Man Helicopter."[6]

This was a subject of keen interest to military men as well as the general public. As early as November 19, 1947, Lieutenant Colonel James D. Hittle had submitted a memorandum to the Commandant, describing the small helicopters of that date. The most promising of these experimental models weighed only 175 pounds, empty, and had an anticipated payload of 250 pounds with maximum speed of 90 miles per hour. Powered by a two-cylinder engine driving two coaxial rotors, this design had a three-wheeled carriage. "One man helicopters of such performance and light weight," commented Hittle, "would appear to offer many possibilities for amphibious operations."[7]

The Board report of April, 1952, conceded that "a one-man machine can be built and successfully flown which would have all the inherent advantages of the larger types." As for its military value, the verdict was that "employment of the one-man helicopter by tactical units shows promise but is dependent upon radical developments in simplicity and economy."[8]

Among the other Marine Corps Schools studies of 1952 were "Use of Smoke in Helicopter Operations," "Composition and Duties of Helicopter Control Units," "Supporting Arms in Helicopter Assault Operations," and "Study on Supply Concept to Support Helicopter-Borne Units."[9]

Helicopter tactics had an entire section devoted to them in *Landing Force Manual 4, Ship to Shore Movement,* the comprehensive publication which was officially "approved and published for the information and guidance of the Marine Corps" in 1952.[10]

Three Marine publications of 1953 were based on the experience gained during the five years since the appearance of *Phib-31,* which still remained a sound work within its limits. *Interim Doctrine for the Tactical Employment of Helicopters* came out in February with these remarks in the preface:

"This landing force bulletin is published for the information and guidance of ground and aviation commanders in planning and executing helicopter operations. It presents only broad governing principles. Since helicopter operations are still in process of development, this bulletin is not intended to limit initiative with respect to details necessary to implement these principles. . . . Users of this bulletin are requested to submit comments and recommendations for changes and additions to the Commandant of the Marine Corps."[11]

Four months later the Marine Corps Development Center sponsored a publication which was "believed to be the most complete document on military helicopter tactics in existence." This appraisal by Colonel Paige seems justified by the scope of *Tactics and Techniques for Helicopter Employment with Ground Forces.* Organization, command relationships, planning, the ship-to-shore movement, helicopter employment in support of ground-to-ground operations and special operations, logistical support, communications, light helicopter operations—every phase of the subject is taken up in this manual.[12] As a companion piece, the Marine Corps Schools brought out a technical study, consisting largely of diagrams, under the title, "Troop Seating in Marine Assault Transport Helicopters."[13]

MORE HELICOPTER SQUADRONS

While these helicopter doctrinal studies were burgeoning, the Marine Corps had been setting up new helicopter units on both coasts in the ratio of three transport squadrons to every division and aircraft wing.

The three Atlantic Coast transport squadrons, based at the Marine Corps Air Station, Cherry Point, N. C., were HMR-261, HMR-262, and HMR-263, of Marine Helicopter Transport Group 26.

Six Pacific Coast squadrons (including HMR-161 in Korea) were based at Santa Ana, Calif.—HMR-162 and HMR-163, of Marine Helicopter Transport Group 16; and HMR-361, HMR-362, and HMR-363, of Marine Helicopter Transport Group 36.

"The East and West Coast helicopter units have spent many long and fruitful hours trying out and improving on the techniques of employing our present type helicopter in the amphibious-airborne ship-to-shore movement," said Colonel Owen A. Chambers, first commanding officer of HMR-261.[14]

A total of 52 large-scale exercises were completed by these squadrons from August, 1951, to June, 1953. Two of the most instructive Atlantic Coast operations were HELEX I and II, conducted by HMR-261 and HMR-262 in co-operation with ground force elements of the 2d Marine Division. Both exer-

cises were made the subject of a detailed analysis submitted
to the Chief of Naval Operations by a Marine board headed
by Major General Field Harris. The other members were
Colonel Chambers, Colonel Roy L. Kline, Colonel Harold B.
Meek, Lieutenant Colonel Irving Schechter, Captain Alexander Wilson, and Captain Thomas B. Owen.

Operations HELEX I and II were initiated when the Board
met on January 2, 1952, and recommended "that two helicopter exercises be conducted during the period 20 January—
1 March, 1952, and that these exercises include the assault lift
of a battalion by helicopter from a CVE to a suitable landing
zone ashore."[15]

The period from January 21 to 24 was utilized for pilot
familiarization and qualification, also for evaluation of the
HRS-1 aircraft and its flight and handling characteristics
aboard the CVE. HMR-261 and HMR-262 were commanded
by Colonel Chambers and Lieutenant Colonel David M.
Danser respectively, the latter having relieved Lieutenant
Colonel William H. Doolen on the 21st. The two squadrons
boarded the USS *Siboney* with a combined strength of 44
officers, 113 enlisted personnel, and 20 HRS-1 aircraft. The
landing force, consisting of 37 officers and 663 enlisted men
of the 1st Battalion, 8th Marines, came aboard on January 28,
and the carrier departed from Norfolk for the Camp Lejeune
exercise area.

The under-way period gave an opportunity for loading and
unloading drills, and limited flight operations were carried out
on the 29th. A small-scale rehearsal on the 30th involved the
loading and launching of 18 aircraft and their flight to the
landing zone. Communications circuits were tested.

HELEX I took place according to schedule on the last day of
the month. H-hour was set for 0800, and by 1225 the 18 helicopters had the last personnel on the beaches. The next two

hours and five minutes were devoted to flying all combat cargo ashore. The two helicopter squadrons then reported to Cherry Point, N.C., and the carrier returned to Norfolk.[16]

On February 12 the Board met again to plan HELEX II in the light of the experience gained in the first exercise. Five days later the Helicopter Evaluation Group boarded the *Siboney* for a four-day period of qualifying new pilots and testing techniques of helicopter operation on a carrier. Again the 1st Battalion of the 8th Marines embarked with HMR-261 and HMR-262. Heavy seas prevented flight operations for two and a half days, but on the afternoon of February 27 a rehearsal was held in the landing zone of Camp Lejeune to test communication nets.

On D-day, the 28th, ABLE flight was launched at 0655. Then BAKER flight was brought up from the hanger deck to be launched at 0730. This flight set up an interval of eight minutes, by returning at a speed of 55 knots, for the purpose of enabling ABLE flight to land, refuel, load, launch, and clear the flight deck. All subsequent personnel waves were landed by flights of eight aircraft or less, and the original time separation remained in force. It was 0801 when the first troops landed, and the last cargo flight was completed at 1400.

Two and a quarter hours after the first landings the 603 assault troops were on the beach. The initial wave of 18 helicopters had been launched while under way at a distance of about 17 miles from the landing zone. The *Siboney* then closed to 12 miles before anchoring at 0730.

Immediately after the troop landings, the supply phase of the operation commenced. Only ten helicopters were equipped with cargo slings, and they were launched in flights of two, three, or four. Thirty-five tons of cargo, loaded internally and in pallets, were lifted 12 miles in about three hours and 55 minutes.

Operations on the *Siboney* ended at 1650 on D-day with the

completion of the shuttle of squadron personnel to Bogue Field. The last six aircraft, loaded with personnel and equipment, departed for Cherry Point.

During the two HELEX operations a total of 3,180 carrier landings were made aboard the *Siboney*. All results were evaluated in detail and submitted to CNO on April 16, 1952, in the final report of the Assault Helicopter Concept Board.[17]

OPERATION LEX BAKER I

This same month saw the completion of the six-day LEX BAKER I Operation on the Pacific Coast by HMR-162, commanded by Colonel Harold J. Mitchener. The landing force consisted of elements of the 3d Marines of the 3d Marine Division.

For purposes of the exercise, it was assumed that aggressor forces, attacking this country through Mexico and Lower California, had succeeded in advancing to a general line between Las Vegas, Nev., and Santa Fe, N. M. Neither the United States nor the aggressor forces had been able to establish air superiority over the battle areas or naval supremacy in the seas off the California coast.

"Subsequent to his initial attacks," continued the HMR-162 report, "aggressor had occupied the offshore islands of San Clemente, San Nicholas, and Santa Margarita . . . in a series of airborne and seaborne attacks and had developed advanced air bases thereon from which to assist the advance from Lower California by attacking U.S. forces and installations along the coastal areas. The bulk of the aggressor ground strength was then known to be concentrating in the area just east of Ensenada in lower California in preparation for a major effort along the Pacific coast line of advance."[18]

It was further assumed that the Commander-in-Chief, U.S. Fleet, had been directed to seize Santa Margarita Island as a base for further air and amphibious operations against the other two islands and to assist U.S. ground forces on the mainland. The 3d Marines was designated as the landing force to "seize, occupy and defend" Santa Margarita, and HMR-162 helicopters had the mission of landing a reinforced infantry company from the USS *Rendova* (CVE 114). The squadron was also given evacuation, resupply, photography, reconnaissance, and scouting missions.

On February 21, 1952, the squadron strength on board the *Rendova* amounted to 29 officers and 144 enlisted personnel with 11 HRS-1 aircraft. All helicopters were flown aboard by a flight echelon of 22 pilots.

On the 22d, D-day, a total of 637 troops with equipment were landed in 131 personnel lifts. Twenty-two resupply cargo lifts were made, two by each aircraft, to transport 13,200 pounds of supplies.

One aircraft crash-landed immediately after taking off from the landing point, where troops had been discharged on the first wave. The accident was attributed to a mechanical failure in the main drive system, but there were no personnel injuries.

Operation LEX BAKER I continued from D-plus-1 to D-plus-6—February 23 to 28—with most of the squadron's efforts being devoted to such missions as evacuations, supply, photography, and reconnaissance.

A total of 302 sorties were made during this six-day period. HMR-162 closed its final CP at 0800 on February 29.[19]

This was but one of twelve operations in which the squadron participated from November 12, 1951, to May 10, 1953. HMR-163 completed a total of five operations from October 1, 1952, to May 10, 1953. The other three Pacific Coast transport squadrons had the following record:

HMR-361—seven operations from October 1, 1952, to June 17, 1953;

HMR-362—five operations from December 2, 1952, to May 6, 1953;

HMR-363—six operations from September 2, 1952, to May 6, 1953.

On the Atlantic Coast the three squadrons at Cherry Point were meanwhile taking part in these exercises:

HMR-261—seven operations from November 13, 1951, to May 29, 1953;

HMR-262—eight operations from November 13, 1951, to March 29, 1953;

HMR-263—two operations from August 11, 1952, to November 12, 1952.

THE A-BOMB IN NEVADA

There could be no question as to the largest helicopter operation ever completed in this country to that time. This distinction goes to Operation DESERT ROCK V, held at Yucca Flat, Nev., on Saturday, April 18, 1953. Elements of four Pacific Coast helicopter transport squadrons took part with a total of 39 HRS-1 helicopters—enough aircraft to lift a Marine infantry battalion ten miles in an hour.

The exercise was held in conjunction with an atomic test at the Nevada proving grounds of the Atomic Energy Commission Command. A new combination of letters with a Scottish burr evolved when 2d MCPAEB*—the 2d Marine Corps Provisional Atomic Exercise Brigade—was activated on March 2 at Camp Pendleton. Two battalions (each minus a rifle company) from the 3d and 8th Marines, plus some supporting arms and the helicopter contingent, brought the total Marine personnel up to 211 officers and 1,956 enlisted men who trained at Camp Pendleton.

Planning began in Nevada early in March while Marine officers studied the terrain and conferred with the director of the exercise, Brigadier General William C. Bullock, USA,

* A far cry from the musical Italian vowels of ANGLICO—Air and Naval Gunfire Liaison Company.

and his staff. "The co-operation received was excellent," said the Marine report, "and continued throughout the concurrent and parallel planning phases, as well as during the conduct of the exercise."[20]

Marine Helicopter Transport Group 16 (MAG(HR)-16)

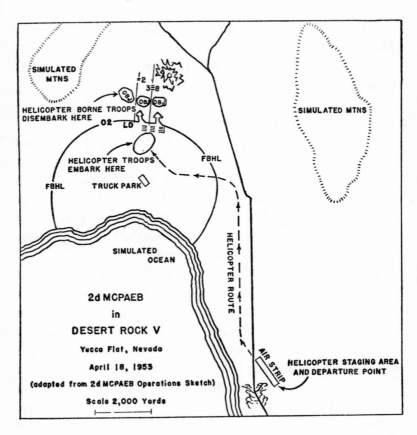

reported for operational control on March 15 with a complement of 79 officers and 141 enlisted men selected from HMR-162, HMR-163, HMR-361, and HMR-362. A rehearsal was held at Pendleton on the 30th for the helicopter phase with the 2d Battalion, 3d Marines.

After arrival at Camp Desert Rock, some 80 miles northwest of Las Vegas, Nev., a final and complete rehearsal of the operation plan took place on April 16. The plan was approved as sound, and the only changes were made in connection with the helicopter lift. It was decided that, due to the altitude and atmospheric conditions, the aircraft could lift only three troops at a time instead of five.

At 1700 on D-1 the 39 helicopters were flown from Camp Desert Rock to the staging area at Yucca airstrip. Pilots and crews were to remain there all night, and it had originally been planned to have Easy Company airborne at the time of the detonation. Restricted predawn visibility was the cause of a new decision to lift the company from the entrenchment area after the shot, thus avoiding the danger of helicopter collisions in the air.

Complete radio silence went into effect at 0230—H-minus-30 minutes. At H-10 minutes the troops were instructed by the loud-speaker to enter their assigned trenches, and to assume a kneeling position at H-minus-2 minutes while braced against the side of the trench toward ground zero.

With a minute left, the helicopters were revving up their engines. The predawn desert cold penetrated to the bones as the grating voice of the loud-speaker continued its chant:

"Four seconds . . . three . . . two . . . one . . ."

The most memorable thing about the detonation was the burst of pale, unearthly light that cast no shadows and turned everything white, even the dark blue helicopters. And then came the shock wave, as if the earth had been struck a heavy blow.

As the huge mushroom cloud formed, two Marine pathfinder helicopters landed in the embarkation area behind the trenches and took aboard radio monitor teams. They were lifted to the objective in four minutes. Next came the lift of Easy Company, which was landed on the objective within the next half hour.

"This time would have been cut down considerably," added the 2d MCPAEB report, "had it not been for rigid safety precautions and limited communications agencies, which restricted control. . . . The employment of helicopters in the exercise did not reveal or develop any new techniques in the embarkation or landing of helicopter borne troops in relation to atomic warfare." New methods of embarking and landing troops were learned, however, which would be applicable to any type of operation. And the conclusion of the report was that "the exercise served to stimulate valuable thought in the tactical field of atomic warfare."

Although a simulated ocean and mountains had been included in the operational plan, these assumptions do not appear to have added much to the execution. At least the four squadrons learned one thing *not* to do when going up against atomic weapons. This negative precept was communicated by the 2d MCPAEB report:

"The employment of helicopters in the exercise revealed the tactical necessity for the selection of alternate routes of approach and objectives when placing helicopter borne forces on objectives in close proximity to ground zero. An uncalculated change in the direction of an atomic cloud can render a route of approach or an objective excessively radioactive and restrict visibility to the extent that operations can be seriously impaired."[21]

1ST MARINE DIVISION RELIEVED

The A-bomb exercise in Nevada crowded Marine operations in Korea off the first page for a few days. Then, on May 5, it was announced that the 1st Marine Division had gone into reserve after being relieved in west Korea by elements of the Eighth Army.

This was news in view of the fact that the Division had put

in a total of 879 days at the front since landing at Inchon on September 15, 1950.

The spring months had been devoted to routine outpost warfare, and HMR-161 completed only two tactical operations, CROSSOVER II, and SILENT REDLINE VI, after its big logistical lift in February, 1953. So far the squadron had maintained intact its amazing record of conducting helicopter operations at the front without losing a single man. Then on February 12, Captain Allen W. Ruggles and his crew chief, Technical Sergeant Joseph L. Brand, Jr., plunged into the sea about 25 miles south of Pusan while flying to a rendezvous with an aircraft carrier that was to take them to Japan. Mechanical trouble was believed to be the cause, and the bodies were never recovered.

On March 25 another fatal accident occurred six miles northeast of Sinchon, Korea. Major Doil R. Stitzel was making a test hop out of Ascom City when his helicopter crashed and burned. The pilot and his two mechanics, Master Sergeant Gilbert N. Caudle and Sergeant Richard L. Parsell, were killed or died of injuries.[22]

VMO-6 helicopter pilots took more risks than their HMR-161 colleagues because of a higher proportion of emergency battlefield evacuations. Scarcely a day passed without one of the flying ambulances returning with bullet holes, yet the squadron had only two more pilots killed in action after the two shot down in 1950. Captain David T. Gooden's death occurred on February 7, 1950; and a fourth name was added with the recovery of Lieutenant Charles Morino's body on July 18, 1953. Several other VMO-6 pilots were still listed as missing in action at the end of the year.[23]

This makes a total of nine operational deaths for Marine pilots and crewmen in Korea. On the strength of this record, it could not be said that the helicopter was unduly vulnerable.

But the Marines had no experience with enemy air opposition in Korea, so that the full story had yet to be told.

Lieutenant Colonel Carey had been relieved as commanding officer of HMR-161 by Colonel Owen A. Chambers before the squadron went into reserve on May 5, 1953. Planning began immediately, at the direction of the Division staff, for a large-scale helicopter landing exercise to be known as MARLEX I.

Major General Edwin A. Pollock, who relieved Selden as commanding general of the 1st Marine Division, initiated the first helicopter assault landing exercises in Korea on a regimental scale. The 5th Marines was designated for a combined landing by air and water to take place on May 13 in the Yongdong-ni beach area of southwest Korea. Unfortunately, no carrier was available at the time; and HMR-161 could assign only six helicopters, supported by the 1st Air Delivery Platoon with its usual loading and unloading missions.

Total enemy strength in the Yongdong-ni area was assumed for purposes of the exercise to be a division consisting of three infantry regiments and an artillery regiment—a total of 10,000 men.

"Approximately 920 troops, one battalion, are presently committed to the defense of the landing area," continued the HMR-161 report. "The enemy has available for tactical air defense missions approximately 1,315 jet fighters and 685 conventional fighters, ground attack planes, and bombers. It is not known what naval defense units are in the area. The coastal defense guns may be manned by a naval defense force."

In view of this allowance, it could never be said that the theoretical enemy had stinted his troops with respect to air support. As the assault force, the 5th Marines was "to land on MARLEX beaches, advance inland, seize force beach headline, protect landing of supporting elements and additional ground forces, advance inland on order and destroy or capture enemy forces in the area. Surface units of COMNAVFE are to direct such naval support as will be necessary to support this amphibious operation."[24]

At 1325 on May 13 the six helicopters took off from inland loading zones with their first waves. A shuttle system was utilized to lift a BLT of assault troops to the two landing sites on RED beach, where Air Delivery Platoon personnel directed the unloading.

"All phases of the problem were accomplished," according to the HMR-161 report, which recommended "that additional operations of this type be assigned for further training of personnel of the 1st Marine Division and HMR-161."[25]

Operation MARLEX II on June 6 was a duplicate in most respects of the first exercise, with the difference that six helicopters landed a BLT of the 7th Marines on the same beaches at Yongdong-ni. The lift of 688 assault troops commenced at H-plus-10 minutes and was completed at H-plus-3 hours and 20 minutes. One helicopter had to be withdrawn after an hour and 50 minutes to evacuate an actual case of acute appendicitis.[26]

This was the last large-scale exercise for HMR-161 in 1953. Although the 1st Marine Division returned to the front early in July, the helicopters had only their usual routine missions down to the armistice of July 27.

RHYME AND STATISTICS

The final statistics of Marine helicopter operations in Korea are impressive. Yet it may be questioned whether the story of the helicopter can be told by rows of figures. These cold fruits of the adding machine can give no idea of the hard-bitten sentimentality and affection which was the tribute of Marine ground forces to the whirlybirds. Tanks and rocket launchers and 155mm howitzers were all held in respect, and you could be happy that they were playing on your team. But there was something almost human about the big-bellied choppers flapping along slowly and awkwardly, close to the ground, with the pilot waving a greeting from his goldfish bowl on top of the six hundred horses which turned the windmill overhead. There was none of the icy, terrible, out-of-this-world perfection of a jet streaking its way across the sky from horizon to horizon. An egg beater seemed earthbound in comparison as it approached for a landing. . . .

> If you listen you can hear her
> Whirling rotors slap the air,
> In a minute she'll come stealing
> Through that valley over there.[27]

These lines are quoted from verses entitled "Angel with a Rotary Wing," written by Bert Herrin—Captain Hubert L. Herrin, of Lemon Grove, Calif. A pilot of HMR-161, he was a contributor to *Equitatus Caeli*, 1951, the informal yearbook written in diary form by the squadron and printed in Japan.

> 'Neath the ridge line, down the gully,
> Fanning tree tops in her wake,
> Like a horse that's gone a flyin'
> To run down Medusa's fake.

From the landing in Korea to the Armistic in the summer of 1953, a total of 18,607 flights were made by HMR-161 pilots in 16,538 flight hours. Personnel were lifted to the number of 60,046, and 7,554,336 pounds of cargo were transported.[28]

> Now she's slower, now she hovers,
> Gently lets her cargo down,
> Then flies sideways to a clearing;
> Lets herself upon the ground.

There were three months in which HMR-161 lifted more than a million pounds of cargo while carrying out all other routine missions. The largest amount transported in any one month was the 2,018,120 pounds during February, 1953; and 8,471 passengers (April, 1952) came first in that category.[29]

Although evacuations ranked as a secondary mission of the transport squadron, 2,748 were carried out successfully during the 23 months from September, 1951, to the end of July, 1953. And VMO-6 flew out a total of 7,067 wounded men during its 35 months of combat.[30]

> From the hillsides' winding trails
> Down the paths they trudge and slide
> Come the men who've earned their passage
> For a helicopter ride.

Altogether, nearly ten thousand evacuation and rescue missions were completed by the two Marine helicopter outfits. It is a safe guess that this total included several thousand Americans whose bones would now be moldering in Asiatic soil if it were not for the choppers, and the ground forces did not fail to show their appreciation.

> Some on stretchers, lowered gently,
> Others manage on their own.
> Bleeding, shattered, broken figures,
> With their courage freedom's sown.
>
> Then they're lifted up inside her,
> All ready—up she'll climb!
> Off the clearing, down the gully,
> Save a life by racing time!

But the Angel with the Rotary Wing was not entirely preoccupied with errands of mercy. She also had her avenging moods, and it is a reasonable speculation that Marine helicopters were directly or indirectly the cause of several enemy casualties for every American life saved. There was often no way of telling just how much damage was done as a result of (a) the photographic mission completed by a Marine helicopter, followed by (b) the Corsair strike which rained fire on the camouflaged artillery position revealed by the picture. Nor was there any way of knowing exactly the losses inflicted after (a) a reconnaissance helicopter spotted a CCF column, and (b) the 155mm howitzers registered on this target of opportunity.

At any rate, the Marine ground forces could and did attest that the flying windmills did their share when it came to hitting the enemy in Korea.

The armistice did not mean an end, or even an interruption, to the helicopter development program of the Marine Corps. Both in this country, and the Far East, Marine helicopter squadrons continued to train at wartime tempo. When the guns became silent on July 27, 1953, the 1st Marine Division remained in front-line positions of the old sector in west Korea. Major General Randolph McC. Pate, who relieved Pollock as commander, kept the helicopters busy at administrative missions, including the transportation of UN delegates to the peace talks at Panmunjom.

Only two weeks after the armistice, the 3d Marine Division sailed from San Diego to Japan under the command of Major General Robert H. Pepper. Three of the West Coast helicopter units—HMR-162, HMR-163, and VMO-2—embarked with the ground forces on August 13, 1953. A fourth squadron, HMR-361, had orders for duty in Hawaii.[31]

THE HELICOPTER ERA

It was too soon to look back at the Korean conflict with the proper historical perspective. But there could be no doubt that the helicopter had been the war's foremost tactical innovation. Again, as in the case of World War II amphibious techniques, the Marine Corps had begun with a concept and developed it into a doctrine and system of tactics.

Perhaps never in American history has there been a less popular military venture. Both the motives and results were confusing to the general public. But if the costly three-year war taught any lesson at all, it was that the Western nations cannot hope to cope with Asiatic communist adversaries on a basis of muscular tactics. Not only do such opponents hold a great potential superiority in human tonnage; they have a further advantage in their cheap evaluation of human life.

The Chinese did not, as newspaper correspondents sometimes reported, resort to "human sea" tactics in Korea. Their night attacks were usually launched with comparatively small units and conducted with skill. But the CCF generals made it evident on many occasions that the man in the ranks was as expendable as a grenade. The eight Chinese divisions which tried unsuccessfully to isolate and destroy the 1st Marine Division in November, 1950, were sent into the objective area with food, ammunition, and supplies for a few days—such amounts as could be transported over mountain roads by the soldiers themselves plus a few pack animals. If these 80,000 troops did not accomplish their mission while the supplies lasted, the penalties of failure would inevitably be drastic in sub-zero weather. Yet they did fail in a 13-day attack, and it is probable that their losses from freezing, malnutrition, and disease equaled the thousands of casualties inflicted by the Marines.

If such a catastrophe had overtaken an American force, the political reverberations would have been comparable to a major earthquake. But Chinese communist leaders did not find it necessary to account for the warm bodies transformed by the chemistry of war into cold bodies. There were always more warm bodies to be conscripted from China's millions.

These military coolies were by no means contemptible opponents. They won some valid victories over better equipped U.S. forces, and our troops were chided by stateside editorial writers seeking an explanation. Mechanized Americans had lost the ability to march, it was charged, as compared to Chinese Reds who covered 30 miles of mountain roads in a winter night while subsisting on a diet of cold boiled rice.

True as this may be, it is questionable whether the fault lay in too much mechanization. Could it be, on the contrary, that the U.S. forces did not carry mechanization far enough? This query is suggested by the results of helicopter operations in Korea. Seldom did the two Marine squadrons bring more than 25 aircraft into action, all told. Yet these helicopters set new time and space standards by reducing battalion troop movements to routine missions and supplying whole regiments at the front.

In view of such achievements, it would appear that reliance on outdated forms of mechanization was the actual handicap of U.S. forces against an Asiatic peasant army. In reality, both trucks and fixed-wing planes were rendered obsolescent by the helicopter for most purposes of front-line supply or troop movements. For if 25 American helicopters could make such a record in Korea, the tactical and logistical potentialities of a thousand are challenging to the imagination.

Early in 1954 it appeared likely that this total would soon be reached in the U.S. armed forces, considering the commitments of all branches to rotary-wing aircraft. The U.S. Navy and Coast Guard having been helicopter-minded since 1943, their programs presented progression rather than expansion. Atomic weapons made necessary a greater degree of dispersion than the fleet ever knew before; and the helicopter promised to solve the resulting new problems of command, liaison, and transportation. In addition, there are such long-recognized Navy and Coast Guard missions as rescue, casualty evacuation, reconnaissance, mine spotting, and submarine detection.

The U.S. Army was primarily interested in the logistical possibilities of vertical flight. A month before the armistice in Korea, the largest helicopter operation of the war occurred in an ROK sector when Army and Marine squadrons combined forces for front-line missions reported in American newspapers:

"EAST CENTRAL FRONT, Korea, June 17 (Delayed by Censor) (AP).—Forty-five United States Army and Marine Corps helicopters flown here on an emergency call are getting their heaviest workout of the Korean war in this sector hit by the Chinese offensive.

"The helicopters are doing the jobs that trucks normally do—or cannot do on the piney ridgelines and narrow valleys.

"Roads are clogged 24 hours daily with trucks rolling to and from the front. Helicopters are the only solution for getting supplies and troops on an emergency basis to distant mainline positions.

"Monday afternoon [June 15, 1953] the helicopters lifted a Republic of Korea battalion of about 800 men 10 miles over mountains to strengthen a weak spot in the line. . . .

"Communist artillery gunners shelled the helicopters when they neared their valley destination, but no planes were lost."[32]

After the armistice, the U.S. Army visioned the helicopter as the successor to the truck. Rotary-wing aircraft, replacing wheeled transport, would move 80 per cent of the Army's troops and equipment within the next few years, according to Colonel William B. Bunker, USA. Addressing the American Society of Mechanical Engineers on December 1, 1953, this officer of the Air Transport Service Division pointed out that the helicopter is not an airplane and is not accepted as one. Machines with a lift of five tons, he asserted, would give the Army a mobility never known before and permit dispersion of troops and supplies against an enemy using atomic artillery.[33]

Prior to the Korean conflict the U.S. Air Force esteemed the helicopter chiefly as a vehicle for ARS (Air Rescue Service) units in all parts of the world. Then Marine combat operations made it evident that vertical-lift aircraft had a definite advantage in accuracy over parachute drops of troops or supplies by such large cargo planes as the C-47 or C-119. Marine demonstrations brought to mind the object lessons of World War II which taught that paratroopers were often too scattered for an effective surprise attack after landing, while supplies dropped by parachute were sometimes damaged or fell out of reach.

In the summer of 1952 a record-breaking Air Force flight added to the evidence of the helicopter's versatility. Instead of crating and shipping two machines destined for an ARS squadron in Germany, the Air Force flew them from a Massachusetts airfield by way of Nova Scotia, Labrador, Greenland, Iceland, Scotland, and England. The two ten-place Sikorsky H-19's (Air Force equivalent of the Marine HRS) were loaded to the limit with extra tanks of fuel and escorted by a C-54 transport plane and a World War II Flying Fortress. With two pilots taking turns in each helicopter, the nonstop distance record of 703.6 miles was broken in the lap from Greenland to Iceland with 137 miles to spare. The flight as a whole covered 3,984 miles in 51 hours and 55 minutes of flying time over a period of 20 July and August days.[34]

Piasecki announced in September, 1953, that its new YH-16A, under construction for the Air Force, was the world's largest helicopter. This twin-rotor transport was an outgrowth of the YH-16, which in turn was an extension of the XH-16, dating back to 1947. It had two Pratt and Whitney engines of 1,650 horsepower each. The YH-16A was designed to cruise at more than 125 miles per hour. Airborne armies had been made a reality, said Piasecki, by a lifting capacity of 40 soldiers, 32 litter patients, or three jeeps.[35]

The Marine Corps had been interested in the XH-16 along with the Air Force in 1947. But General Shepherd announced on September 10, 1953, that the Marines had their ideal transport helicopter in the XHR2S being tested by Sikorsky.[36]

The Commandant and other high-ranking Marine officers

attended the demonstration held at Bridgeport, Conn., on January 18, 1954. Two Pratt and Whitney R2800 aircraft engines, similar to those which powered the F4U Corsair and F47 Thunderbolt fighters, were slung outboard on short wing stubs. This left room in the fuselage for 26 combat-equipped Marines or 3 jeeps.[37]

Although the XHR2S was the largest helicopter ever put into regular production, size was of secondary importance to the Marine Corps as compared to dimensions permitting orderly stowage on the hangar decks of aircraft carriers. Power from the two engines was transmitted to the five-blade main rotor and vertical tail rotor, both of which folded for handling aboard carriers. The XHR2S carried an automatic pilot for instrument flight, and the two rotors had de-icing equipment.

Spectators were impressed by the clean lines of the first helicopter ever built with retractable landing gear. This feature contributed to a top speed of well over 150 miles per hour. And since the two engines were outboard, practically all the space in the fuselage could be utilized for passengers and cargo. Rounded doors beneath the pilots' cabin opened wide enough to admit jeeps or howitzers over a ramp.

Designed and built to satisfy Marine requirements, the aircraft was "a prime example of the development of Marine equipment through Navy sources," according to the Marine announcement of January 18, 1954. "The U.S. Army has shown interest in the future employment of the XHR2S and has contributed financially to the program."[38]

Igor Sikorsky, president of the Sikorsky Aircraft Division, said that the XHR2S would be mass-produced in a new plant being built at Stratford, Conn. After military orders had been filled, commercial models would be available in two years.[39]

Marine officers watching the demonstration of the new aircraft must have reflected that the helicopter had come a long way since 1948. It was no coincidence, moreover, that aeronautical progress had kept pace with tactical development. Aircraft designing is so expensive that military demands, evolving from the tests of combat, are sometimes the only means of footing the bill for major changes. Thus the Marine operations in Korea gave rotary-wing aircraft an impetus comparable to the influence of World War I on the conventional plane. From the biplane of 1914, an overgrown kite with scarcely enough range for a crossing of the English Channel, military aircraft of that war progressed in four years to the stage of bombers capable of flying half a ton of explosives from northern France to Berlin. But such revolutionary advances were achieved only at the cost of unstinted millions spent for development.

The evolution of the helicopter in the Korean conflict has not been as dramatic. Yet the Marine officers watching the demonstration of the XHR2S probably recalled that February day in 1948 when the first two HO3S aircraft landed at Quantico. These machines had a practical lifting capacity of about 500 pounds as compared to the estimated 6,500-pound payload of the XHR2S only six years and one war later.*

Even so, it is the conviction of American and European designers that the helicopter of 1954 is at the threshold of its development. Jet-propelled helicopters have been proved feasible, and even more exciting prospects are opened by experiments seeking to combine the versatility of the helicopter with the speed and stability of the fixed-wing plane.

"The most dramatic progress will be increased speed of vertical-lift aircraft," said Frank N. Piasecki in a forecast of helicopter advances during the next half century. "This will come from two directions: helicopter designers will add speed to their machines; conversely, airplane designers will add

---

* The exact payload was not disclosed, but this estimate of 6,500 pounds is based upon an allowance of 250 pounds for each of the 26 battle-equipped Marines.

vertical-lift capabilities to their high-speed aircraft. The result will be a blending of the two types of flight into machines fully capable of both helicopter flight as we know it today and high-speed flight at velocities far beyond today's experimental supersonic speeds. . . .

"The size and capacity of the helicopter shows no inherent tactical limit. Larger and heavier machines, capable of lifting heavier and heavier loads, can and will be built as the basic workings of commercial economics and military planning dictates. Even today we can foresee the design of helicopters over 200,000 pounds in weight.[40]

The military future of the helicopter is filled with so many potentialities that few men are in a position to predict what may happen during the coming decade, let alone the next fifty years. Nobody could be better qualified, however, than General Lemuel C. Shepherd, Jr., Commandant of the Marine Corps. Not only was he a member of the Special Board of 1946 which formulated the Marine helicopter concept; he was commanding general of FMFPac in Korea when vertical-wing aircraft had their first tests in combat. As early as the Inchon-Seoul amphibious operation of 1950, it may be recalled, General Shepherd's evaluation was expressed in a dispatch to Marine Headquarters at Washington:

"No effort should be spared to get helicopters . . . helicopters in any form, to the theater at once, and on a priority higher than any other weapon."[41]

There were at the time no vertical-wing aircraft in Korea which could lift more than two men in addition to the pilot. It was a tremendous leap, therefore, from the HO3S of 1950 to the XHR2S of 1954 with its capacity of 26 battle-equipped Marines. The new Sikorsky and Piasecki models provided the U.S. armed forces with their first true transport helicopters; and General Shepherd indicated that the Marine Corps had not swerved from its original concept of the helicopter as the vehicle of vertical envelopment in the amphibious warfare of the Atomic Age. Addressing the National Security Industrial Association at Washington on September 10, 1953, he said:

"Seven years have passed since the development of the helicopter as a troop carrier was begun, but in the fall of 1951, in the bleak Korean countryside, the worth of the ungainly looking craft was finally proved. Just as the amphibian tractor came to the fore as a troop carrier over the reefs of Pacific atolls during World War II, so the helicopter became the greatest single innovation during the Korean conflict as a tactical and humanitarian medium of transportation. . . .

"The fact that we have a suitable helicopter transport now in sight, coupled with the answers arrived at during our last participation in the atomic exercises as Desert Rock, leaves us with a sense of confidence. I believe that the Marine Corps, with our skilled close air support and our own helicopters to pave the way for the amphibious landing, is capable of following up an atomic attack with the most powerful assault punch possessed by any nation in the world today."[42]

APPENDIX A

Glossary of Military and Aeronautical Terms

Including Abbreviations Used in Chapter Notes

Able Phonetic symbol for the letter A.

ADC Assistant Division Commander.

Aircraft Designations See end of Glossary, where this entry has been relegated because of its length.

AirDelPlt Air Delivery Platoon.

AKA Attack Cargo Ship.

ARS Air Rescue Service units of U.S. Air Force.

Asst Assistant.

Baker Phonetic symbol for the letter B.

BAR Browning automatic rifle.

Biaxial Disposed on separate axles, either laterally or longitudinally.

BLT Battalion landing team.

Bn Battalion.

Brig Brigade.

Brig Comdr Brigade Commander.

BuAer U.S. Navy Bureau of Aeronautics.

Cannibalize To strip an aircraft (or other equipment) of parts to be used in repairing another aircraft of the same type.

CCF Chinese Communist Forces (used more often as an adjective than a noun).

CG   Commanding general

Ch   Chief

CinCLant   Commander in Chief, Atlantic Fleet.

CinCPac   Commander in Chief, Pacific Fleet.

CMC   Commandant of the Marine Corps.

CMCS   Commandant Marine Corps Schools.

CNO   Chief of Naval Operations.

Co   Company.

CO   Commanding officer.

Coaxial   One rotor above the other on the same axle.

Combat loading   The method of loading a military unit and its equipment and supplies on a transport in such a manner that they can be discharged from the ship according to tactical considerations.

Comdr   Commander.

Contrarotating   Rotating in opposite directions.

CP   Command Post.

CV   The letters designating an aircraft carrier. Third letters are added to distinguish various types:
> CVA for an attack aircraft carrier;
> CVB for a large aircraft carrier;
> CVE for an escort aircraft carrier;
> CVL for a small aircraft carrier; and
> CVS for a seaplane carrier.

DCNO   Deputy Chief of Naval Operations.

D-day   The term denoting the unnamed day on which a previously planned military operation is to commence.

Defilade   Protection by natural or artificial obstacles from enemy observation and fire.

Disp   Dispatch.

Div   Division.

DUKW   An amphibious truck (usually called "duck") which operates as a powerboat on water and a vehicle on land to transport men and supplies in amphibious operations.

Encl Enclosure.

EUSAK Eighth U.S. Army in Korea.

FBHL Force Beachhead Line; the objective prescribed for the purpose of fixing the limits of the beachhead and establishing a tentative ·MLR for further advances.

FE Far East.

FLEX Fleet landing exercise.

FMF Fleet Marine Force.

FMFLant Fleet Marine Force, Atlantic.

FMFPac Fleet Marine Force, Pacific.

G-2 Designation of the military intelligence section of the general staff of a division or larger unit. G-1 refers to the personnel section; G-3 to the operations and training section; and G-4 to the supply and evacuation section. The letter "S," when substituted for "G," denotes a military unit smaller than a division. The letter "A" is used in the same way for an air wing.

H-hour The term denoting the unnamed hour at which a previously planned military operation is to commence.

Hist History.

HMR Marine Corps Transport Helicopter Squadron.

HMX Marine Corps Experimental Helicopter Squadron.

HQMC Headquarters U.S. Marine Corps.

JCS Joint Chiefs of Staff.

JTF Joint Task Force.

KIA The designation used in casualty reports to denote Killed in Action. WIA means Wounded in Action, and MIA stands for Missing in Action.

KMC Korean Marine Corps units trained by U.S. Marines.

Knot One nautical mile (6080.20 feet) per hour.

Landing Boat All craft designed for landing operations which are shipborne.

LEX Landing Exercise.

LCVP   Landing Ship, Vehicle, Personnel.

LD   Line of Departure: the line from which an attack is launched.

LST   Landing Ship, Tank: the famous U.S. Navy workhorse of World War II and the Korean conflict.

Ltr   Letter.

LVT   Landing Vehicle, Tracked.

MAG   Marine Aircraft Group.

MarBrig   Marine Brigade.

MarDiv   Marine Division.

MATS   Military Air Transportation Service.

MAW   Marine Aircraft Wing.

MCAS   Marine Corps Air Station.

MCDC   Marine Corps Development Center.

MCEB   Marine Corps Equipment Board.

MCEC   Marine Corps Educational Center.

MCPAEB   Marine Corps Provisional Atomic Energy Brigade.

MCS   Marine Corps Schools.

Memo   Memorandum.

Mission   In the military sense, a specific task or duty assigned to an individual, weapon, or unit.

MLR   Main line of resistance: the line where the first determined effort is made to stop an enemy attack.

MSR   Main supply route.

NA   National Archives.

NAS   Naval Air Station.

NCO   Noncommissioned officer.

NK   The abbreviation applied to the North Korean armed forces.

NRMC   Naval Records Management Center.

NRS   Navy Records Section.

Obj   Objective.

Op Plan   Operations plan.

Pack Howitzer   A 75mm or other small howitzer which can be taken apart and transported by pack animals, motor vehicles, or aircraft.

Pallet   A portable platform used for loading and transporting supplies which are said to be "palletized."

Pres   President.

Prog Rpt   Progress Report.

R   The letter "R" denotes Reserve (USNR, for example, or USMCR) as distinguished from a regular or career officer.

Radio Frequency   The frequency at which radio waves useful for communication can be produced. The "spectrum," as established by the Federal Communications Commission, consists of seven bands ranging from Very Low Frequency to Superhigh Frequency. Medium, High and Very High frequencies (MHF, HF and VHF) are used for tactical air-ground communication.

Radius   The maximum distance along a given route which an aircraft can travel, with normal load and without refueling, and return to its base.

RCT   Regimental combat team.

Ready Room   The compartment of an aircraft carrier or room of an airfield installation where pilots assemble for briefing and flight orders.

Recon   Reconnaissance.

Recon Co   Reconnaissance Company.

ROK   Republic of Korea (used both as a noun and adjective).

Rpt   Report.

RS   Record Section.

S&C   Secret and Confidential Files Section.

SAR   Special Action Report.

SecNav   Secretary of the Navy.

Ser   Serial.

SOP   Standard Operating Procedure.

Sqdn   Squadron.

TF   Task Force.

UN   United Nations.

Unit of Fire   A quantity of ammunition used as a measure. The term usually refers to the amount which a military unit may be expected to use up, on the average, in one day of combat.

USA   United States Army.

USAF   United States Air Force.

USMC   United States Marine Corps.

USMC Historical   Historical Branch, G-3, Headquarters U.S. Marine Corps.

USN   United States Navy.

VMF   Marine Fighter Squadron.

VMO   Marine Observation Squadron.

Aircraft Designations   This is a subject complicated by differences in terms. The Army and Air Force use "C" to denote a cargo or transport plane, while "R" is preferred by the Navy and Marine Corps. Only a few symbols, such as "F" for fighter and "B" for bomber, are accepted by all U.S. armed forces. This category includes the letter "X," reserved for experimental aircraft, while "Y" indicates more advanced experimental types.

In Navy and Marine Corps usage, the first one or two letters denote the primary function of the aircraft and the next letter identifies the manufacturer. Thus "OP-1" stood for the initial observation aircraft of Pitcairn manufacture to be tested by the Marine Corps, and the Navy more properly added the prefix "X" to indicate that its XOP-1 was experimental. It would take too much space to cover in detail the differences between Army-Air Force and Navy-Marine Corps terminology, but a few examples may be helpful for illustration. Not only does "B-17" refer to an Army bomber but also the fact that it was the seventeenth design of this bomber. When the B-17 was succeeded by the B-29, it meant that the Army Air Corps had accepted or rejected as many intervening designs for a new and improved bomber as the difference between those numbers.

The Navy and Marine Corps give more information in their designations. Taking the F4U-5 as an example, "F" stands for fighter, "4" for the fourth fighter built by "U," meaning Chance Vought of United Aircraft, and "5" calls attention to the number of comparatively minor changes or improvements made in the famous Corsair. Manufacturers are not always identified by the first letter of the company name, since "F" refers to Grumman and "O" to Lockheed. Thus the F7F-3P Tiger Cat is the seventh Grumman fighter, a machine with three minor changes which has been adapted to photographic missions. But "P" means photographic only when it is a suffix; as a prefix it indicates a patrol aircraft. These explanations, of course, hardly scratch the surface, and the reader desiring further enlightenment is advised to consult one of the manuals devoted to a complex subject.

APPENDIX B

U.S. Marine Corps Helicopter Units and Commanding Officers (to 31 July 1953)

MARINE HELICOPTER SQUADRON 1 (HMX-1)
  Commissioned 1 December 1947 at MCAS, Quantico, Va.
  Commanding Officers:
    Col Edward C. Dyer, 1Dec47-25Jun49
    LtCol John F. Carey, 26Jun49-9Jul50
    Col Keith B. McCutcheon, 10Jul50-20Nov51
    LtCol John H. King, Jr., 21Nov51-24Jan52
    LtCol George W. Herring, 25Jan52-23Jun52
    LtCol Edward V. Finn, 24Jun52-31Jul53

HEADQUARTERS MARINE HELICOPTER TRANSPORT GROUP 16 (MAG(HR)-16)
  Commissioned 1 March 1952 at MCAF, Santa Ana, Calif.
  Commanding Officers:
    Col Harold J. Mitchener, 1-23Mar52
    Col William D. Roberson, 24Mar52-2Jun52
    Col Harold J. Mitchener, 3Jun52-31Jul53

HEADQUARTERS SQUADRON, MARINE HELICOPTER TRANSPORT GROUP 16 (Hedron, MAG(HR)-16)
  Commissioned 1 March 1952 at MCAF, Santa Ana, Calif.
  Commanding Officers:
    Capt Paul L. Robinson, 1Mar52-31May52
    Capt Raymond D. Dallam, 1Jun52-16Oct52
    Maj William L. Gunness, 17Oct52-13Jun53
    Maj John N. Wester, 14Jun53-27Jul53
    Maj Joseph L. Freitas, Jr., 28Jul53-31Jul53
234

MARINE AIR BASE SQUADRON 16 (MABS-16)
Commissioned 1 March 1952 at MCAF, Santa Ana, Calif.
Commanding Officers:
Maj William L. Gunness, 1Mar52-30Jun52
Capt Donald H. Foss, 1-31Jul52
Maj Perry P. McRobert, 1Aug52-30Jun53
Maj George F. Bauman, 1Jul53-25Jul53
LtCol Robert R. Ayres, Jr., 26Jul53-31Jul53

MARINE AIRCRAFT MAINTENANCE SQUADRON 16 (MAMS-16)
Commissioned 1 March 1952 at MCAF, Santa Ana, Calif.
Commanding Officers:
Maj Tillman E. Bishop, 1Mar52-16May52
Maj Edwin E. Shifflett, 17May52-31Jul53

MARINE HELICOPTER TRANSPORT SQUADRON 161 (HMR-161)
Commissioned 15 January 1951 at MCAF, Santa Ana, Calif.
Commanding Officers:
LtCol George W. Herring, 15Jan51-18Dec51
Col Keith B. McCutcheon, 19Dec51-6Aug52
LtCol John F. Carey, 7Aug52-15Mar53
Col Owen A. Chambers, 16Mar53-31Jul53

MARINE HELICOPTER TRANSPORT SQUADRON 162 (HMR-162)
Commissioned 30 June 1951 at MCAF, Santa Ana, Calif.
Commanding Officers:
Col Harold J. Mitchener, 30Jun51-29Feb52
Maj George H. Linnemeier, 1Mar52-31Jul52
Maj Tillman E. Bishop, 1Aug52-31Oct52
LtCol James M. Johnson, 1Nov52-13May53
LtCol Wallace J. Slappey, Jr., 14May53-27Jul53
Maj Dwain L. Lengel, 28Jul53-31Jul53

MARINE HELICOPTER TRANSPORT SQUADRON 163 (HMR-163)
Commissioned 1 December 1951 at MCAF, Santa Ana, Calif.
Commanding Officers:
Col William D. Roberson, 1Dec51-25Feb52
Maj Lynn E. Midkiff, 26Feb52-29May52

Maj Gerald R. Graff, 30May52-30Jun52
Maj Homer L. Daniel, 1Jul52-30Jun53
Maj Victor A. Armstrong, 1Jul53-31Jul53

HEADQUARTERS MARINE HELICOPTER TRANSPORT GROUP 26 (MAG(HR)-26)
Commissioned 16 June 1952 at MCAS, Cherry Point, N. C.
Commanding Officers:
Col Owen A. Chambers, 16Jun52-28Jul52
LtCol Frank H. Collins, 29Jul52-4Jan53
Col Martin A. Severson, 6Jan53-30Mar53
LtCol Frank H. Collins, 31Mar53-31July53

HEADQUARTERS SQUADRON, MARINE HELICOPTER TRANSPORT GROUP 26 (Hedron, MAG(HR)-26)
Commissioned 16 June 1952 at MCAS, Cherry Point, N. C.
Commanding Officers:
Capt William C. Hosch, 16Jun52-16Nov52
Capt Wallace Wessel, 17Nov52-9Apr53
Capt Marion J. Daane, 10Apr53-31Jul53

MARINE AIR BASE SQUADRON 26 (MABS-26)
Commissioned 16 June 1952 at MCAS, Cherry Point, N. C.
Commanding Officers:
Capt William O. Smiley, 16-27Jun52
Maj Virgil D. Olson, 28Jun52-31Jul52
Maj William W. Eldridge, 1-21Aug52
Maj Roy T. Dasher, 22Aug52-24Feb53
Maj Ray T. Lemmons, 25Feb53-2Mar53
LtCol Vernon O. Ullman, 3Mar53-31Jul53

MARINE AIRCRAFT MAINTENANCE SQUADRON 26 (MAMS-26)
Commissioned 16 June 1952 at MCAS, Cherry Point, N. C.
Commanding Officer:
Maj James T. Cotton, 16Jun52-31Jul53

MARINE HELICOPTER TRANSPORT SQUADRON 261 (HMR-261)
Commissioned 5 April 1951 at MCAS, Cherry Point, N. C.
Commanding Officers:
LtCol Owen A. Chambers, 5Apr51-15Jun52

Maj Stanley V. Titterud, 16Jun52-24Feb53
Maj Roy T. Dasher, 25Feb53-31Jul53

MARINE HELICOPTER TRANSPORT SQUADRON 262 (HMR-262)

Commissioned 1 September 1951 at MCAS, Cherry Point, N. C.
Commanding Officers:
LtCol William H. Doolen, 1Sep51-20Jan52
LtCol David M. Danser, 21Jan52-27Mar52
LtCol Frank E. Hopper, 28Mar52-9Sep52
Maj Robert L. Rathbun, 10Sep52-31Jul53

MARINE HELICOPTER TRANSPORT SQUADRON 263 (HMR-263)

Commissioned 16 June 1952 at MCAS, Cherry Point, N. C.
Commanding Officers:
Maj William L. Crapo, 16Jun52-14Jun53
LtCol John P. Newlands, 15Jun53-31Jul53

HEADQUARTERS MARINE HELICOPTER TRANSPORT GROUP 36 (MAG(HR)-36)

Commissioned 2 June 1952 at MCAF, Santa Ana, Calif.
Commanding Officers:
Col William D. Roberson, 2Jun52-15Jan53
LtCol Charles J. Prall, 16Jan53-11Jun53
Maj John K. Sinderholm, Jr., 12Jun53-27Jul53
LtCol Wallace J. Slappey, Jr., 28Jul53-31Jul53

HEADQUARTERS SQUADRON, MARINE HELICOPTER TRANSPORT GROUP 36 (Hedron, MAG(HR)-36)

Commissioned 2 June 1952 at MCAF, Santa Ana, Calif.
Commanding Officers:
Capt James P. Bruce, 2-4Jun52
Capt Rodney E. Montgomery, 4Jun52-17Jul52
Capt Kerwin W. Jacobs, 18Jul-31Jul52
Maj Herbert J. Lewis, 1Aug52-19Sep52
Capt John H. Magouyrk, Jr., 20Sep52-29Sep52
Maj Dwain L. Lengel, 30Sep52-31Oct52
Maj Samuel M. Sampler, Jr., 1Nov52-9Feb53
Capt John H. Magouyrk, Jr., 10Feb53-31Jul53

MARINE AIR BASE SQUADRON 36 (MABS-36)
Commissioned 2 June 1952 at MCAF, Santa Ana, Calif.
Commanding Officers:
Capt Robert W. Allen, 2Jun52-1Sep52
Maj John K. Sinderholm, Jr., 1Sep52-20Mar53
Capt James H. Dorough, 21Mar53-9Apr53
Capt Floyd A. Wines, 10Apr53-30Jul53
Maj Earl W. Langston, 31Jul53

MARINE AIRCRAFT MAINTENANCE SQUADRON 36 (MAMS-36)
Commissioned 2 June 1952 at MCAF, Santa Ana, Calif.
Commanding Officers:
Maj M. D. Hill, 2Jun52-29Sep52
Maj James A. Sawyer, 30Sep52-31Oct52
Maj Albert W. Simmons, 1Nov52-4Feb53
Maj Andrew Y. McVicars, 5Feb53-23Jul53
Maj Walter T. Scarborough, 24Jul53-31Jul53

MARINE HELICOPTER TRANSPORT SQUADRON 361 (HMR-361)
Commissioned 25 February 1952 at MCAF, Santa Ana, Calif.
Commanding Officers:
Col William D. Roberson, 25Feb52-23Mar52
Maj John L. Mahon, 24Mar52-1Jun52
Maj Donald S. Osen, 2Jun52-31Oct52
Maj Charles C. Samis, 1Nov52-31Jul53
Assigned to MAG(HR)-16, 24Mar52; Assigned to MAG(HR)-36, 27Jul53

MARINE HELICOPTER TRANSPORT SQUADRON 362 (HMR-362)
Commissioned 30 April 1952 at MCAF, Santa Ana, Calif.
Commanding Officers:
Maj William R. Rozier, 30Apr52-31Oct52
Maj James A. Sawyer, 1Nov52-26Jan53
Maj Edward I. Lupton, 27Jan53-3Mar53
Maj Arthur O. Hellerude, 4Mar53-31Jul53

MARINE HELICOPTER TRANSPORT SQUADRON 363 (HMR-363)

Commissioned 2 June 1952 at MCAF, Santa Ana, Calif.

Commanding Officers:

Maj Andrew L. McVicars, 2Jun52-31Oct52
Maj Dwain L. Lengel, 1Nov52-13Mar53
LtCol Robert R. Ayres, Jr., 14Mar53-26Apr53
Maj Dwain L. Lengel, 27Apr53-24Jul53
Maj Jesse E. Morrison, 25Jul53-30Jul53
Maj John J. Doherty, 31Jul53

MARINE OBSERVATION SQUADRON 1 (VMO-1)

Received helicopters September 1951. Attached to 2dMar Div.

Commanding Officers:

LtCol Robert W. Teller, 15Jul49-29Dec51
LtCol George L. Hollowell, 31Dec51-31Jul53

MARINE OBSERVATION SQUADRON 2 (VMO-2)

Received helicopters July 1951. Attached to 3dMarDiv.

Commanding Officers:

LtCol William E. Abblitt, 15Jun51-31Oct52
Maj William G. MacLean, Jr., 1Nov52-31Jul53

MARINE OBSERVATION SQUADRON 6 (VMO-6)

Received helicopters July 1950. Attached to 1stMarDiv.

Commanding Officers:

Maj Vincent J. Gottschalk, 3Jul50-4Apr51
Maj David W. McFarland, 5Apr51-30Sep51
Maj Kenneth C. Smedley, 1-31Oct51
Maj Edward R. Polgrean, 1Nov51-30Jan52
Maj Kenneth C. Smedley, 1-10Feb52
Maj William G. MacLean, Jr., 11-26Feb 52
LtCol William T. Herring, 27Feb52-9May52
Maj Wallace J. Slappey, Jr., 10May52-9Sep52
LtCol Elkin S. Dew, 10Sep52-1Feb53
LtCol William A. Cloman, 2Feb53-30Jun53
LtCol Earl E. Anderson, 1-31Jul53

CHAPTER NOTES

CHAPTER ONE

1. War Plans Section, Division of Operations and Training, USMC, op plan 712, "Advanced base operations in Micronesia," prepared by Maj Earl H. Ellis, USMC, 23 Jul 21. War Plans Section (General Plans) Files, USMC Historical (hereafter referred to as USMC Hist).
2. USMC Historical, interview with Maj Gen Merrill B. Twining, USMC, 26 Aug 53. Helicopter Material, Monograph and Comment File, USMC Hist. Hereafter the above file will be cited as Helicopter, USMC Hist.
3. "Army-Navy joint action," quoted in Eli K. Cole, "Joint overseas operations," *U. S. Naval Institute Proceedings*, 55:930 (Nov 1929).
4. John H. Russell, "The birth of the Fleet Marine Force," *Ibid.*, 72:51 (Jan 1946).
5. Jeter A. Isely and Philip A. Crowl, *The U. S. Marines and amphibious war* (hereafter cited as Isely and Crowl), 35-37.
6. *Ibid.*, 67.
7. J. F. C. Fuller, *The Second World War*, 207.
8. LtGen Roy S. Geiger, USMC, ltr to CMC, 21 Aug 46, ser 0265-46. Copy in Helicopter, USMC Hist.
9. USMC Historical, interview with Col Victor H. Krulak, USMC, 18 Nov 53. *Ibid.* Hereafter, in addition to its usual meaning, the abbreviation *ibid.* will also serve to indicate the document location cited immediately before.
10. Archie J. Clapp, "Their mission is mobility," *Military Review*, 38, no. 5:12 (Aug 1953).
11. HMX-1, *Operation Packard Two: amphibious command post exercise, 10-26 May 1948*. Copy in Aviation Semi-Annual Historical Report File, USMC Hist. Hereafter the above file will be cited as Aviation S-A, USMC Hist.
12. HMX-1, sqdn hist, 1 Dec 47-30 Jun 49. *Ibid.*
13. Encl (1) to Landing Force Bulletin No. 4, "Interim doctrine for the tactical employment of transport helicopters," 26 Apr 53, ser 03A12654. Copy in USMC Hist.
14. USMC Historical, interview with LtGen Gerald C. Thomas, USMC, 18 Nov 53. Helicopter, *ibid.*

CHAPTER TWO

1. F. Alexander Magoun and Eric Hodgins, A *history of aircraft* (hereafter

cited as Magoun and Hodgins), 223; C. B. F. Macauley, *The helicopters are coming* (hereafter cited as Macauley), 33.

2. Eugene K. Liberatore, *ed.*, *Rotary wing aircraft handbooks and history* (hereafter cited as Liberatore), 1:7; Magoun and Hodgins, 224.
3. Devon Francis, *The story of the helicopter* (hereafter cited as Francis), 23; Macauley, 33.
4. H. F. Gregory, *Anything a horse can do* (hereafter cited as Gregory), 10; Liberatore, 1:20.
5. Francis, 26-27; Macauley, 34-35.
6. Gregory, 12.
7. Magoun and Hodgins, 235; Macauley, 36.
8. Charles Lester Morris, *Pioneering the helicopter* (hereafter cited as Morris), 31; Magoun and Hodgins, 237; Macauley, 32.
9. Gregory, 17.
10. Liberatore, 2:56-57; Francis, 39-40; Gregory, 16-30.
11. Gregory, 32-36.
12. *Ibid.*, 37-38.
13. Ch BuAer (Maj Walter H. Sitz, USMC, by direction) ltr to J. E. Meredith, 21 Mar 31; BuAer telg to Pitcairn Aircraft, Inc., 6 May 31. BuAer File VV-2, Navy Records Section, National Archives (hereafter referred to as NRS, NA).
14. Plans Division, BuAer, memo for Material Division and USMC Aviation, 8 Oct 31. *Ibid.*
15. USMC Aviation ltr to Pitcairn Aircraft, Inc., 8 Feb 32. USMC Aviation File A4-1, *ibid.*
16. USMC Historical, interview with Col Frank M. June, USMC, 22 Oct 52. Helicopter, USMC Hist.
17. *Ibid.*; see also Lynn Montross, "The Marine autogiro in Nicaragua," *Marine Corps Gazette*, 37, no. 2:56-61 (Feb 1953).
18. "Press News Translations, Nicaragua." Area Subject File, USMC Hist.
19. *Ibid.*
20. *Ibid.*
21. Capt Harold C. Major, USMC, 1stLt Paul A. Putnam, USMC, and 2dLt Frank M. June, USMC, rpt to CO Aircraft Squadrons, 2dMarBrig, Managua, Nicaragua, 19 Nov 32. USMC General File 1165-15, NRS, NA.
22. *Ibid.*
23. *Ibid.*
24. USMC Historical, interview with Col June, *op. cit.*
25. Capt Francis E. Pierce, USMC, ltr to MGC, 6 Nov 33. USMC Aviation A4-1, NRS, NA.
26. NAS, Anacostia, D. C., flight test rpt on XOP-1, quoted in AsstCh BuAer memo for AsstSecNav, 29 Oct 31. BuAer VV-2, *Ibid.*
27. Material Division, BuAer, memo for AsstCh, BuAer, 22 Mar 32. *Ibid.*
28. LtComdr Robert E. Thomas, USN, memo for RAdm William A. Moffett, USN, 21 May 31. *Ibid.*
29. AsstCh BuAer ltr to Manager, Naval Aircraft Factory, Philadelphia, Pa., 15 Aug 32. *Ibid.*
30. BuAer, memo for record, 17 Aug 37. *Ibid.*
31. Gregory, 82-87.
32. CO Aircraft One, 1stMarBrig, FMF, Quantico, Va., memo for Brig Comdr, 16 Jul 36. USMC Aviation A4-1, NRS, NA.

CHAPTER THREE

1. Francis, 42-43, 99; Liberatore, 2:54.
2. Francis, 42; Liberatore, 2:190.
3. Gregory, 34-35.
4. Morris, 40.
5. Gregory, 83.
6. Ibid., 92-99.
7. Ibid., 102.
8. Ibid., 105.
9. Ibid., 112, 119-122; Liberatore, 3:200.
10. Macauley, 4-5.
11. Liberatore, 12:173.
12. Ibid., 174-175.
13. Richard Bradberry, "The RAF's helicopters," American Helicopter, 2, no. 5:31 (Apr 1946); Air Section, British Joint Services Mission, Washington, D. C., "Brief historical note on no. 529 squadron." Helicopter, USMC Hist.
14. Bradberry, op. cit., 32, 43.
15. Gregory, 219, 221.
16. Ibid., 223.
17. Ibid., 201-206.
18. Ibid., 233-234.
19. Aviation Training Division (Op-31), DCNO (Air), encl (A) to hist rpt of World War II activities. World War II Histories File, Air History Unit, DCNO (Air).
20. Ibid.
21. Op plan 712, op. cit.
22. Ibid.; John N. Rentz, Marines in the central Solomons, 6.
23. John L. Zimmerman, "The Marines' first spy," Saturday Evening Post, 23 Nov 46, 99.
24. Reprinted in Marine Corps Gazette, 8:252 (Dec 1923).
25. "Army-Navy joint action," loc. cit.
26. John H. Russell, loc. cit.
27. Isely and Crowl, 36.
28. The Army's doctrine on amphibious warfare was embodied in Field Manual 31-5, Landing operations on hostile shores, published in 1942.
29. Isely and Crowl, 64, 68.
30. Ibid., 69.
31. Robert D. Heinl, Jr., "Naval gunfire training in the Pacific," Marine Corps Gazette, 32, no. 6:11 (Jun 1948).
32. Marine Corps aviation general—1940, 49.
33. Robert Sherrod, History of Marine Corps aviation in World War II, 22-27.
34. Isely and Crowl, 64-66.
35. Op plan 712, op. cit.
36. Isely and Crowl, 67.
37. U. S. Strategic Bombing Survey, "The effects of the atomic bombing of Hiroshima and Nagasaki," cited in Chairman Special Board, CMC encl (B) to rpt to CMC, 16 Dec 46, ser 004. Records Section, Marine Corps Educational Center, Marine Corps Schools (hereafter referred to as RS, MCEC, MCS).
38. Washington Post, 14 Jan 46.

39. Chesly Manly in Chicago *Daily Tribune*, 25 Jan 46.
40. Statement by VAdm William H. P. Blandy, USN, in New York *Times*, 2 Jul 46.
41. James E. Warner in New York *Herald Tribune*, 7 Jul 46.
42. Statement by VAdm William H. P. Blandy, USN, in New York *Times*, 15 Jul 46.
43. Hanson W. Baldwin in New York *Times*, 30 Jul 46.
44. LtGen Roy S. Geiger, USMC, ltr to CMC, 21 Aug 46, *op. cit.*

CHAPTER FOUR

1. CMC ltr to CNO, Ops 06L, 23, 30M, 34D, 34H, 34J, and 416 of OCNO, CinCPac, CincLant, CMCS, Pres MCEB, CG Air FMFPac, CG 1stMarDiv, CG 2dMarDiv, Comdr Air West Coast, CG 1stMAW, CG 2dMAW, and CO 6th Marines. Copy in Helicopter, USMC Hist.
2. CMC ltr to Chairman Special Board, CMC, 13 Sep 46, ser 03A25646. *Ibid.*
3. USMC Historical, interview with MajGen Twining, *op. cit.*
4. CMC ltr to Chairman Special Board, CMC, 13 Sep 46, *op. cit.*
5. Franklin A. Hart, "Marine Corps Schools at Quantico," *Army Information Digest*, 7, no. 2:39 (Feb 1952).
6. *Ibid.*, 36.
7. *Ibid.*, 33, 39.
8. CNO jt ltr to CMC, *et al.*, 6 Jun 46, ser 1107P34. USMC File 1165-15, General Files Section, HQMC (hereafter referred to as General Files, HQMC).
9. Clayton C. Marcy, "Operation Crossroads," *American Helicopter*, 4, no. 12:37 (Nov 1946).
10. CNO ltr to ComOpDevFor, 23 Jul 46, ser 1641P34. Copy in USMC 1165-15, General Files, HQMC.
11. NAS, Lakehurst, N. J., supp hist, 1 May-31 Dec 46. Naval Air Stations Histories File, Air History Unit, DCNO (Air).
12. CG FMFPac ltr to CMC, 29 Jul 46, ser 28640. USMC 1165-15, General Files, HQMC.
13. CMCS ltr to CMC, 9 Aug 46, ser 4195. *Ibid.*
14. USMC Historical, interview with Col Edward C. Dyer, USMC, 30 Jul 53. Helicopter, USMC Hist.
15. CMC memo for VAdm William H. P. Blandy, USN, 4 Oct 46, ser 08A27746. Secret and Confidential Files Section, HQMC (hereafter referred to as S&C, HQMC).
16. LtCol Loren E. Haffner, USMC, ltr to Lynn Montross, 15 Jan 53. Helicopter, USMC Hist.
17. *Ibid.*
18. USMC Historical, interview with Col Dyer, *op. cit.*
19. *Ibid.*
20. Chairman Special Board, CMC, encl (C) (part I) to rpt to CMC, 16 Dec 46, *op. cit.*
21. *Ibid.*
22. USMC Historical, interview with Col Dyer, *op. cit.*
23. Chairman Special Board, CMC, encl (C) (part I) to rpt to CMC, 16 Dec 46, *op. cit.*
24. *Ibid.*, part III.

25. CMC ltr to CMCS, 19 Dec 46, ser 008A35346. Secret and Confidential Files Section, Marine Corps Schools (hereafter referred to as S&C, MCS).

CHAPTER FIVE

1. CNO ltr to CMC, 30 Apr 47, ser 00127P34. Secret and Confidential Files, Naval Records Management Center, Alexandria, Va. (hereafter referred to as NRMC, Alexandria).
2. Marine Corps Schools, Amphibious Warfare School (Junior Course), *Tentative doctrine for employment of helicopters in amphibious operations 12 April 1948.*
3. *Address to graduates . . . Marine Corps Schools,* 19 Sep 53.
4. *United States Navy regulations,* 1948, 39.
5. USMC Historical, interview with MajGen Twining, *op. cit.*
6. *Id.,* interview with Col Dyer, *op. cit.*
7. *Id.,* interview with MajGen Twining, *op. cit.*
8. *Id.,* interview with Col Dyer, *op. cit.*
9. Encl to CMCS ltr to CMC, 10 Mar 47, ser 001120. S&C, MCS.
10. *Ibid.*
11. CNO disp 221351z to CMC, Nov 47. NRMC, Alexandria.
12. USMC Historical, interview with Col Dyer, *op. cit.*
13. CMC ltr to CO MCAS, Quantico, Va., 3 Dec 47, ser 007A33547 and DA-0022470. S&C, MCS.
14. USMC Historical, interview with Col Dyer, *op. cit.*
15. HMX-1 sqdn hist, 1947-1949, *op. cit.*
16. *Ibid.*
17. USMC Historical, interview with Col Dyer, *op. cit.*
18. Gregory, 138-149.
19. Information derived from the author's informal conversations with personnel of HMX-1.
20. *Ibid.*
21. HMX-1 sqdn hist, 1947-1949, *op. cit.*
22. HMX-1, *Operation Packard Two, op. cit.*
23. USMC Historical, interview with Col Krulak, *op. cit.*
24. HMX-1, *Operation Packard Two, op. cit.*
25. *Ibid.*
26. USMC Historical, interview with Col Dyer, *op. cit.*
27. HMX-1, *Operation Packard Two, op. cit.*

CHAPTER SIX

1. HMX-1 sqdn hist, 1947-1949, *op. cit.*
2. *Ibid.*
3. *Ibid.*
4. Information derived from the author's informal conversations with personnel of HMX-1.
5. HMX-1 sqdn hist, 1947-1949, *op. cit.*
6. *Ibid.*
7. *Ibid.*
8. Marine Corps Schools, *Amphibious operations: employment of helicopters (tentative).*
9. HMX-1 prog rpt, 1 Oct-31 Dec 48. NRMC, Alexandria.
10. Marine Corps Schools, *Amphibious operations: employment of helicopters (tentative), op. cit.*

11. *Ibid.*
12. *Ibid.*
13. Isely and Crowl, 36.
14. HMX-1 sqdn hist, 1947-1949, *op. cit.*
15. *Id.*, prog rpt, Oct-Dec 48, *op. cit.*
16. *Id.*, sqdn hist, 1947-1949, *op. cit.*
17. CO Air FMFPac ltr to CNO, 15Jun48, ser 1555. USMC 1165-15, General Files, HQMC.
18. USMC Historical, interview with Maj Wallace D. Blatt, USMC, 28 Jan 53. Helicopter, USMC Hist.
19. HMX-1 prog rpt, 1-30 Jan 49. S&C, MCS.
20. *Id.*, sqdn hist, 1947-1949, *op. cit.*
21. *Id.*, prog rpt, Jan 49, *op. cit.*
22. Encl to CG 2dMarDiv ltr to CMC, 26 Apr 48, ser 7507. USMC 1165-15, General Files, HQMC.
23. CO HMX-1 ltr to CMC, 22 Nov 48, ser 207-48. *Ibid.*
24. Division of Plans and Policies memo for Director USMC Aviation, n.d., file 1165-15/AO-3-des. *Ibid.*
25. J. W. Bunkley, "The U. S. Navy's helicopter program," *American Helicopter*, 11, no. 7:11 (Jun 1948).
26. Senior member board to study and submit recommendation on a transport helicopter program for the Marine Corps rpt to CMC, 14 Oct 49, ser 91841. NRMC, Alexandria.
27. HMX-1 prog rpt, 1 Jul-31 Dec 49. *Ibid.*
28. *Ibid.*
29. *Id.*, prog rpt, 1 Feb-30 Jun 50. S&C, MCS.
30. *Ibid.*
31. Id., prog rpt, 1 Jul-31 Dec 50. S&C, MCS.
32. *Id.*, prog rpt, Feb-Jun 50, *op. cit.*
33. *Id.*, prog rpt, Jul-Dec 50, *op. cit.*
34. *Ibid.*
35. Brigade rpt, 1stProvMarBrig special action rpt, 7 Jul-6 Sep 50. Special action reports are hereafter cited as SAR's, and copies of each are in the SAR File, USMC Hist.
36. HMX-1 prog rpt, Jul-Dec 50, *op. cit.*
37. See A. von Boguslawski, *Tactical deductions from the War of 1870-1871, passim.*

CHAPTER SEVEN

1. For a brief review of the activities of VMO-6 in Korea, see Lynn Montross, "Flying windmills in Korea," *Marine Corps Gazette*, 37, no. 9:20-23 (Sep 1953).
2. Annex Oboe (VMO-6 rpt) to 1stProvMarBrig SAR, Jul-Sep 50, *op. cit.* Hereafter this section of this report will be cited as Annex Oboe, Jul-Sep 50.
3. LtCol Vincent J. Gottschalk, USMC, transcript of informal remarks at HQMC, 17 May 51. Copy in Helicopter, USMC.
4. Annex Oboe, Jul-Sep 50.
5. *Ibid.*
6. LtGen (ret) Edward A. Craig, USMC, ltr to Lynn Montross, 18 May 53. Helicopter, USMC Hist.
7. FMFPac SOP 3-5, "VMO squadrons," 28 Nov 49, cited in Annex Oboe, Jul-Sep 50, *op. cit.*

8. Gottschalk, informal remarks, 17 May 51, *op. cit.*
9. *Ibid.*
10. Marine Corps Board, *An evaluation of the influence of Marine Corps forces on the course of the Korean War (4 Aug 50-15 Dec 50),* 1:II-A-11-II-A-15. Encl to ser 07A21352, S&C, HQMC. For a general coverage of early Marine Corps actions in Korea, see Lynn Montross, "The Pusan perimeter," *Marine Corps Gazette,* 35, no. 6:30-39 (Jun 1951); Ernest H. Giusti, "Marine air over the Pusan perimeter," *ibid.,* 36, no. 5:18-27 (May 1952); and Andrew Geer, *The new breed* (hereafter cited as Geer), 1-73.
11. Craig to Montross, 18 May 53, *op. cit.*
12. Annex Oboe, Jul-Sep 50.
13. Maj Victor A. Armstrong, USMC, ltr to Lynn Montross, 23 Jul 50. Helicopter, USMC Hist.
14. Craig to Montross, 18 May 53, *op. cit.*
15. Marine Corps Board, *op. cit.,* 1:II-A-11.
16. Annex How (5th Marines rpt) to 1stProvMarBrig SAR, Jul-Sep 50, *op. cit.*
17. USMC Historical, interview with Capt Nicholas A. Canzona, USMC, 21 Dec 53. Helicopter, USMC Hist.
18. Craig to Montross, 18 May 53, *op. cit.*
19. *Ibid.*
20. *Ibid.*
21. Annex Oboe, Jul-Sep 50.
22. LtCol Vincent J. Gottschalk, USMCR, ltr to Lynn Montross, 26 Aug 53. Helicopter, USMC Hist.
23. Annex Oboe, Jul-Sep 50.
24. Gottschalk, informal remarks, 17 May 51, *op. cit.*
25. Marine Corps Board, *op. cit.,* 1:II-A-21-24.
26. *Ibid.*
27. Craig to Montross, 18 May 53, *op. cit.*
28. Annex Oboe, Jul-Sep 50.
29. Gottschalk, informal remarks, 17 May 51, *op. cit.*
30. Craig to Montross, 18 May 53, *op. cit.*
31. Brigade rpt, 1stProvMarBrig SAR, Jul-Sep 50, *op. cit.*
32. Annex Oboe, Jul-Sep 50.
33. See Ernest H. Giusti, "Minute men—1950 model," *Marine Corps Gazette,* 35, no. 9:22-31 (Sep 1951).
34. Lynn Montross, "Fleet Marine Force Korea," *U. S. Naval Institute Proceedings,* 79:835 (Aug 1953). See also Lynn Montross, "The Inchon landing," *Marine Corps Gazette,* 35, no. 7:26-35 (Jul 1951); and Ernest H. Giusti and Kenneth W. Condit, "Marine air over Inchon-Seoul," *ibid.,* 36, no. 6:18-27 (Jun 1952).
35. Annex Queen Queen (5th Marines rpt) to 1stMarDiv SAR, 15 Sep-7 Oct 50.
36. Annex Mike Mike (1stShorePartyBn rpt), *ibid.*
37. Annex Peter Peter (1st Marines rpt), *ibid.*
38. Annex Baker (G-2 rpt), *ibid.*
39. Annex William William (VMO-6 rpt), *ibid.* Hereafter this section of this report will be cited as Annex William William, Sep-Oct 50.
40. 1stMAW diary, Sep 50. Monthly diaries of Marine Corps units are hereafter cited as diaries, and copies of each are in the Diary File, USMC Hist.

41. Annex William William, Sep-Oct 50.
42. Division rpt, 1stMarDiv SAR, Sep-Oct 50, *op. cit.*
43. Annex William William, Sep-Oct 50.
44. *Ibid.*
45. *Ibid.*
46. Gottschalk, informal remarks, 17 May 51, *op. cit.*
47. Annex William William, Sep-Oct 50.
48. *Ibid.*
49. *Ibid.*
50. LtGen Oliver P. Smith, USMC, ltr to Lynn Montross, 28 Jul 53. Helicopter, USMC Hist.
51. Annex William William, Sep-Oct 50.
52. *Ibid.*

CHAPTER EIGHT

1. See Lynn Montross, "Wonsan to the reservoir," *Marine Corps Gazette,* 35, no. 10:31-32 (Oct 1951); and Geer, 192-195.
2. VMO-6 diary, Oct 50.
3. *Ibid.*
4. USMC Historical, interview with Maj Blatt, *op. cit.*
5. Craig to Montross, 18 May 53, *op. cit.*
6. Gottschalk, informal address, 17 May 51, *op. cit.*
7. BrigGen Clayton C. Jerome, USMC, jt memo for VAdm Cassady, RAdm Soucek, RAdm Duckworth, RAdm Pride, and RAdm Coe, 19 Sep 50. USMC VV, General Files, HQMC.
8. VMO-6 diary, Oct 50.
9. Geer, 202.
10. Annex Roger Roger (7th Marines rpt) to 1stMarDiv SAR, 8 Oct-15 Dec 50.
11. VMO-6 diary, Nov 50.
12. *Ibid.*
13. Geer, 194 ff.
14. Marine Corps Board, *op. cit.,* 1:II-C-31-33.
15. *Ibid.,* II-C-34-38.
16. Smith to Montross, 28 Jul 53, *op. cit.*
17. Annex Charlie Charlie (Air Observers rpt) to 1stMarDiv SAR, Oct-Dec 50, *op. cit.*
18. Marine Corps Board, *op. cit.,* 1:II-C-37-39.
19. Armstrong to Montross, 23 Jul 53, *op. cit.*
20. Marine Corps Board, *op. cit.,* 1:II-C-38-42.
21. Smith to Montross, 28 Jul 53, *op. cit.*
22. VMO-6 diary, Nov 50.
23. *Ibid.*
24. *Ibid.*
25. USMC Historical, interview with Maj Blatt, *op. cit.*
26. Lynn Montross, "Breakout from the reservoir," *Marine Corps Gazette,* 35, no. 11:35 (Nov 1951). See also Kenneth W. Condit and Ernest H. Giusti, "Marine air covers the breakout," *ibid.,* 36, no. 7:18-25 (Jul 1952).
27. Montross, "Breakout from the reservoir," *op. cit.,* 27-30.
28. LtCol Raymond G. Davis, USMC, ltr to Lynn Montross, 17 Jan 53. Helicopter, USMC Hist.

29. USMC Historical, interview with Col Homer L. Litzenberg, USMC, 27-30 Apr and 10 Jul 51. Interview File, USMC Hist.
30. Ibid.
31. Annex Nan Nan (1st EngrBn rpt) to 1stMarDiv SAR, Oct-Dec 50, op. cit.
32. BrigGen Oliver P. Smith, USMC, ltr to MajGen Merwin H. Silverthorn, USMC, 10 Jan 51.
33. Annex Nan Nan, op. cit.
34. Annex Baker (G-2 rpt) to 1stMarDiv SAR, Oct-Dec 50, op. cit.
35. Annex William William (VMO-6 rpt), ibid.
36. Ibid. For an account of Marine action in this area, see Lynn Montross, "Ridgerunners of Taktong Pass," Marine Corps Gazette, 37, no. 5:16-23 (May 1953).
37. Col Edward H. Forney, USMC, special after-action rpt to X Corps, 19 Aug-31 Dec 50. Copy in SAR File, USMC Hist. See also Lynn Montross, "The Hungnam evacuation," Marine Corps Gazette, 35, no. 12:18-27 (Dec 1951); and "All in a day's work," op. cit., 30.
38. Comdr Amphibious Group One (CTF-90) action rpt, 9-25 Dec 50, "Hungnam redeployment." SAR File, USMC Hist.
39. 1stMarDiv diary, Jan 51. See also Lynn Montross, "The Pohang guerrilla hunt," Marine Corps Gazette, 36, no. 1:18-27 (Jan 1952).
40. Smith to Montross, 28 Jul 53, op. cit.
41. Ibid.
42. VMO-6 diary, Feb 51.
43. Ibid.
44. Eighth Army command rpt, Mar 51. Adjutant General's Office, Departmental Records Branch, Alexandria, Va. (hereafter referred to as AGO, DRB).
45. See Lynn Montross, "Buttoning up the offensive," Marine Corps Gazette, 36, no. 2:30-39 (Feb 1952).
46. Smith to Montross, 28 Jul 53, op. cit.
47. Ibid.
48. See Lynn Montross, "Advance to the 38th parallel," Marine Corps Gazette, 36, no. 3:18-27 (Mar 1952).
49. Eighth Army command rpt, Apr 51. AGO, DRB.
50. See Lynn Montross, "Advance to the Punchbowl," Marine Corps Gazette, 37, no. 8:14-23 (Aug 53).
51. VMO-6 diary, Mar 51.
52. Ibid.
53. Ibid.
54. VMO-6 diary, Apr 51.
55. Ibid.
56. VMO-6 diaries, Jan-Jun 51.
57. Capt Eugene R. Hering, (MC) USN, address to the U. S. Association of Military Surgeons, New York, 9 Oct 51.
58. USMC Historical, interview with LtComdr John H. Craven, (CHC) USN, 8 Sep 52. Interviews File, USMC Hist. See also Lynn Montross, "They make men whole again," Marine Corps Gazette, 36, no. 12:42-49 (Dec 1952).
59. CO USS Consolation rpt to COMNAVFE, 26 Jan 52. Copy in Helicopter, USMC Hist.
60. Ibid.

CHAPTER NINE

1. HMR-161 diary, Jan 51.
2. *Id.*, diary Jul 51.
3. *Id.*, diary Sep 51.
4. 1stMarDiv type "C" rpt on employment of assault helicopters, 4 Oct 51. SAR File, USMC Hist.
5. *Ibid.*
6. 1stShorePartyBn diary, Sep 51.
7. *Ibid.*; USMC Historical, interview with LtCol Harry W. Edwards, USMC, 29 Dec 53. Helicopter, USMC Hist.
8. 1stMarDiv type "C" rpt on assault helicopters, 4 Oct 51, *op. cit.*
9. *Ibid.*
10. 1stShorePartyBn diary, Sep 51.
11. HMR-161 diary, Sep 51.
12. *Ibid.*
13. 1stMarDiv rpt on assault helicopters, 4 Oct 51, *op. cit.*
14. *Id.*, diary, Sep 51.
15. 1stReconCo diary, Sep 51.
16. 1stShortPartyBn diary, Sep 51.
17. HMR-161 diary, Sep 51.
18. *Ibid.*
19. 1stMarDiv rpt on assault helicopters, 4 Oct 51, *op. cit.*
20. HMR-161 diary, Sep 51.
21. USMC Historical, interview with LtCol F. Brooke Nihart, USMC, 31 Dec 53. Helicopter, USMC Hist.
22. HMR-161 diary, Sep 51.
23. 1stShorePartyBn diary, Sep 51.
24. HMR-161 diary, Sep 51.
25. *Ibid.*
26. 1stMarDiv type "C" rpt on employment of assault helicopters, 16 Nov 51. SAR File, USMC Hist.
27. *Ibid.*
28. *Ibid.*
29. *Ibid.*
30. *Ibid.*
31. 1stMarDiv diary, Oct 51.
32. HMR-161 diary, Oct 51.
33. CG 1stMAW disp 1601127 of Oct 51, quoted in HMR-161 diary, Oct 51.
34. 1stReconCo diary, Oct 51.
35. HMR-161 diary, Oct 51.
36. *Ibid.*
37. 1stMarDiv rpt on employment of assault helicopters, 16 Nov 51, *op. cit.*
38. HMR-161 diary, Oct 51.
39. 1stMarDiv rpt on assault helicopters, 16 Nov 51, *op. cit.*
40. *Ibid.*
41. HMR-161 diary, Oct 51.
42. 1stShorePartyBn diaries, Oct-Nov 51; and HMR-161 diary, Nov 51.
43. HMR-161 diary, Nov 51.
44. *Id.*, diary, Dec 51.
45. *Ibid.*
46. *Ibid.*

47. Col Keith B. McCutcheon, USMC, ltr to Lynn Montross, 20 Jul 53. Helicopter, USMC Hist.
48. LtCol William P. Mitchell, USMC, ltr to Lynn Montross, 21 Jul 53. *Ibid.*
49. 1stAirDelPlt diary, Dec 51.
50. USMC Historical, interview with LtCol George W. Herring, USMC, 28 Aug 53. Helicopter, USMC Hist.
51. HMR-161 diary, Jan 52.
52. *Ibid.*
53. *Ibid.*
54. *Id.,* diary, Feb 52.
55. *Ibid.*

CHAPTER TEN

1. VMO-6 diaries, Jul-Dec 51.
2. Maj William G. MacLean, Jr., USMC, ltr to Lynn Montross, 3 Sep 53. Helicopter, USMC Hist.
3. VMO-6 diaries, Jan-Dec 52.
4. *Id.,* diary, Sep 51.
5. HMR-161 diaries, Sep 51-Sep 52.
6. Capt Robert F. Warren, USMC, ltr to CG AirFMFPac, 18 Aug 53, encl to MajGen Christian F. Schilt, USMC, ltr to Lynn Montross, 19 Aug 53. Helicopter, USMC Hist.
7. HMR-161 diary, Feb. 52.
8. McCutcheon to Montross, 20 Jul 53, *op. cit.*
9. *Ibid.*
10. HMR-161 diary, Mar 52.
11. *Ibid.*
12. *Ibid.*
13. *Id.,* diary, Apr 52.
14. McCutcheon to Montross, 20 Jul 53, *op. cit.*
15. HMR-161 diary, Apr 52.
16. *Ibid.*
17. *Id.,* diaries Apr and May 52.
18. *Id.,* diary, June 52.
19. McCutcheon to Montross, 20 Jul 53, *op. cit.*
20. HMR-161 diary, Jun 52.
21. *Ibid.*
22. *Ibid.*
23. *Id.,* diary, Jul-Dec 52.
24. *Id.,* diary, Jul 52.
25. *Ibid.*
26. USMC Historical, interview with LtCol Herring, 28 Aug 53, *op. cit.*
27. Maj Lynn E. Midkiff, USMC, ltr to Lynn Montross, 8 Jul 53. Helicopter, USMC Hist.
28. See Peter Braestrup, "Outpost warfare," *Marine Corps Gazette,* 37, no. 11:32-36 (Nov 53).
29. VMO-6 diaries, Jul-Aug 52.
30. HMR-161 diary, Aug 52.
31. *Ibid.*
32. *Ibid.*
33. *Id.,* diary, Sep 52.

34. *Ibid.*
35. *Ibid.*
36. *Ibid.*
37. *Id.*, diary, Oct 52.
38. *Id.*, diary, Sep 52.
39. *Id.*, diary, Feb 53.
40. *Ibid.*
41. *Ibid.*
42. *Ibid.*
43. *Ibid.*

CHAPTER ELEVEN

1. Col Henry R. Paige, USMC, ltr to Lynn Montross, 27 Jul 53. Helicopter, USMC Hist.
2. Marine Corps Schools, Marine Corps Landing Force Development Center, Landing Force Tactics and Techniques Board, "Study on employment of assault transport helicopters, 5 January 1951." S&C, MCS.
3. *Id.*, "Study on Marine helicopter transport program, 28 February 1951." *Ibid.*
4. Director MCS Atomic Warfare Committee interim rpt no. 1 (5 Jan-31 Mar 1951) to CMC, 19 Apr 51, ser 00114-51. *Ibid.*
5. Marine Corps Schools, Marine Corps Landing Force Development Center, Landing Force Tactics and Techniques Board, "Study to determine the requirements of the Marine Corps for flying crane type helicopter, 14 April 1951." *Ibid.*
6. *Id.*, "Study of a Marine Corps requirement for a one-man helicopter, April 1952." *Ibid.*
7. LtCol James D. Hittle, USMC, ltr to CMC, 19 Nov 47, ser 83386. NRMC, Alexandria.
8. Marine Corps Schools, Marine Corps Landing Force Development Center, Landing Force Tactics and Techniques Board, "Study . . . flying crane type helicopter, 14 April 1951," *op. cit.*
9. *Id.*, "Supporting arms in helicopter assault operations, June 1952," and "Study on supply concept to support helicopter-borne units, November 1952;" Director MCDC to CMC, 20 Sep 52, ser 01632-52, "Use of smoke in helicopter operations," and 19 Nov 52, ser 01988-52, "Clarification of composition and duties of helicopter control units." S&C, MCS.
10. USMC, *Amphibious manual: ship-to-shore operations*, sec. 13, 1-12.
11. Marine Corps Schools, Marine Corps Landing Force Development Center, Landing Force Tactics and Techniques Board, "Interim doctrine for the tactical employment of helicopters, February 1953," later issued under the same title as Landing Force Bulletin 4, 26 Apr 53, ser 03A12653. USMC Hist.
12. *Id.*, "Tactics and techniques for helicopter employment with ground forces, June 1953." S&C, MCS.
13. Marine Corps Schools, Marine Corps Landing Force Development Center, Marine Corps Equipment Board, "Test report: troop seating in Marine assault transport helicopters, 26 June 1953." *Ibid.*
14. Col Owen A. Chambers, USMC, ltr to Lynn Montross, 31 Aug 53. Helicopter, USMC Hist.
15. MajGen Field Harris, USMC, ltr to CMC, 7 Apr 52, ser 00104. RS, MCEC, MCS.

16. FMFLant final rpt on Helex I and II, 7 Apr 52. *Ibid.*
17. *Ibid.*
18. AirFMFPac special rpt of helicopter participation in Lex Baker, I, 1 May 52, ser 0387. USMC Hist.
19. *Ibid.*
20. CG 2dMCPAEB rpt to CMC, 19 May 53, ser 120053. S&C, HQMC.
21. *Ibid.* See also Louis E. Hudgins, Jr., "AEC's shot V," *Marine Corps Gazette*, 37, no. 7:36-38 (Aug 1953).
22. Maj Archie J. Clapp, USMC, ltr to CMC (attn: Lynn Montross), 28 Aug 53. Helicopter, USMC.
23. VMO-6 diaries.
24. HMR-161 diary, May 53.
25. *Ibid.*
26. *Id.*, diary Jun 53.
27. *Id.*, 1951 yearbook, encl to diary, Jun 52.
28. *Id.*, diaries Sep 51-Jul 53.
29. *Id.*, diaries Feb and Apr 53.
30. VMO-6 diaries, Aug 50-Jul 53.
31. VMO-2, HMR-162, 163, and 361 diaries, Aug 53.
32. Washington *Post*, 17 Jun 53.
33. New York *Herald Tribune*, 2 Dec 53.
34. Vincent H. McGovern (as told to Hugh Morrow), "We flew the Atlantic in helicopters," *Saturday Evening Post*, November 1, 1952: 22-23, 82-84.
35. *Time*, September 21, 1953: 100.
36. Address . . . *National Security Industrial Association*, 10 Sep 53.
37. USMC Division of Information, "Fact sheet on the XHR2S," released 18 Jan 54. Copy in USMC Hist.
38. *Ibid.*
39. New York *Herald Tribune*, 19 Jan 54.
40. *Army-Navy-Air Force Register*, 26 Dec 53.
41. Jerome to Cassady, *et al.*, 19 Sep 50, *op. cit.*
42. *Address*, 10 Sep 53, *op. cit.*

BIBLIOGRAPHY

PRIMARY SOURCES

This volume is based chiefly upon official records. Inasmuch as references to primary source materials in the text have been of a bibliographical nature, giving precise location and file designations for each document cited, it is not deemed necessary to repeat this detailed information here. This note on primary sources will be confined, therefore, to a listing of general groups of records consulted.

U.S. NAVY
Records of the Bureau of Aeronautics, 1921-46.
Historical records and reports of Naval Aviation units and installations, 1944-48.

U.S. MARINE CORPS
Records, correspondence, and reports of Headquarters, U.S. Marine Corps, 1921-53:
> Commandant of the Marine Corps; the General Staff Sections and their predecessors (viz., the Division of Operations and Training, and the Division of Plans and Policies); the Division of Aviation; the Division of Information; and Headquarters Battalion (Photographic Section).

Records, correspondence, reports, and studies of Marine Corps research and development activities, 1946-53:
> Marine Corps Schools; Marine Corps Amphibious Warfare School (Senior and Junior Courses); Marine Corps Landing Force Development Center; Marine Corps Landing Force Tactics and Techniques Board; Marine Corps Equipment Board; and Special Boards of the Commandant of the Marine Corps, and the Commandant of the Marine Corps Schools.

Records and reports of Marine Corps field units, 1946-53:
> Historical diaries, semiannual historical reports, progress reports, exercise reports, and special action reports.

U.S. AIR FORCE
General Files records of Headquarters, U.S. Army Air Corps, 1941-46.

SECONDARY SOURCES

Robert B. Anderson. *Address to graduates of 22d Special Basic Course and the Eighth Officer Candidate Course, Marine Corps Schools, Quantico, Va., Saturday, 19 September 1953.* (Mimeographed; copy in Division of Information, HQMC.)

A. von Boguslawski. *Tactical deductions from the War of 1870-1871*. Translated by Lumley Graham. London: H. S. King, 1872.

Richard Bradberry. "The RAF's helicopters." *American Helicopter*, 2, no. 5:30-32 (Apr 1946).

J. W. Bunkley. "The U.S. Navy's helicopter program." *American Helicopter*, 11, no. 7:10-11 (Jun 1948).

Archie J. Clapp. "Their mission is mobility." *Military Review*, 38, no. 5:10-18 (Aug 1953).

Eli K. Cole. "Joint overseas operations." *U.S. Naval Institute Proceedings*, 55:927-937 (Nov 1929).

Devon Francis. *The Story of the helicopter*. New York: Coward-McCann, 1946.

J. F. C. Fuller. *The Second World War, 1939-1945: a strategical and tactical history*. London: Eyre and Spottiswoode, 1948.

Andrew Geer. *The new breed: the story of the U.S. Marines in Korea*. New York: Harper, 1952.

H. F. Gregory. *Anything a horse can do: the story of the helicopter*. New York: Reynal and Hitchcock, 1944.

Franklin A. Hart. "Marine Corps Schools at Quantico." *Army Information Digest*, 7 no. 2:31-39 (Feb 1952).

Robert D. Heinl, Jr. "Naval gunfire training in the Pacific." *Marine Corps Gazette*, 32, no. 6:10-15 (Jun 1948).

Louis E. Hudgins, Jr. "AEC's shot V." *Marine Corps Gazette*, 37, no. 7:36-38 (Aug 1953).

Jeter A. Isely and Philip A. Crowl. *The U.S. Marines and amphibious war: its theory and its practice in the Pacific*. Princeton: Princeton Univ. Press, 1951.

John A. Lejeune. "The United States Marine Corps; delivered at the Naval War College, Newport, Rhode Island, December 14, 1923." *Marine Corps Gazette*, 8:243-254 (Dec 1923).

Eugene K. Liberatore, ed. *Rotary wing aircraft handbooks and history*. Eighteen unpublished volumes in the files of the Rotary Wing Section, Directorate of Laboratories, Wright Air Development Center, Wright-Patterson Air Force Base, Dayton, Ohio. (Project done by Prewitt Aircraft Company, Clifton Heights, Pa., on contract for the Air Matériel Command, U.S. Air Force.)

C. B. F. Macauley. *The helicopters are coming*. New York: McGraw-Hill, 1944.

Vincent H. McGovern (as told to Hugh Morrow). "We flew the Atlantic in helicopters." *Saturday Evening Post*, November 1, 1952: 22-23, 82-84.

F. Alexander Magoun and Eric Hodgins. *A history of aircraft*. New York: McGraw-Hill, 1931.

Clayton C. Marcy. "Operation Crossroads." *American Helicopter*, 4, no. 12:8-9, 36-38 (Nov 1946).

Lynn Montross. "Fleet Marine Force Korea." *U.S. Naval Institute Proceedings*, 79:829-841, 995-1005 (Aug-Sep 1953).

―――. "The Marine autogiro in Nicaragua." *Marine Corps Gazette*, 37, no. 2:56-61 (Feb 1953).

―――. "Ridgerunners of Toktong Pass." *Marine Corps Gazette*, 37, no. 5:16-23 (May 1953).

Charles Lester Morris. *Pioneering the helicopter*. New York: McGraw-Hill, 1945.

William A. Reavis. "The transport helicopter." *Marine Corps Gazette,* 36, no. 7:54-60 (Jul 1952).

John N. Rentz. *Marines in the central Solomons.* Washington: U.S. Govt. Print. Off., 1952.

John H. Russell. "The birth of the Fleet Marine Force." *U.S. Naval Institute Proceedings,* 72:49-51 (Jan 1946).

Lemuel C. Shepherd. *Address to the Washington Group, National Security Industrial Association, Washington, D.C., 10 September 1953.* (Mimeographed; copy in Division of Information, HQMC.)

Robert Sherrod. *History of Marine Corps aviation in World War II.* Washington: Combat Forces Press, 1952.

Joseph H. Strain and James M. Brannaman. "Cavalry of the air." *Marine Corps Gazette,* 36, no. 3:30-35 (Mar 1952).

U.S. Marine Corps. Preliminary studies of the Marines in Korea, prepared in the Historical Branch, G-3, Headquarters, U.S. Marine Corps, and printed in the *Marine Corps Gazette,* 1951-53.

Kenneth W. Condit. "Marine artillery in Korea." 36, no. 11:26-33 (Nov 1952).

———. "Marine supply in Korea." 37, no. 1:48-55 (Jan 1953).

——— and Ernest H. Giusti. "Marine air at the Chosin reservoir." 36, no. 7:18-25 (Jul 1952).

Ernest H. Giusti. "Marine air over the Pusan perimeter." 36, no. 5:18-27 (May 1952).

———. "Minute men—1950 model: the reserves in action." 35, no. 9: 22-31 (Sep 1951).

——— and Kenneth W. Condit. "Marine air covers the breakout." 36, no. 8:30-27 (Aug 1952).

———. "Marine air over Inchon-Seoul." 36, no. 6:18-27 (June 1952).

Lynn Montross. "Advance to the Punchbowl." 37, no. 8:14-23 (Aug 1953).

———. "Advance to the 38th parallel: the Marines in Operation Ripper." 36, no. 3: 18-27 (Mar 1952).

———. "All in a day's work: the engineers and shore party in Korea." 36, no. 9:24-31 (Sep 1952).

———. "Breakout from the reservoir: Marine epic of fire and ice." 35, no. 11:22-37 (Nov 1951).

———. "Buttoning up the offensive: the Marines in Operation Killer." 36, no. 2:30-39 (Feb 1952).

———. "The capture of Seoul: battle of the barricades." 35, no. 8:26-37 (Aug 1951).

———. "Flying windmills in Korea." 37, no. 9:16-25 (Sep 1953).

———. "The Hungnam evacuation: amphibious landing in reverse." 35, no. 12:18-27 (Dec 1951).

———. "The Inchon landing: victory over time and tide." 35, no. 7:25-35 (Jul 1951).

———. "March of the iron cavalry: Marine tanks in Korea." 36, no. 10:46-54 (Oct 1952).

———. "The Pohang guerrilla hunt: 1,600 square miles of trouble." 36, no. 1:18-27 (Jan 1952).

———. "The Pusan perimeter: fight for a foothold." 35, no. 6:30-39 (Jun 1951).

———. "Red China on the offensive." 37, no. 7:16-24 (Jul 1953).

————. "They make men whole again: the medical battalion and chaplains in Korea." 36, no. 12:42-49 (Dec 1952).

————. "Wonsan to the reservoir: Red China enters the fight." 35, no. 10:30-39 (Oct 1951).

U.S. Marine Corps. *Amphibious manual: ship-to-shore operations.* Quantico: Marine Corps Schools, 1951. (Amphibious, *i.e.*, Landing Force, Manual 4).

U.S. Marine Corps. *Marine Corps aviation general—1940.* Washington: U.S. Govt. Print. Off., 1940.

U.S. Marine Corps. Marine Corps Board. *An evaluation of the influence of Marine Corps forces on the course of the Korean War (4Aug50-15Dec50).* 2 v. (Processed; copy in USMC Historical.)

U.S. Marine Corps. Marine Helicopter Squadron One (HMX-1). *Operation Packard Two: amphibious command post exercise,* 10-26 May 1948. Quantico, Va.: Marine Corps Air Station, 1948.

U.S. Marine Corps Schools, Amphibious Warfare School (Junior Course). *Tentative doctrine for employment of helicopters in amphibious operations,* 12 April 1948. (Mimeographed; copy in RS, MCDC.) Later published as *Amphibious operations: employment of helicopters (tentative),* Quantico: Marine Corps Schools, 1948. (Phib-31.)

U.S. Navy Department. *United States Navy regulations,* 1948. Washington: U.S. Govt. Print. Off., 1948.

U.S. Navy Department. Office of Naval Operations. *Tentative landing operations manual,* 25 May 1935. (Mimeographed; copy in USMC Historical.)

U.S. War Department. *Basic field manual: landing operations on hostile shores,* 2 Jun 1941. Washington: U.S. Govt. Print. Off., 1942. (Field Manual, 31-5.)

John L. Zimmerman. "The Marines' first spy." *Saturday Evening Post,* November 23, 1946: 19, 97-99.

INDEX